Text-book for Coaches, Instructors
and Sports Teachers

Swimming

By Dr Gerhard Lewin
in collaboration with nine contributors

Sportverlag Berlin 1979

Published under the auspices of the Department for Swimming Events of the Leipzig College of Physical Culture (DHfK)

Contributors:
Dr Walter Hentzschel
Dr Lothar Kipke
Heidi Leopold
Dr Hanno Mertens
Karl-Heinz Rasenberger
Heinrich Rothe
Siegmar Schöne
Dr Eberhard Schramm
Dr Christine Wagner

Chief Editor: Dr Gerhard Lewin

© Sportverlag Berlin
First Edition
Licence No.: 140 355/20/79
Sub-editor: Peter Schulze
Translators: Ruslan Tulburg, Ilia Moser (Chap. 7, 8, 9)
Title of the German Original: Schwimmsport
Illustrations: Hans Hausmann
Cover Design: Marianne Baußat
Printed in the German Democratic Republic
Printers:
Copy Dead Line: June 1st, 1978
671 382 3

Contents

1. The Role of Swimming in the GDR

Growing numbers of people from all walks of life and of all ages in the GDR go in for swimming. Participation in sports has become an integral part of life for many people and they regularly participate in organized exercises, training sessions and contests.

People taking part in organized swimming are normally members of the Deutscher Schwimmsport-Verband (DSSV), an association which sponsors children's and youth aquatic sports activities and competitive sports in the GDR. The fact that the DSSV has more members than the other sports associations in the GDR reflects the broad participation in this sport.

Large sections of the population avail themselves of the opportunities of participating in regular swimming instruction and exercises. They include the entire school population (swimming is mandatory in GDR schools), students taking part in collegiate sports and groups participating in leisure and recreational sports. A high level of proficiency in swimming is the basis of various special training programmes, including life-saving and skin diving.

The large number of people going in for swimming also includes those who sporadically but frequently swim in their leisure time or when on holiday.

If we sum up all these people we find that at present about 25 per cent of the GDR population take part in one form of swimming or another, be it in order to improve their performance or to stay fit and thus get more enjoyment out of life. This is an important aspect in the development of all-round and harmonious socialist personality.

Swimming is an excellent sport for developing these and other character traits, and it is this aspect that largely determines the significance of swimming in the social sphere in the GDR. The development of swimming as a sport is a part of the overall development of physical culture and sports and it is guaranteed by the Constitution of the GDR.

The Socialist Unity Party of Germany has consistently patronized this development. The fundamental significance and the objectives of physical culture and sports in the steady development of the advanced socialist society in the GDR were reaffirmed at the 9th Congress of the Socialist Unity Party. The programme adopted by the 9th Congress reads in part: „Healthy living habits, physical culture and sports are an integral part of the socialist way of life. The Socialist Unity Party of Germany promotes and supports the development of physical culture and sports as an important social need. Regular participation in sports promotes health, relaxation and enjoyment of live and helps people to stay fit. Physical culture and sports help promote the all-round development of the individual in socialist society. The Socialist Unity Party of Germany supports all endeavours aimed at advancing the further development of sports among children and young people, of the Spartakiad movement, of leisure and recreational sports among working people and of training, exercises und competitions organized by the German Sports and Gymnastics Union (DTSB) of the GDR. It promotes the people's athletic talents and individuals' efforts to attain record achievements, which serve the cause of socialism and peace." According to the Directive of the 9th Congress of the Socialist Unity Party of Germany to the Five-Year Plan for the Development ot the National Economy of the GDR, continuous development in this field is a task for the whole society to tackle. Essential measures are concretely discussed with a view to strengthening mass participation in physical culture, measures which can be taken only on the basis of increased production and greater national wealth.

Public recreation and physical culture and sport will continue to be developed in line with the developing productive capacity of the socialist economy. Physical culture and sports in their turn have a positive bearing on the development of the economy by raising working people well-being, performance, creative power, joy of life and on other factors. All sports make a contribution in this way.

The differences that do exist between the sports people go in for in the GDR are more in terms of degree than in terms of principle; they correspond to the specific features of the sports in question. The main specific features involved in swimming ar as follows:

– The beneficial influence of swimming on the human body is particularly important. This influence is produced even if the swimmer does not tax his energies very much. Swimming offers many people of all ages, including those who cannot go in for any of the „dry" sports at all or only to a limited degree, an opportunity to improve their vital functions and to raise their resistance to disease.

– Such character traits as courage, cooperation, strength of mind, etc., are required and trained already in the initial phases. The psychological boosts one gets in the process have a strong positive influence on the personality. They are achieved when the beginner starts to master the initial problems in an element which had been alien to him up to then and they are a source of joy, justified pride and self-reliance when the swimmer qualifies for the beginner's, ordinary and advanced level swimming badges.

– In the course of further improving swimming proficiency the swimmer develops endurance, coordination as well as will power.

– To those who learn how to swim properly this sport is a very good way to compensate for a sedentary occupation or for those normally doing mental work, and it also helps people exposed to severe nervous strain to relax.

The successes a country scores in the Olympics and in other high-level competitions reflect its level of development in swimming. High achievements in swimming and efforts on the way to achieving them have played and will continue to play an important role in building up a good image of our socialist state abroad, they serve to promote better understanding among peoples and to safeguard peace. The good example given by socialist athletes, especially by our top sportsmen, for our young people to follow promotes the development of healthy habits, regular participation in sports, aspiration for better achievements in one's personal and in social life and one's readiness to contribute an equal share for our socialist cause.

1.1. Significance of swimming for young generation

Systematic and collective participation in any sports helps to form an all-round personality. Physical training has an undisputed educational effect. The task of the sports instructor in the GDR is not only to develop the young athletes' physical faculties but also to help them become socially conscious people who actively take part in socialist construction, honourably representing their workers' and farmers' state, cultivating friendship with all peace-loving peoples and being committed to the tenets of socialist morality as a guideline for their personal lives.

Regular participation in sports helps to develop positive character traits. These can be consciously and systematically promoted by certain exercises. Every educational influence is connected with man actively coming to grips with his environment. The training of will power is particularly important here. This is what *Meinel* wrote in this connection: „All forms of training and forming a strong will simply make it necessary to face and overcome ever greater obstacles and resistances, which are given in a particularly clear form and in all degrees of difficulty in sports." [52]

Swimming helps to promote a strong will power in various ways. One's first encounter with water as a new element in one's experience requires quite some will power on the part of the swimmer. Persistent efforts are needed before one is able to execute the swimming movements properly, for only through unflagging training can one attain the goal. Whether one reaches one's objective will, in the final analysis, depend on one's „I will" attitude.

Once the beginner has passed through the initial stage of basic instruction he feels safe in water, his confidence in his own ability becomes stronger and deep water will no longer instil fear in him.

The act of jumping into the water plays an important role throughout the basic training phase. Resolution, courage and self control are promoted through the act of jumping into the water, at first in an unrestrained way. Springboard and firmboard diving, which are governed by rules on carriage and execution, require a great deal of concentration and fast reactions. Due to the fact that in the case of springboard and firmboard diving the beauty of execution is the main criterion of performance, this sport helps to develop one's sense of good body carriage and graceful of movement. Synchronized swimming, in which grace and precision must harmonize with music and form one harmonious entity, has a similar influence aesthetic education.

Physical training is almost always done collectively. This is true of basic training as well as of intermediate and advanced training in groups. As a member of his team the individual athlete tries to improve his performance. In this process the individuals concerned must show mutual regard, and they must help and respect each other. Trying to emulate the best athletes in diligence, courage, perseverance and discipline in sport and to act as a model for the weaker ones is the mainspring of collective upbringing, which the individual member of the team becomes aware of as his performance improves. Satisfaction and disappointment also manifest themselves clearly in a training group. An experienced sports teacher can channel satisfaction with an athletic success or disappointment as a result of a defeat in such a way as to spur the whole team or some of its members on to more diligent training and greater commitment.

Water polo, which is the swimmers' ball game, embraces the educational values of all the other popular ball games. The development of a team spirit, the subordination of the individual to the interests of the team, ranks first among them. But the special feature of water polo is that it demands from the players a greater measure of self discipline, fairness and honesty, because due to restricted visibility, which is often the case with this sport, the referee cannot always spot foul play under water, which can lead to serious injury. On the other hand this sport requires not only good control of the ball and a command of the tactics of this game, but also a high level of swimming skill, endurance and strength. To achieve these the player must train very hard, he must condition his willpower and possess a good measure of self control.

There is hardly another sport like swimming when it comes to helping a person develop a humanist outlook and to act accordingly. Although efforts are being made by various quarters to enable everybody to join the ranks of the swimmers – these efforts being vigorously supported by the GDR Government – the percentage of non-swimmers among the population is still felt to be too great. Each year in summer, when great masses of people throng to lakes and rivers to spend a holiday or just relax for a few hours after work, hundreds of cases of narrow escapes from drowning are recorded. In most cases such accidents happen during bathing or boating. To reduce the danger of drowning to a minimum the German Red Cross has set up a network of life guard stations. A large number of lifeguards are on duty during the swimming season.

In addition a department of the German Red Cross specializing in rescue activities, training courses for life guards are conducted. Basic courses for training young life-savers have been included in the gym training programme in the GDR's general comprehensive secondary schools. All gym and sports teachers in the GDR are expected to qualify for the life-saver's certificate before they take their state examinations.

And finally we should like to mention the great significance of swimming in developing proper habits of hygiene. The importance of thorough body hygiene before swimming and of proper measures after swimming, which depend on the place, season and the weather, is pointed out to the beginners from the very first training session.

1.2.   Role of various swimming sports

The various swimming sports comprise a broad range of exercises, each of which requires different control and skill of movement. They also differ considerably from each other in purpose. That is why different swimming sports organizations specialize in specific swimming sports.

Deutscher Schwimmsport-Verband (German Swimming Sports Association) (DSSV) of the German Democratic Republic is the parent organization of all swimming sports in the GDR. The DSSV is an organic part of Deutscher Turn- und Sportbund (German Sports and Gymnastics Union of the GDR, also known by its abbreviation DTSB) and comprises all members of the DTSB who go in for swimming on an organized basis.

Swimming, diving, water polo, and synchronized swimming are the swimming sports represented in the DSSV. The first three of the four swimming sports mentioned are Olympic disciplines. Swimming is the basis of all swimming sports and for this reason it plays a particularly important role. This explains why swimming is second only to track and field in terms of the number of contestants and events that account for in the Olympic Games.

Although synchronized swimming is not among the Olympic events it plays an important role in women's sports. Many exercises in this sport are also ideally suited for leisure and recreation activities.

The articles of association of the German Swimming Sports Association of the GDR lay down the tasks the Association has set itself and rules governing membership, organizational structure, finances and organizational principles of the DSSV. The following are among the tasks set:

– Swimming is to be promoted among the population, special attention being paid to attracting young people;

– standard contest rules are to be worked out on the basis of FINA articles of association;

– championships, cup games and test matches are to be sponsored and participation in national and international contests is to be organized or sponsored;

– teaching and research work being conducted by institutions in relevant fields is to be supported and cooperation with them is to be promoted;

– the building of new indoor swimming pools is to be promoted and help is to be given in the associated project planning work.

In the field of competitive sports one of DSSV's special tasks is to sponsor the training of athletes who represent the GDR at the Olympic Games, world championships, European championships, international competitions and at other major international events.

In keeping with the principles and objectives of the DTSB, the DSSV endeavours to help bring up its athletes as upright and active citizens of the German Democratic Republic, to develop in them high moral values and to educate them in the spirit of the Olympic ideal.

Organizationally, the most important branch of life saving is the "Wasserrettungsdienst" (Water Rescue Service), which is a special department of the German Red Cross. The Water Rescue Service's job is to train life-savers, to set up and man life guard stations at bathing facilities and to watch over the sports boat traffic.

The members of the Water Rescue Service are aware of the humanitarian objectives of the Red Cross societies and are guided by them in their own work in which they are actively supported by the authorities of the socialist state.

The central commission of the Water Rescue Service and its county and district commissions are attached to the Presidium of the German Red Cross and its county and district committees in whose work they participate in an advisory capacity. Members of these commissions are appointed to the committees by virtue of their expertise and administrative abilities. The Water Rescue Service conducts courses in life-saving.

Scuba diving (diving with self-contained underwater breathing apparatus) is a relatively young sport which has many practical uses, the most important ones being underwater filming and photography, research, underwater search and rescue work and minor underwater repair work.

Scuba diving is one of the sports pursued by the Gesellschaft für Sport und Technik (Society for Sports and Technology).

The equipment used in diving sports are snorkels, flippers, goggles (referred to here as ABC equipment) as well as breathing apparatus) compressed air and oxygen equipment).

Chart 1 Swimming sports and the organizations associated with them

Deutscher Schwimmsportverband der DDR (DSSV)	Deutsches Rotes Kreuz (DRK) Spezialdienst Wasserrettungsdienst (WRD)	Gesellschaft für Sport und Technik (GST)
German Swimming Sports Association of the GDR	German Red Cross Special Water Rescue Service	Society for Sports and Technology

Swimming	Lifesaving	Skin diving
Diving		Swimming with flippers
Water Polo		
Synchronized Swimming		

There are various relations and connections between the different swimming sports and the various fields of application. So, e.g., exercises from all the sports can be used in leisure and recreational activities. Similar connections with other areas of practical use could also be mentioned; such connections need not exist with all the swimming sports in each individual case.

Interrelations exist also between the sports and the fields of application. This is perhaps best illustrated by the role of swimming in all other swimming sports; but there is also an obvious interrelation between life-saving swimming and scuba diving. On the other hand the connection between the fields of application is readily recognizable; the importance of swimming instruction in school and pre-school swimming instruction being particularly great by virtue of its fundamental nature.

The sports instructor, gym teacher or coach, irrespective of the swimming sport in which he specializes, should always be aware of the relations and interrelations mentioned above; this will help to make his instruction interesting and varied, to organize the training programme on a broad scope and to mediate the complex nature of training for the swimming sports.

2. Influence of Swimming on Human Organism

2.1. Physiological and biological factors

Many attempts have been made to list physical exercises and sports according to their biological effectiveness. Such an attempt was made by *Lorenz* in 1938, for instance, who gave swimming 42 points (as compared with only 25 points for track and field) and placed it clearly in front of all other sports. Although the principles used in setting up this list lacked a scientific basis, it can still be said without exaggeration that swimming is a particularly healthy sport.

The influences of water, air and sun to which the human body is exposed in practising this sport act on the organism in manifold ways. Swimming is a favourite sport not only among competitive athletes but also for holiday-makers, and those seeking rest and recreation go swimming to relax, to collect fresh strength and to toughen their body.

The prophylactic and curative value of swimming and bathing in all weather was recognized in antiquity.

A saying in ancient Greece put the learning of swimming and of writing on an equal footing. Today we have gone one step further and the trend is first to teach children to swim and then to write.

The favourable influence of swimming on the development of the organism shows how important swimming is for children.

The influence of water, air and sun

Any athletic activity produces stimuli which have a positive bearing on physical and mental development. Movement markedly stimulates the development of muscles and in this way it plays a vital role in determining the body's form.

In any athletic activity the human body is more or less exposed to the natural weather conditions, but in swimming the body is exposed only to water and its temperature. It is not possible to protect the body against low temperatures with clothing. The only thing that can be done in this connection is to adjust the water temperature to the body temperature in indoor swimming pools.

Even at relatively high temperatures of 24 to 28 °C the body's temperature regulating capacity is considerably taxed, but this too has a beneficial influence on the body. A properly functioning temperature regulating system is the basis of toughening. Physical hardening promotes the human organism's adaptability, stability and endurance and its resistance to harmful environmental influences.

Toughening is one of the principal components of physical training, because it helps to develop a healthy, resistant and viable body. It is one of the most important ways of protecting public health. Toughened people are more seldom ill than those not.

The processes of toughening takes place

mainly in the capillaries of the skin, because the wind, cold, warmth, sun, moisture, etc. act directly on them. Inurement is the training of the vasomotors (nerves of the autonomous nervous system, which control the blood vessels). The process of toughening should be gradual and started in earliest youth. It should be adjusted to an individual's endurance, resistance, his physical development, constitution, etc. Each person, without applying a rigid system of rules, should do something daily for improving or preserving his or her resistance to harmful environmental influences. And swimming is most effective here.

The control mechanism of the cutaneous vessels plays the main role. The amount of heat a body emits depends on its blood supply to the skin. The cutaneous vessels can be greatly dilated ensuring a good blood supply to the skin then exposed to the relatively low water temperature as a conditioning stimulus. This is the case with the body's increased warmth generation. The capillaries can also be greatly constricted as a result of the body's diminished warmth production or exposure to very low temperature.

But the stimulus produced by the water temperature is not proportional to the blood vessel diameter. Strong stimuli produced by low temperatures can initially result in a constriction of the capillaries, which, in turn, results in a higher rate of metabolism and a correspondingly higher heat generation; then the vessels are dilated again and the supply of blood to the skin is improved. If the body is exposed to low water temperatures for excessively long periods the capillaries are constricted once again and the person feels cold. This is a sign that the generation and the liberation of heat on the surface of the body are out of balance. If the excitation by low temperature is increased, the vessels become dilated once

again, because at this stage a paralysis of the vessels sets in, which can result in organic damage. This phenomenon can also be observed when swimming in cold water. Cold baths are not tolerated well by people under 16 years of age due to inadequate development of vasomotor reactions (reactions of vascular nerves) and by people over 50 years of age in general. Such exposure can result in spasmodic contractions of cerebral vessels at old age, which can produce considerable organic damage. But short cold baths are salubrious during puberty and in the active age.

Twenty-five per cent of the body heat is produced in the periphery at rest and 70 per cent is produced there while swimming. This also suggests that the additional heat produced in the periphery can be dissipated faster and in greater quantities. The heat produced internally is transmitted only by convection, i. e., by the circulating blood, because tissue is a bad heat conductor. This is why peripheral circulation plays a major role.

This means that if the blood supply to the skin is poor the insulating effect increases, while better blood supply results in more heat being given off to the peripheral regions. Under normal conditions the human body gives off two to three times as much heat in the water as in the air at the same temperature. Another example that can be mentioned in this connection is that the body loses 75 per cent more heat in water than in the air given an equal temperature of 32 to 33 °C. An experiment has been conducted to show the body's different reactions in water and in the air: When the body is immersed in water at 36 °C the periphery warms up very evenly, which is not the case in the air. In this way a higher ambient temperature is simulated to the body's temperature control centre than the actual temperature acting on the body's heat regulating system. Due to this discrepancy the body slowly becomes cold despite the slight temperature difference, which explains why one begins to feel cold after a prolonged stay in water even at a temperature of 36 °C.

Knowing this some rules have been drawn up for swimmers to follow. Bathing or swimming training should be stopped before one starts freezing. Wet clothing worn in the open also causes very rapid cooling due to the fact that a great deal of heat is lost by the body through evaporation. This fact is often disregarded, resulting in colds that could otherwise be avoided. (Cf. *Landois-Rosemann:* Lehrbuch der Physiologie des Menschen. Verlag Urban und Schwarzenberg, München/Berlin 1962, p. 528.)

Children up to 10 years of age should be allowed to bathe naked whenever possible. Temperature regulating processes causing increased production of body heat through increased metabolic rate are the reason for the great amount of energy used up when swimming. Swimmers always head the list of people engaged in different types of sport when it comes to the daily calorie requirements. A system that can very accurately balance heat production and heat output is trained through regular swimming. The body's heat regulating mechanism that is therapeutically conditioned by the tried and tested method of contrast baths is also conditioned through swimming.

The production of vitamin D, which is particularly important for the development of the skeletal system in children, is activated only by UV rays to which swimmers are exposed out of doors in the summer.

Influence on heart and circulatory system

Training with effective training stimuli brings about what is known as the sportsmen's heart and raises the efficiency of the circulatory system. Since swimming requires a great deal of energy the circulatory system is also exposed to substantial strain (Chart 2). O_2 consumption is higher in swimming than in other sports. But there are no essential differences in the circulatory values between swimmers and athletes engaged in other sports requiring a great deal of endurance such as long-distance running, rowing and cycling. Manifest differences can be observed, however, in the capillarization of the muscles, in the O_2 utilization rate and in the oxygen difference between arterial and venous blood in muscle groups used in swimming. Since swimming is an endurance sport, regular swimming training leads to the development of a typical sportmen's heart featuring greater muscular strength (hypertrophia) in the auricles and vertricles and of a regulatory expansion of the heart's hollow spaces (dilatation). In this way the human organism is better able to raise the minute output (stroke volume Vs × heart rate), which is a performance-limiting factor, more

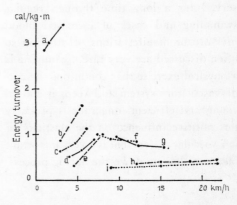

Chart 2 Energy turnover involved in different kinds and speeds of motion (after Müller, A. A.: „Die Physiologie der körperlichen Leistungsfähigkeit", cf. Landois-Rosemann: „Lehrbuch der Physiologie des Menschen", Verlag Urban und Schwarzenberg, München/Berlin 1962, p. 528)

a – Swimming; b – Rowing (fixed seat); c – Rowing (rolling seat); d – Walking; e – Paddling; f – Skiing; g – Running; h – Ice skating; i – Cycling through economical pressure volume action than through an uneconomical increase in the heart rate. *Reindell* found heart volumes of about 900 ml in swimmers. Heart volume in ml divided by body weight in kg yields heart volume/body weight quotients of about 13. Our own tests on athlete swimmers, some of which still belonged to the junior class, showed considerably higher values than those obtained in the case of other young people of the same age. Heart volume/body weight quotients of over 15 have been observed, and the heart volumes were around 1,000 ml. In recent years it has been possible faster to achieve circulatory values that could be said to be those of well-trained athletes by using modern training methods in swimming, which include serial interval training and various forms of endurance training.

Swimming training acts not only on the heart but also on the peripheral circulatory system. Systolic pressure drops and diastolic pressure increases somewhat at rest, which results in a diminished blood pressure amplitude. Vascular elasticity is preserved for a long time through regular swimming and cases of increased blood pressure or manifestations of attrition so often discussed are very rare. Swimming is a physical exercise that conditions the cardiovasculatory system and keeps it elastic, young and efficient longer. It is precisely this positive influence on the elasticity of our vascular system that is a very important factor in slowing down the ageing process.

Influence on respiratory organs

Swimming strongly taxes the respiratory system because it increases the intake of oxygen and the giving off of carbon dioxide. There is a certain period of adaptation from the time a person begins exercising, during which oxygen consumption is greater than oxygen intake. During this period the organism must meet its energy requirements from anaerobic energy supplying processes which require no oxygen. The oxygen deficit is then compensated after the exercise has been completed by the body's taking in more oxygen in the course of a few minutes after the exercise than it would at rest. Oxygen compensation is always quantitatively greater than the oxygen deficit (Chart 3).

It has been observed that the maximum oxygen intake capacity is increased through regular swimming training as a result of enlarged vital capacity (the volume of air taken in by the lungs at the deepest inhalation), heart minute output and an optimum adjustment of the circulatory system. Increased O_2 diffusion capacity and haemoglobin, improved O_2 utilization, increased oxygen compensation tolerance, improved blood supply to the muscles involved through increased capillarization, also help to adapt the circulatory system to the higher performance (40). In view of the aforementioned facts it is very important to pay attention to proper breathing when swimming. Very often a swimmer is handi-

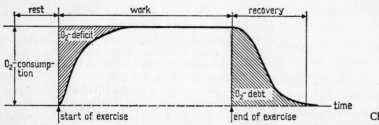

Chart 3

capped from the very outset as a result of a faulty breathing technique. For instance, if too little time is taken for exhaling, the exchange of gas in the lungs cannot take place effectively owing to the fact that sufficient air is inhaled but not enough is exhaled. This leads to increased pressure in the chest, which in turn causes blood to be dammed up in front of the heart. This can cause cardiovascular damage. Let us take crawling to illustrate this point.

A crawler who cannot exhale into the water and who uses the relatively short period of time in which his mouth is above the surface of the water for inhaling and exhaling will soon feel pressure building up in his chest which leads to diminished performance capacity as a results of a faulty breathing technique. In view of this the instructor, coach or gym teacher has the very important responsibility of paying special attention to this aspect of teaching people how to swim properly.

Proper breathing techniques taught in swimming are also often used for preventive and therapeutic purposes in connection with respiratory, heart and circulatory disorders. The correct breathing rhythm which is synchronized to the movement rhythm, and the overcoming of water resistance have a very beneficial influence on such disorders.

Influence on musculature and locomotor system

Training brings about greater capillarization in the musculature, which results in better blood supply and an enlargement of the muscle cross-sections. But a swimmer develops his strength not only by swimming but also through gymnastics, cord work, weightlifting, etc. The development of stamina is important, whereas the development of one's maximum strength should only be regarded as the basis of the former. Proper combination of dynamic and isometric heavy exercises is very important here. But it should always be borne in mind that the muscles must be kept loose; this is achieved by looseningup and stretching exercises, massage and by swimming itself. This type of training results in a general development of the musculature, which has a very positive bearing on the posture.

Thanks to the fact that the muscles of the left and right halves of the body are always used symmetrically (axially symmetrical in the case of breaststroke and butterfly and centre symmetrical in the case of crawl and backstroke), swimming is gaining in importance also in the body posture and carriage training of children and in remedial training to correct defects in posture and orthopaedic diseases.

Influence on Metabolism

We have already pointed out that swimming requires the mobilization of a great deal of energy in the body. For this reason the metabolic system must work extremely economically in order to meet the performance requirements. The body must get the necessary amount of calories in the form of food. The diet has a decisive influence on sustained performance capacity. It has been shown experimentally that trained persons were able to work two to three times as long when put on a pure carbohydrate diet than when put on a pure fat diet. Care should be taken that an athlete gets wholesome food and that there is a proper balance between fat, carbohydrate and proteins. According to *Gräfe*, a top-rate athlete should get approximately the following quantities of the three main types of food:

proteins	175 g
carbohydrates	820 g
fats	105 g

But proper quantities of vitamins and of alkalis and trace elements should also be included in the diet.

Swimming requires a great deal of calories. A top-rate swimmer, for instance, needs about 6,000 kcal per day. In this connection it is important to note that if the training programme is reduced a corresponding reduction should be made in the calories a person gets in order to avoid excessive weight gains.

An athlete's weight could be checked to control the training load to metabolism ratio. Eventually an equilibrium will be established, which will show regular fluctuations in the course of the day. Should this average weight rise, the calorie intake should be reduced, if it should drop, the calorie intake should be raised. In the latter case imbalances will be observed also in other body functions and a consultation with a sports physician is indicated. A drop in performance usually accompanies both rises and drop in weight. This shows that the weight check is an important method of seeing whether an athlete's eating and living habits follow a regular pattern (Chart 4).

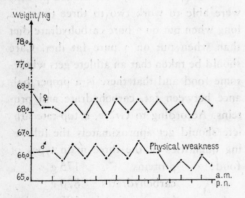

Weight/kg

Chart 4

Influence on nervous system

Any physical activity results in added strain on the nervous system. Locomotion is one of the main characteristics of life itself. A decision – an act of will – precedes each voluntary movement. This is particularly apparent in sports, since in sports every movement is voluntary, even though a certain degree of automation of movement is achieved.

Although it is the central nervous system that plays the main role in the process of learning and executing the movements which are required for swimming and although it is the CNS that responds to the stimuli encountered by the body in water by forming new conditioned reflexes and broadening its range of variation, it is the autonomous nervous system that is chiefly responsible for the process of toughening, which is promoted particularly by swimming. In this way swimming contributes considerably to the development of the nervous system as a whole.

2.2. Medical aspects of swimmer's training

On endurance training

The development of endurance is just as important in swimming as in any other endurance sport for achieving high performance. Performance depends on various factors also requiring adequate training stimuli. Appropriate training stimuli are just as essential for developing basic endurance as they are for improving specific endurance and speed. That is why diverse methods should be used in training.

The development of basic endurance should

be the basis that would enable the swimmer to exercise over prolonged periods without tiring. The rhythm of exercise and the alternating stress and relaxation of the muscles are very important here. A muscle in which the working and relaxation phases are properly balanced could work indefinitely, an example of this being the heart and muscles of the respiratory system. But since it is the higher performance that matters in sports exercises, fatigue invariably sets in sooner or later, depending on how fit an athlete is. For this reason it is important that the athlete should get accustomed to using the proper technique from the very start, making sure that the rhythm of movement is preserved and that the swimmer relaxes properly during the recovery phases of the swimming movement in developing his or her general endurance. In this manner the muscles can reach a high pitch of efficiency by rationally utilizing all energy substances and a fast discharge of metabolic waste products can be achieved.

But a well-functioning and properly trained cardiovascular system is required for this purpose. These requirements also determine the methods to be used for developing basic endurance. The organism achieves a high degree of economy through an even rhythm of movement in the course of endurance training. This method could be used to prepare an athlete for attempting a new record, because there is a constant balance between the performance and the energy input. In the course of such training an athlete is in a relatively "steady state" (stationary condition having the character of a dynamic equilibrium that can be maintained only through a constant energy input).

But it happens quite often in competitive meets that an athlete must depart from the steady state and then readjust to it very quickly. This ability to readjust quickly requires certain forms of training. A method known as interval training is suited for this purpose. Interval training is also an excellent method for training the whole cardiovascular system, because this is the best way to develop a sportsman's heart.

The cardiovascular system's adaptability and biochemical processes are developed in a particularly effective manner and great resistance against fatigue is achieved through basic endurance training.

Specific endurance training is carried out on the basis of a highly developed basic endurance and its purpose is to develop endurance for a special stroke and distance. A special rhythm of the body's physiological processes is conditioned by using a combination of competition simulation training, interval training and training in specially selected distances. Whether a swimmer has faultlessly coordinated movements and whether he or she develops an automatically functioning movement rhythm, stroke rate, power input and other factors depends on the precision of the nervous control processes. These processes, in conjunction with changes brought about in the cardiovascular system mainly through basic endurance training, enable the swimmer's body to work economically in the stroke and distance for which the swimmer trains.

Developing speed

The development of speed, by which is generally meant the ability to overcome resistances at high rates of speed, also calls for special training. Prolonged basic endurance training, in which often relatively long distances are swum at speeds below those common in competitive swimming, often develops in an athlete a stereotype movement pattern, which is then difficult to readjust to fast movement patterns.

These slow rhythms of movement and the associated sequence of biochemical and nervous processes tend to become stereotype enabling the swimmer effortlessly to swim long distances but not to increase his or her speed to a maximum. The motor-dynamic stereotype (a characteristic functional complex in which the action of individual stimuli depends on constantly recurring situations) adjusts itself to the swimming speeds that are slower than those common in competitive events. A swimmer that has undergone this type of training is often heard saying after a competitive event that he did not feel exhausted but that he just could not develop higher speeds. This is an indication that such a swimmer has been unable to "break through" the stereotype developed through prolonged basic endurance training. That is why the formation of a motor-dynamic stereotype for relatively slow movement patterns should be counteracted by having the athlete swim shorter distances at maximum speeds. It is also important to bear in mind in this connection that the athlete should practice a variety of swimming styles and concentrate more on strokes other than those for which he is training in the course of conditioning his or her basic endurance.

Strength training

The strength an athlete needs for swimming cannot be developed by swimming alone. A variety of exercises on land are needed to strengthen the musculature. Great emphasis is laid on stamina in such exercises. But special care must be taken to make sure that the swimmer's muscles stay loose when developing his muscular strength, because loose muscles are important in swimming. For this reason it should be kept in mind that it is important to keep a proper balance between training in and out of the water. This is very difficult to do, because there are no hard and fast rules one can follow. For this reason the training programme should be worked out for each athlete individually. Unfortunately the main criteria involved here have not been established yet, so that the different methods cannot be put to the test. Empirical data gathered by individual coaches is still the only thing we have to go by.

The basis of stamina is "maximum strength", which should be developed mainly in the preparatory period and, through appropriate exercises, preserved in the main period. Muscle cross-sections and muscle fibres are enlarged, enabling the athlete to develop greater strength through maximum strength training. It is important to bear in mind that exercises designed to develop an athlete's maximum strength should be wisely proportioned and that they should by no means be continued over prolonged periods or performed against great resistances in training athletes for endurance sports and especially in training swimmers, because otherwise the diffusion paths for oxygen become too extensive enabling the owners of such muscles to move heavier loads but making them fatigue very quickly.

Isometric and dynamic training methods can be used, relatively heavy loads are recommended. In developing an athlete's stamina the loads should be reduced but the number of repetitions of an exercise should be enlarged to produce a pronounced effect especially on the biochemical processes. The instructor should see to it that a proper balance between muscular tensioning and relaxation is maintained.

It is particularly important to make sure that the rate at which an athlete trains with pulley weights or on friction resistance equipment corresponds as nearly as possible to the frequency used in the swimming event he or she is training for.

Physiological experiments have proved that muscles work differently when an athlete exercises on a pulley weight and friction resistance equipment than when swimming and that if the rate of exercise is too high there is no adequate alternation between muscular tensioning and relaxation, and inadequate alternation does not produce the desired results in training. In such cases an athlete's muscles are in a constant state of contraction, and instead of achieving stamina such exercises train the athlete's maximum strength, although this too is not done effectively, for metabolic waste accumulates very rapidly in this way and the formation of muscular hypertrophy (enlargement of the muscles) is prevented.

It is essential that loosening up, stretching and relaxation exercises should be performed after or even during strength training.

Testing effectiveness of training stimuli

In any training programme the question that keeps recurring is whether a swimmer is overtaxed or undertaxed. The question of balancing the exercises properly is one of the most difficult to answer, and the trainer who has the greater stock of experience to draw on is more likely to see his fledgelings to success than his less experienced colleague. Unfortunately there are few aids a trainer can use to help him test the effectiveness of a training programme.

But it is known that endurance essentially depends on the organic pre-conditions. Certain parallels can be drawn: If the heart volume increases, so does the oxygen intake capacity, while the heart rate at rest drops. During exercise, the minute volume of a trained athlete's heart is maintained through volume pressure regulation, which is more economical than frequency regulation, which implies that increased heart rate can be seen as an indicator of general fatigue.

Pulse checks are essential during interval training. A trainer is often found labouring under the misconception that he is teaching interval training, which on closer scrutiny proves to be nothing else but alternate training, or the athlete is outside the effective training range. According to *Reindell* in interval training an athlete's heart rate should rise to about 180/min after exercising and drop to 120/min during the relaxation phase, which should then be followed by another exercise phase.

Greater difficulties are encountered in monitoring these phases if interval training is performed in groups. It can happen on the one hand that the best swimmers in such a group are not taxed sufficiently to achieve the results that would normally be expected from interval training and on the other hand that the weaker ones, altogether contrary to the rules of interval training, are unable to get enough rest during the relaxation phases and are overtaxed through what is to them a very intensive form of endurance training. For this reason it has proved to be a good practice in basic training to organize training in such a way that swimmers of equal performance are trained over specific distances.

To sum up this section we should stress once again the importance of checking the pulse as a training aid, any technique from palpation to telemetric methods being suitable for this purpose. More advanced swimmers can also take their own pulse.

3. History of Swimming

3.1. Development of swimming in human society

Swimming can be traced back a long time in history. Swimming, not as a sport but as a useful practice, has played an important role in all societies and on all continents where people lived near lakes, rivers or oceans. Apart from the role played by swimming in seeking food or in overcoming water obstacles encountered in hunting or during hostilities, another important reason why swimming is such a popular activity is the hygienic and salubrious influence of bathing and swimming.

This review of the historical development of swimming is designed to help the reader understand the dependence of the developments in this field of physical culture on the conditions of production prevailing during the periods of development under consideration and on the class forces acting during these periods. In the course of this review we shall also discuss the trends in development of the techniques and methods in use in all swimming sports in order to enable sports educationalists to work in such a way as to bring maximum benefits that can be derived from swimming to as many people in the German Democratic Republic as possible and to train our swimmers in such a way as to give them an opportunity to play a role in international swimming competitions commensurate with their social development.

3.1.1. Swimming in primitive society

In their constant struggle to obtain food people were compelled to come to grips with various difficulties posed by their environment. Collective hunting and, in the case of tribes living near lakes, rivers or oceans, collective fishing were an important way of getting food. For these people swimming and diving were vitally important physical activities, which called for a certain measure of constant training on the part of those who possessed these skills.

Assyrian and Egyptian cave drawings, seals and stone statues stemming from prehistoric times testify to how wide spread swimming was; they also tell us something about the techniques of locomotion in water used in those times. Different forms of alternate stroke swimming predominate in almost all representations connected with swimming from those times. Swimming skills, just as all other physical exercises, were not limited to any one section of the population in primitive society, differentiation began to appear in the period of transition to a class society, i. e., in the period of military democracy. Physical exercises began to play an increasingly important role in preparations for belligerent confrontations. Most drawings dealing with this subject that have survived through the ages show swimming in connection with river crossing operations with chariots, crossing water obstacles with the aid of inflated animal skins, transporting war machinery and similar military operations.

3.1.2.   Swimming in slave society

In slave society, which was the first historical form of class society, swimming was one of the most popular sports pursued by the aristocracy and freemen. In Greece and Rome, the two leading slave-holding states in antiquity, swimming was a popular pastime and bathing was at the height of its popularity.

The swimming pond ("Colymbethra") was an integral and the most important part of the gymnasiums, which were the public educational institutions of the free Greeks. Swimming had become an important component of physical training of the sons and daugthers of the well-to-do. Swimming also played a vital role in the military conditioning of young men.

But swimming contests were still an exception rather than the rule (they were not included even in the Olympic programme). It can be assumed that the main reason for this was there was no suitable water in the vicinity of the site of the Olympic Games.

Homer makes frequent reference in his „Iliad" and „Odyssey" to the great swimming feats of the Greeks; the love story of Hero and Leander has achieved particular fame. Bathing was a favourite pastime among the ancient Romans. Crowds of well over one thousand are said to have frolicked in their thermae (heatable swimming pools up to 70 metres in length). Swimming was part of the physical education of young people and played a particularly important part in the physical conditioning of young men belonging to the ruling class for military service. But the Romans just as the ancient Greeks did not take to swimming as a competitive sport. The fall of the Roman Empire as a slave-holding state marked the beginning of a steady decline of the thermae, which became establishments of moral decadence. They were neglected and gradually fell into ruin.

Swimming among tribes and peoples in Northern, Central and Eastern Europe

Around the beginning of the Christian era, northern and central Europe, which has many lakes and rivers, was inhabited by numerous Germanic tribes and peoples, which were in a process of transition from primitive to feudal society and which were subjects to a certain amount of influence from the declining Roman slave-holding society.

Owing to the fact their settlements were situated near lakes and rivers and to the necessity of crossing streams and rivers when hunting or in times of war, swimming was a very popular sport of practical value. Both men and women went in for swimming. Judging from old myths and sagas there is reason to believe that there were also swimming contests. The east European regions were inhabited mainly by Slavic tribes in those times. They too preferred to build their settlements near lakes and rivers and they too regarded swimming as a useful art. No conclusive evidence or myths exist at present about the techniques of locomotion in water or about swimming contests being held by them.

Swimming on other continents

Historical studies show that the art of swimming and diving was also widespread in Asia and America. About Japan it is known, for instance, that some of the inhabitants of that island state were excellent swimmers and that they were able to dive considerable depths mainly in pursuit of fish or when looking for pearls. Swimming feats were often demonstrated in public shows held at the royal court in China; the art of swimming also played a role in military training for the purpose of crossing rivers.

Little is known about the swimming skills of the aborigines of Central and South America. A party crossing a river in boats is supposed to have been attacked by some 10,000 Inca warriors belonging to the Muso-Chucho tribe. It is also known that forms of swimming belonged to the religious ritual of the Chibchas Indians of Colombia. No authentic evidence is available as yet about the swimming techniques used in that part of the world.

3.1.3. Swimming in feudal society

Knights, burghers and peasants practised different forms of physical culture, but swimming played a certain role with all of them. Peasants practised swimming as part of popular exercises, while the burghers were very fond of their public baths. Among the knights swimming was regarded as an important part of the system of exercises known here as the "seven agilities". As the exploitation of the peasants and lower strata of the urban population became more and more severe they had less and less leisure time at their disposal. As a result it became almost impossible for them to go in for sports. The situation was aggravated by the fact that sports in general were prohibited under the influence of scholasticism, and bathing and swimming were particularly combated because they were connected with the unveiling of the body. Owing to the fact that immorality began to spread in the bathing establishments, which were open only to the well-to-do sections of the population, they fell into disgrace

and were closed. Bathing and the art of swimming ceased to be practised, and those who were caught violating the bathing prohibitions were punished. Reporting about those times *Friedrich Ludwig Jahn* wrote that boys who were unable to resist the temptation and went swimming were canned. But the people preserved the art of swimming through tradition, and noted personalities continued to propagate the teaching of swimming.

3.1.4. Swimming in the era of Humanism and Enlightenment

The intellectual era of humanism dawned in Central and Western Europe at the turn of the 15th century. The development of the early capitalist mode of production and the associated rise of the progressive middle class lay at the root of this development. In keeping with this trend people began to look up to the energetic, optimistic man. It is understandable that more attention was paid again to physical exercise. In the field of swimming the first steps were extremely timid. The world's first swimming manual, "Colymbetes", was published in 1523, but the aim of the author and humanist *Nicolaus Wynmann* [74] was not so much to renew the teaching and learning of swimming as a form of physical fitness training as to reduce the danger of drowning. Nevertheless the book contained some basics about the techniques and methods of swimming in general and breaststroke in particular. But the book could not gain the broad distribution it deserved owing to the social conditions prevailing at that time and the objectives pursued by the author. The era of enlightenment, which took root in England towards the end of the 16th century, had a more powerful influence on the spread of swimming as a means of physical training and toughening. *Locke, Rousseau* and the philanthropists *Basedow, Salzmann* and *GutsMuths* were the eminent champions of this movement. People who worked as salt miners and labourers in the salt works of Halle in that period also contributed a great deal to the spread of swimming. [29] In times of unemployment they worked as fishermen and boatsmen, and as a result of always being close to water in this occupation they developed a liking for swimming. It is said that salt miners at Halle whose sons reached the age of three or four took them along when they went swimming in the Saale River. *Fulda* also mentions this fact in his Philonexia. [24]

The salt miners of Halle are also frequently referred to as the "fathers of modern swimming". Their influence on broad sections of the population was much more effective than that of the humanists, who were more given to theorizing.

The opening of the first public baths in Paris in 1760, in Frankfurt am Main in 1774 and in other cities in Western and Central Europe dates from that period. The seaside and mud-bath resort of Heiligendamm near Doberan was opened in 1793. It was the first German seaside resort and many more followed suit.

As the capitalist mode of production developed, people increasingly focused their attention on life on earth instead of in heaven. Stimulated by philanthropists, farsighted educationalists and medical men, more attention was again paid to the physical education of young people, and especially of middle class youth.

Swimming, which had been practised clandestinely for a long time, was again recognized as an excellent method of physical training and its teaching was introduced again in progressive philanthropic educational institutions. Even the powerful influence of the church, which for a longer time had continued to oppose this development could not stem this movement.

The pedagogic activities of *Johann Christoph GutsMuths* at Schnepfenthal had a particularly positive influence on the development of swimming in Germany towards the end of the 18th century. He creatively analysed the experience of the salt miners of Halle and founded a system of swimming instruction. He devoted a considerable part of his work entitled "Gymnastik für die Jugend" [27] to swimming, emphasizing the development of valuable character traits in connection with swimming skills and abilities. He wrote down his training method, which had been tried in practical work, in a self-teaching booklet entitled "Kleines Lehrbuch der Schwimmkunst zum Selbstunterricht", which appeared in 1798. [26] *GutsMuths* wanted to see swimming become "a principal component of education".

3.2. Development of swimming as a sport

The development of swimming as a sport is closely connected with the further development of the capitalist mode of production. Great Britain, the most highly developed industrial state in the 19th century, became the "mother country" of modern sport. At first it was a privilege enjoyed exclusively by the ruling class, i.e., the bourgeoisie. Being forced to work twelve to fourteen hours a day it was practically impossible for the proletariat to engage in sports and on the other hand the sports clubs protected themselves against an influx of workers by imposing high membership fees and restrictive provisions in their articles of association.

Only towards the end of the 19th century,

when the working people had managed to get their working hours reduced and when extensive exploitation was replaced more and more by intensive exploitation as a result of rationalized production, did working people start going in for sports. Swimming became a popular sport among the working people because it entails little expense and brings a great deal of enjoyment. The sport began to spread also in other industrial countries in Europe. Manifold forms of physical training, which had been created by the people but which had been more or less suppressed or forgotten over prolonged periods, were modified and organized under the influence of capitalist development. Many sports clubs were also founded in Germany towards the end of the 19th century.

Swimming became an increasingly popular sport, especially among young people. The people's growing interest in this sport was also stimulated by the building of swimming pools and improved methods used in teaching swimming.

At the turn of the 19th century the bourgeois swimming associations, following the example of other sports, united into a world federation. FINA (Fédération Internationale de Natation Amateur) was founded in London in 1908. It consisted of ten national swimming associations. In the course of time FINA has developed into one of the world's biggest sports federations. At present it is composed of over 100 national swimming associations irrespective of the forms of state or society of the member countries.

The sports which have crystallized in the course of development of aquatic sports are swimming, water polo, diving and synchronized swimming. The first three swimming sports are included in the programme of Olympic events, swimming having been added to the Olympic events list in 1896 (the first Olympic Games), water polo in 1900 and high diving in 1904.

Continental federations were formed within FINA in order to stimulate international competitions. They include LEN (Ligue Européenne de Natation) which was founded in 1927 and whose members include the GDR's Deutscher Schwimmsport-Verband, which joined LEN in 1952.

FINA's main tasks are to organize and monitor international swimming competitions (Olympic Games, world and continental cup competitions), to issue uniform statutes and rules of competition and to keep a list of world and continental records.

Development of swimming sports in the German Democratic Republic

After the destruction of fascism the gymnastics and sports organizations in Germany had to be built up from scratch. Most of the sports facilities, notably indoor and outdoor swimming pools, had been destroyed or had fallen into ruin. The young generation of German athletes had been decimated and many young people were crippled.

In Directive No. 23 the Allied Control Council banned all fascist organizations, including the "Nationalsozialistische Reichsbund für Leibesübungen" and all its affiliated associations. In addition all sports which were part of military training, swimming included, were banned for the time being.

The ban was gradually relaxed and community-level sports were permitted again. Old swimming officials from the worker's sports movement and others progressive actives in this fields, who had learned from past experience, went about jointly putting the swimming sports movement back on its feet in many parts of Germany and especially in the former bastions of swimming. They were aware of the great educational and health value of swimming, especially for the young people whose development had been so seriously hampered by the war and its aftermath. Their aim was to build up a sports movement that was to be free from the pernicious influences of the past and which was to comply with the Olympic spirit expressed by Baron de Coubertin.

The political divisions of Germany, brought about by the reactionary forces of Germany and promoted by the western occupation forces, also brought about divergent developments of objectives and organization of the sport.

In the western occupation zones, where initially anti-fascist athletes had been in charge of organizing sports associations in the Länder, former Nazi sports officials soon elbowed their way into leading positions of the new sports associations, which were assuming the old forms.

The Deutsche Schwimmverband, which sees itself as the successor of the former bourgeois Deutsche Schwimmverband with all its aims and traditions, was one of the first swimming sport associations to be formed there after the war.

On the territory of the former Soviet Occupation Zone, sports were organized in accordance with the principles of the Potsdam Agreement. The old Nazi and militarist influence was abolished and all athletes, and especially the young generation, was brought up in the spirit of building a new anti-fascist democratic order.

Initially sports were organized at community level. Although this basis proved to be too narrow later on the unfold sports activities on a central scale, at the time the community-level sports organized fulfilled the task of collecting and activating the available people willing to take part in the process of reconstruction. For this reason the community-level sports organization should be viewed as a transitional phase.

Anti-fascist community swimming divisions came into life especially in the old swimming centres of Leipzig, Halle, Magdeburg and Dresden. The first functionaries who went about reviving German swimming sports and giving it a new purpose in the spirit of the anti-fascist democratic order included *Heinz Deininger,* who has for many years been the president of the swimming section of the Deutscher Sportausschuss and of the Deutscher Schwimmsport-Verband and who is now its honorary president.

Länder executives for swimming were set up, and the first "East Zone Championships" in swimming and high diving were held in 1948 after a great deal of preparatory work. Zeitz was the venue picked for the championships. Athletes from twenty-five communities took part, and many of the athletes that participated in the competitions are today seasoned officials and coaches of the Deutscher Schwimmsport-Verband of the GDR.

"Deutscher Sportausschuss" (German sports committee), a central sports organization sponsored jointly by the Free German Youth organization and the Confederation of Free German Trade Unions (the two leading young people's and labour organizations in the GDR), was set up on 1 October 1948.

"Sparte Schwimmen" (swimming division) of the Deutscher Sportausschuss was founded in January 1949. It set itself the task of bringing up sportsmen as staunch anti-fascists and democrats, of developing swimming into a national sport and of achieving international standards in competitive swimming. In keeping with the traditions of worker's swimming clubs, another body set up was the Wasserrettungsdienst (water rescue service); many swimming athletes were trained as life-savers, who conscientiously watched over the safety of people bathing in sea, lake und river baths. To meet the constantly growing standards in international sports Sparte Schwimmen constituted itself into the "Nationale Sektion Schwimmen" (national swimming section) in May 1951.

The articles of association of the Sektion outlines the following objectives:

"Peaceful cooperation with all peoples; popularization of swimming as a sport and of all fields of activity connected with it; teaching as many peoples as possible to swim and training lifeguards; promoting school and children's sports; promoting competitive sports."

A new presidium was elected at the meeting of the presidium of the Nationale Sektion Schwimmen held in May 1952. The structure of the presidium, which is in keeping with the principle of democratic centralism and which consists of a president, vice-president, general secretary, coach council and committee chairmen, has proved to be equal to the task and it was retained later on when the Sektion Schwimmen was reorganized as the Deutsche Schwimmsport-Verband der DDR (German Swimming Sports Association of the GDR). The county and district branches had a similar structure adapted to the local conditions.

"The Law on the participation of young people in building the German Democratic Republic and the promotion of young people at school and at work, in sports and recreation" passed by the People's Chamber in February 1950 was an essential condition for the rapid development of democratic sports on a large scale. The introduction of the athletic performance badge "Bereit zur Arbeit und zur Verteidigung des Friedens", the resolution to reduce fares of athletes travelling to and from sports events and the founding of the Deutsche Hochschule für Körperkultur (German College of Physical Culture) have also helped promote sports

in the GDR. Swimming as a sport has become a field of scientific training and research at the German College of Physical Culture (also known here by its abbreviation DHfK) and at institutes of physical training, which later became sport science departments at colleges and universities. The training of students and research work in various fields of swimming as a sport have helped considerably to promote swimming sports at schools, as a leisure activity and recreation and as a competitive sport.

Restoration of open-air baths and indoor swimming pools, the building of new swimming facilities, notably of standard public swimming pools, the introduction of mandatory swimming instruction at schools and centralized promotion of young sportsmen were some of the other relevant results that followed in the wake of the Youth Act.

"Nationale Sektion Schwimmen", which later became "Deutscher Schwimmsport-Verband der DDR" (also known here by its abbreviation DSSV) gained world-wide recognition as a result of this systematic development of swimming sports. GDR sportsmen could always rely on fraternal backing from sports supporters in the Soviet Union and other socialist states.

The following is a *sketch of the stages of development* in their chronological order:

1951: First successes achieved in the 9th Academic Summer Games within the framework of the World Festival in Berlin.

1952: Nationale Sektion Schwimmen der DDR granted membership of FINA and LEN.

1954: Two gold medals won at the European Championships in Turin, in which a GDR team took part for the first time.

1956: Six GDR swimmers take part in a joint German team at the 16th Olympic

Summer Games in Melbourne were they win a bronze medal (Eva-Maria ten Elsen – 200-metres Breaststroke event).

1958: "Nationale Sektion Schwimmen" becomes "Deutscher Schwimmsport-Verband" (DSSV) as sports in the GDR undergo a general reorganization. Physical culture and sports reached a high pitch of development by 1957 and Deutscher Turn- und Sportbund (DTSB) is set up as a unified sport organization of the GDR. The improved standard of performance of the GDR's swimmers is demonstrated at the 9th European Championship held in Budapest in 1958. The GDR team wins fifth place in the national score in both the women's (Bredius Cup) and the men's (European Cup) events and ahead of West Germany in both events.

1960: Olympic Games in Rome; Deutscher Schwimmsport-Verband supplies over half of the sportsmen for the joint German team. Two gold and three bronze medals are won by swimmers from the GDR.

1962: Efforts of the DSSV crowned with success: The GDR team comes first at the jubilee European Championships held in Leipzig. All association members demonstrate their enthusiasm.

1964: 23rd Summer Olympics in Tokyo. Swimmers of the DSSV make up two thirds of the athletes of the joint German tram thus demonstrating the uninterrupted progress made in the GDR's swimming sports. They return from Tokyo with a gold medal, five silver medals and other good results achieved in competitions with the world's best athletes.

1966: GDR's swimming athletes again demonstrate their leading role in Europe at the 11th European Championships in Utrecht. Only the Soviet team which is in an excellent condition outswim the GDR-athletes, who get 4 gold, 6 silver and 5 bronze medals.

1968: At the Olympic Games in Mexico the GDR has its own independent team of athletes. The medals won by the swimmers put them in third place behind the USA and Australia.

1970: The 12th European Championships are held in Barcelona. The DSSV's persistent work with the up-and-coming generation of young athletes produces the best results achieved at the championships of our continent to date. A total of 16 gold, 9 silver and 9 bronze medals put the GDR's swimmers and divers in a clear lead, followed by the Soviet team (6 gold, 4 silver and 8 bronze medals) and the FRG (4 gold, 6 silver and 4 bronze medals).

1972: GDR athletes compete in the Olympic Games in Munich as equals among equals. The 2 gold, 5 silver and 2 bronze medals won in swimming events and 2 bronze medals in high diving prove the steadily improving standard of performance of the GDR's swimmers. Numerous young athletes who came into prominence through the Spartakiad movement in the GDR advance into the finals and win medals.

1973: Men's and women's European Cups as well as the European Cup in high diving are won by GDR athletes.

The first world swimming championships are held in Belgrade. The 12 gold, 6 silver and 7 bronze medals and 290 points won by GDR athletes in swimming events put our team in second place behind the USA with 346 points. GDR athletes also secure second place behind the USA's springboard and firmboard divers (USA 36, GDR 30, Italy 26 points).

1974: GDR's swimmers consolidate their lead at the European Championships in Vienna. They get 17 gold, 14 silver and 4 bronze medals in swimming events and a silver medal in diving.

1975: The 2nd World Championships are held in Cali in Colombia. The DSSV team is placed 2nd behind the USA with 11 gold, 7 silver and 5 bronze medals.

1976: Olympic Games in Montreal. GDR's athletes win 20 medals, of which 11 are gold, 6 silver and 2 bronze in swimming events and achieve farther good results in the finals.

Similar successes were scored at these top-level competitions also in other important events, including rowing and canoe races, track and field, soccer, shooting, and many other events. They were possible thanks to the comprehensive promotion of sports by the Socialist Unity Party of Germany and by the socialist government of the GDR and the support by various public organizations.

The Constitution encourages all citizens to take part in and promote sports. A mass popular sports movement which includes mass participation by children and young people develops on this basis, the Sparta-kiad movement being its concrete expression. Nearly all GDR athletes who won medals at the 21st Summer Olympics in Montreal came up through the Spartakiad movement; this applies without exception to the GDR's athletes taking part in the swimming events.

The role of the water rescue service in the GDR is commensurate with its importance. The water rescue service, which had been run by the Deutscher Sportausschuss till 1952, became a special service operated by the German Red Cross which was re-established that year. A tight network of life-saving stations along the Baltic Sea coast and along the shores and banks of lakes and rivers helps protect many of our citizens from the danger of drowning. Courses for lifeguards are regularly being held in order to enable more and more people to save others from drowning.

The development of swimming in the German Democratic Republic shows the im-portance attached and promotion given to this sport in socialist society, which is so important for public health.

3.3. Development of modes of instruction for swimming

Not only swimming in general but also the methods used to develop the abilities and skills of a swimmer depend on the stage of social development and on the progress made in natural sciences.

In the first swimming manual, "Colymbe-tes", which we mentioned in the preceding section, the author instructed the reader in the art of swimming in the form of a dialogue. Breaststroke movements are in the foreground, the instructor, standing in the water, actively supporting the learner. The author recommended reed bundles, cork belts, animal bladders and other swimming aids, but he pointed out that these "buoyant aids" impede the swimmers movements and that through diligent exercise the learner should soon be able to do without them. Confidence exercises through which the learner gets used to water are not mentioned.

A work by the Italian author *de Bernardi* entitled: "A complete concept of swimming instruction based on new studies of the specific gravity of the human body", whose translation appeared in Germany in 1797, gave swimming instruction a fresh impetus. [11] *De Bernardi's* teaching was based on his physical research into buoyancy in water. He said that the beginner should first be convinced of the buoyancy of water and that buoyant aids such as animal bladders, cork, bottles, rushes, etc., tended to dishearten the novice.

But he was unable to assume a leading role in promoting the teaching of swimming because of fundamental errors in his system. One of these errors was his assumption that the human body is one eleventh lighter than an equal volume of water, which, owing to insufficient knowledge, he applied to all people without exception. He also objected to keeping the body in a horizontal position in water, which the thought was very unhealthy ("the internal organs and the arteries are subject to intense pressure, the chest is constricted"). He said that the swimmer should keep his body in water much as he does on land, namely in its natural, erect position. He rejected any movement to keep the body afloat because he was of the opinion that the body's buoyancy was enough to keep it on the surface. He thought that wrong movements could prejudice man's innate facility. The natural thing is the state of rest, movement is needed only for propelling the body through the water, he said. And yet de Bernardi can be regarded as the first known proponent of swimming instruction without the use of aids.

GutsMuths' outstanding merits in connection with teaching swimming should again be mentioned here. The method of swimming instruction he tried out in practical work in Schnepfenthal was described in a booklet entitled "Kleines Lehrbuch der Schwimmkunst zum Selbstunterricht" (Little textbook of the art of swimming for self-instruction), which appeared in 1798. In it GutsMuths described de Bernardi's method and the use of buoyant aids. For his part he preferred the latter method and developed the "angle" to protect the swimming instructor from the harmful effects of standing in water for prolonged periods. It also enabled the instructor to keep better watch over the swimmer and to correct him. GutsMuths also devised dry swimming aids with a view to facilitating the teaching of breaststroke movements and movements used for the more popular backstroke. But

he failed to take into account the different workings of the law of gravity, the reactive forces and the moment of inertia, which, due to differences in density and specific gravity between water on the one hand and air and solid ground on the other, require completely different muscular activity and strength patterns, although the movements are similar in form. He did realize though, that the swimmer should first build up a certain degree of confidence. For this reason he used the following three-tier system: water adjustment, land exercizes; swimming exercises in the water. His water adjustment phase was designed mainly to help the learner overcome the "unpleasant impressions" associated with water. He did not realise that one could help the learner get used to the new element and let him experience buoyancy through confidence-building exercises. GutsMuths' method of instruction was in keeping with the spirit of the time he lived in. Tuition was given mainly on an individual basis.

The angle technique of instruction developed by GutsMuths was regarded suitable and perfected by Pfuel for use in military training. Pfuel dispensed with all forms of confidence-building exercises and laid the emphasis on dry exercises and stylized swimming in accordance with a time beat. Parts of this method have survived and are still in use today because it is very convenient for the instructor and requires little paedagogic ability.

Seen in retrospect, Pfuel's merit lies mainly in the fact that he recognized the necessity of swimming instruction in the army and of young people in general and that he introduced important conditions to this end. Under his influence numerous military swimming facilities were built, the training of swimming instructors was encouraged and swimming instructions elaborated.

But drawbacks in Pfuel's method were recognized as early as the mid-19th century. In his Philonexia published in 1843 *Fuda* objected to the land exercises and buoyant aids: "Preliminary indoor exercises . . . are at least as useless. Moreover, I emphatically reject all kinds of swimming belts, swimming boards, cork vests, pig's bladders and reed bundles. They are superfluous in instruction, they are an impediment in self-instruction and they are dangerous if one relies on them." [24]

In his textbook "Ladebeck's Schwimmschule", which appeared in 1878, *Hermann Ladebeck,* who was a swimming instructor in Leipzig, described a method which completely dispensed with buoyant aids and which in many respects agrees with modern notions. [41] He had beginners carry out their first exercises in the non-swimmers' pool, their purpose being to get the learner used to water. The exercises comprised piking, straddle, diving and vigorous leg action in supine position. Ropes and ladders were used as aids. Ladebeck also recognized the value of the backstroke in instructing beginners. But *Ladebeck's* efforts did not produce the response hoped for, and *Pfuel's* drill method of instruction continued to predominate just as did gymnastic exercises after *Spiess.*

The technique of building up the beginner's confidence in shallow water began to be propagated by *Wiessner* only after the First World War. Prompted by the works of *Gaulhofer* and *Streicher* on "natural gymnastics" he wrote a book in 1925 entitled "Natürlicher Schwimmunterricht" (natural swimming instruction). Apart from the idealist stance taken by the bourgeois school reformers in their search for "natural" movements and their theory of man's spontaneous development, this reformist movement offered a real alternative to the method of instruction in the field of physical education that had prevailed up till then.

It became possible through *Wiessner's* work to conduct group instruction and to develop the basics of swimming in children in their first years of school, taking into account child psychology. The instruction pattern described in "Natürlicher Schwimmunterricht" shows that the author also recognized the need for multiform swimming instruction. According to his method, the learner starts out with confidence-building exercises, games, diving and other collective forms of basic exercises and then goes on to learn swimming techniques, the choice of simultaneous or alternating stroke forms being optional.

The problems involved in the teaching of swimming continued to be a source of controversy among swimming experts for a long time, the question of whether swimming tuition should be given with or without the use of buoyant aids continued to dominate the debate and in some cases it still has not been resolved. The most widely accepted concept that has evolved in the GDR can be described as follows:

1. Basic swimming instruction is sub-divided into two stages, which are closely interrelated. The basic skills connected with swimming, which are diving, jumping into the water, breathing, gliding and locomotion, which build confidence and which are the basis on which the beginner builds his or her ability to swim are taught in the first stage. The 2nd stage is designed mainly to develop swimming techniques with elementary co-ordination and to teach the associated starts and simple forms of turning.

2. Aids are used in such a way as to encourage the learner to come to grips with the new element and to make him aware of its physical properties.

3. Swimming aids worn on the trunk create a wrong notion in the learner's mind about his body's true behaviour in water and prevents the development of a sense of

buoyancy, for this reason they are not very suitable for use in basic instruction.

Boards, balls or other swimming aids can be used for arms in exercises in which only the legs are involved to enable the learner to concentrate on his leg movement.

4. Concessions can be made in cases of physically handicapped or mentally inhibited learners or where the local conditions prohibit the use of the principles mentioned in the foregoing.

And finally we should like to describe the main difference between the notions of the proponents of the method of teaching swimming with the help of swimming aids worn on the trunk (which is usually done in conjunction with land exercises) and of adherents of the method whose first and most important phase is adapting the learner to water. The former regard the main objective as exercising specific movement patterns, i. e., their main aim is developing the skill of "locomotion" using a certain swimming technique. The adherents of the latter approach assign priority in training to the beginner's coming to grips with water as an element in a variety of ways in order to enable him to develop the right way of acting in and under water. The techniques of swimming are then taught on this basis.

4. Swimming as a Sport

4.1. Development of different strokes, starts and turns

Strokes

There is evidence in literature and other forms of art handed down from centuries before the Christian era proving that strokes resembling our present swimming techniques were used in antiquity. The oldest descriptions of swimming on record and some pictures from antiquity suggest that strokes similar to those used today were used for propelling the body through the water. In *Homer's* "Odyssey" the author describes how "Odyssey spreads his arms in water" in order to propel himself. This suggests that he used a technique resembling the breaststroke. The crawl in use today is also described in records handed down to us from the past. It can be assumed that the backstroke was also used in antiquity, but no records or drawings describing how the stroke was executed have been found to date.

All strokes and swimming techniques were completely forgotten in Europe during the Middle Ages.

In Germany, the *breaststroke* technique is mentioned for the first time in 1538 by *Nicolaus Wynmann* in his book "Colymbetes". It is assumed that the movements used in the breaststroke as described in the book imitated those of frogs in the water. As the sport developed in Europe the process of differentiation of the techniques of swimming progressed.

The first reports about the *"side stroke"* came from Great Britain in 1840. The legs executed a scissors kick while the arms moved in the water. Later on one arm was swung forward above the water.

In 1873, *Trudgen,* an Englishman, brought a new technique to Europe from South America in which the scissors movement of the legs is retained but the swimmer propels himself through the water through alternate overarm movements.

This stroke gave rise to the development in Germany of the technique known here as the overhand stroke in which the swimmer used the alternate overhand movement but in which he executed the breaststroke kick.

Healy, an Australian, showed *a new crawl technique* during a swimming festival in Hamburg in 1906. He co-ordinated the alternate overhand movement with the leg kick, which he also executed alternately, raising his calves above the water and vigorously kicking his shins and insteps against the water. This technique then evolved as the crawl stroke. The last major improvement in the crawl was made in 1912 by *Kahanamoku.* He executed the alternate kick, which became known as the flutter kick, with both legs completely immersed in water. This technique has survived without any fundamental changes up to this day (cf. Fig. Crawl technique).

The *backstroke* has been developing along

with the breaststroke since the 18th century. GutsMuths taught both in the course of his 30-odd years of swimming tutorship at Schnepfenthal. The movements made while the swimmer lies face upward, especially the kick, resemble those used with the breaststroke. While the legs execute a breaststroke kick, the arms are brought outward and sideways in the water and pressed vigorously towards the thighs. This form of swimming, which is still known here as the "popular backstroke", has evolved into the old English backstroke. The kick remained unchanged, but the arms were later thrown back from the shoulders and pressed towards the thighs to be swung back again simultaneously above the water to repeat the cycle.

As the crawl stroke became known at the beginning of the 20th century the backstroke technique was developed into *back crawl*. *Hebner,* an American, showed this new technique for the first time in Europe at the Olympic Games in Stockholm in 1912. His winning time was clocked at 1:21.2, which put him 1 second ahead of *Fahr,* a German swimmer, who still used the simultaneous stroke. The back crawl stroke was used more and more in competitive sports. The old English backstroke became one of the forms of popular swimming. The simultaneous kick is particularly important in life-saving work. The basic features of the back crawl stroke have remained unchanged since that time.

The development of the *butterfly stroke* started in 1930. Athletes and coaches sought new ways to improve the breaststroke technique in order to achieve better times. The development of the butterfly started when swimmers moved their arms down to their thighs and then swung them forward toward the wall above the water before turning and before reaching the finish. This series of movements was repeated and the new butterfly stroke came into being. At first it was used only over short distances – mostly at the beginning or in the final sprint – in breaststroke events. This technique was given official recognition by FINA on 1 January 1935.

But improved methods of training enabled swimmers to swim increasing distances with butterfly in breaststroke events and there was the danger of the traditional breaststroke disappearing from the programme of competitive events altogether. Another change was made in the rules of competition to halt this development. The breaststroke and the butterfly became two independent strokes.

Further efforts were made after the FINA resolution of 1935 to improve the butterfly technique.

Jack *Sieg,* a swimmer from the University of Iowa tried a new leg movement in 1935 by kicking his feet up and down at the same time in a manner resembling the movement of a dolphin's tail. Working together with *Armbruster,* his coach, he was able to tie this kick in with the butterfly arm movement. He swam the 100-yard event in 1:00.2.

Fejer and *Tumpek,* both Hungarian swimmers, played a major role in developing the butterfly stroke in Europe by introducing the so-called dolphin movement.

The dolphin movement was co-ordinated with the butterfly stroke and became an independent swimming style. The use of the dolphin movement in competitive events was approved by FINA in 1953.

The basic features of the breaststroke technique hardly changed at all in the centuries that passed since it was rediscovered by *Wynmann.* The sequence of movements was slightly improved only in 1925/26. The long sideways pull of the arms gave way to a *short pull of the arms,* which enabled a faster sequence of movements to be introduced. The wide straddle kick was replaced by the *lower leg swing movement*.

This improvement, just as the butterfly stroke mentioned earlier, came into being as a result of efforts to achieve better times within the constraints of existing rules of competition. After the decision had been taken by FINA to include the two independent swimming styles in the competition progamme, efforts were continued to raise the speed of the breaststroke by improving the technique. Prompted by Japanese swimmers, who dived over considerable distances in competitive breaststroke events, athletes in almost all countries in which there was competitive swimming practised the *underwater breaststroke* (Japanese style). After diving the swimmer pulled his arms down to his thighs and then recovered by moving them up close to his body and stretching them. The leg action remained unchanged.

This modification meant a further change in the orthodox breaststroke. From May 1957 FINA prohibited prolonged swimming under water and introduced stricter rules on the breaststroke under which the swimmer was allowed only *one* dive stroke after the start and after each turn, the rest of the time the swimmer's head had to stay above the water.

In the breaststroke just as in all other fields of competitive sports efforts to improve performance are continuing by modifying the technique within the framework of existing rules of competition and by improving training methods. There are also other interactions between the training method and the swimming technique.

Experience gathered in raising the stroke frequency in alternate-stroke swimming styles was made use of in the breaststroke. In some cases the stroke frequency was increased to the point where the gliding phase

so typical of the breaststroke disappeared almost entirely. There are several technique variants between this form, in which the arm movement is more vigorous and the legs are thrust back in short calf movements directed more towards the rear rather than being swung out so far, and the old orthodox form characterized by the long passive gliding phase, shorter arm movements and wide calf swing. It is only natural that the trend towards faster stroke frequency has asserted itself, but the body is in a fully stretched position at the end of each stroke cycle.

Starts

The start has also gone through a series of evolutionary phases before it reached its present form. In the old days of competitive swimming the swimmers started from a swimming position. In Germany, the racing dive was introduced for members of the "Deutscher Schwimmverband" in 1912. Swimmers organized in the "Deutsche Turnerschaft" continued to use the old push-off start in swimming position until 1920, while swimmers belonging to the "Arbeiter-Wassersport-Verband" used the racing dive start, except in the case of the backstroke, which they also started from the swimming position.

The racing dive from the edge of the pool was used with all swimming styles in Germany from 1920; four years later the start in backstroke events was changed back to the swimming position.

The starting command has also experienced numerous changes. Today the command is only an acoustic signal or a flag signal (in the case of deaf athletes) preceded by the starter's comand "Take your marks!".

At the 1952 Olympic Games in Helsinki some athletes started by pushing off from the gutter. It resembled a backward jump start. But the international rules of competition (FINA) put a stop to this and prescribed he backstroke start used today, in which both feet must be fully immersed. The start from the starting block has been in general use in all other swimming styles since the Olympic Games of 1936.

Turns

The internationally valid standard lane length is 50 metres. Records are recognized only if they are swum in lanes of this length. Lanes are usually shorter in most indoor swimming pools (33^1/$_3$ metres, 25 metres or even less).

In most events the distance to be swum is a multiple of the standard lane length, which means that the swimmers must change their swimming direction by 180 degrees one or several times in the course of a race, i.e., they have to "turn". A 1500-metres event, for instance, involves 29 turns. This fact stresses the importance of *turns* in swimming competitions. Each badly done turn costs time. Changes in pool design (pools shallow on one side, beam borders, pools of even depth, etc.) have had a telling effect on the development of turn styles and turning techniques.

A wide range of factors, which have been taken into account in the rules of competition, have played a role in the quest for more effective techniques from the stand-up and beam turns used years ago to the deep turns used today. The swimmers must touch the wall with one or both hands, depending on the swimming style, or only with any part of the body (in the case of freestyle). Between the time they touch the wall with their hands and push off with their feet they may execute any movement or turn. The push-off from the wall must be executed with both legs. The turns authorized for all swimming styles can be classified into three groups. The main feature of the turn is the position of the head in relation to the surface of the water during the turn. Thus, depending on the head position, turns are grouped into high turns, flat turns and deep turns (cf. "Definitions", p. 260)

Any of these turns can be used with the four swimming styles and with set-style swimming. But since there is still plenty of room for improvement in the turning technique, the sequences of movement used in turns will continue to be subject to frequent changes in efforts to improve records.

4.2. Basic swimming instruction

Objectives of basic swimming instruction

The object of basis swimming instruction is to teach people how to swim, i. e., to enable them to feel safe in water and to propel themselves through water in the desired direction. This instruction will give the learner the fundamental skills and abilities, which he can improve or in which he can specialize according to his inclinations or objective requirements in a special field or area of application (cf. Chart 2 on p.). To achieve this objective the learner must undergo a comprehensive programme of swimming instruction consisting of *two stages,* between which there is no fixed delineation but which differ in the subject matter of instruction. In the *first stage* the novices are taught the five basic swimming skills (diving, jumping into the water, gliding, locomotion and breathing), which give the beginner a sense of security in water and which form the basis of the art of swimming.

In the *second stage* the techniques used in swimming styles, starts and turns are in the foreground.

It is essential that the conditions under which swimming instruction is to be given are checked to make certain that the learners are not endangered in any way; this applies to all forms of tuition (continuous instruction over an extended period or training courses), of the athletic facilities available (indoor or open-air swimming pools, deep or shallow water) and to all ages and both sexes of learners. The following "organizational notes" are designed with this objective in mind.

Organizational notes

All advantages and beneficial effects of swimming are forfeited unless good sense and discretion are used. Overexertion and lack of discipline can bring disastrous consequences not only to those concerned but also to others. The following is a summary of the basic rules to be observed in bathing and swimming:

Swimming rules

1. Do not swim by yourself.
2. Cool off by wetting face, armpits and chest before immersion.
3. Do not stand still, move around vigorously when in water.
4. Do not stay too long in the water; blue lips, violent shivering and goose-pimples are indications to come out.
5. Dry well after swimming, take off wet swimming suit and put on warm clothing. Gymnastics and games help to warm up the body again.
6. Do not bathe or swim if you do not feel well.
7. Do not go into the water on a full stomach.
8. Do not overexert yourself.
9. Do not scream or romp in the water. Do not call for help in fun; do not dip or push others into the water.
10. Do not leave the area marked off for bathing.
11. Always obey the instructions of persons in charge.

But the instructor (sports or swimming instructor, coach, trainer) must know more than just these rules. It is his task to help educate young people in the spirit of our social development, in which the communist education of the young generation is particularly important. His duties include feeling responsible for the lives of young people entrusted to him. If he or she fails to meet these obligations he or she will have to face the full consequences.

Instructor's duties

Under the legal liability stipulations, the instructor is responsible for the safety of his pupils. The instructor is expected to use all his physical and professional abilities, the most progressive methods of education and to have the highest sense of responsibility in order to avert any possible danger to the learners.

All teachers assigned to watch over the safety of others during swimming instruction must have well-founded knowledge, abilities and skills in the field of life-saving and in resuscitation and they must constantly try to improve them. Analogously this also applies to all persons in charge who accompany groups of children on excursions, hikes go swimming or bathing with them. [8] In addition to the basic briefings which the person in charge should give the young athletes before commencing swimming training, the following should be taken into account:

1. The state of health of pupils entrusted to an instructor must be checked by a physician (school medical officer or sports physician). Special attention should be paid to the heart and the ears. Persons with contagious diseases, skin rashes, festering wounds are not allowed to swim. If the instructor neglects his obligation to watch over the children's safety and if it is proved that a disease is aggravated as a result of a

learner being exposed to water or that other persons are contaminated he can be made liable.

2. Preliminary familiarization with the swimming pool, checking and repairing equipment and aids are part of the preparatory work that must be done before starting swimming instructions.

This means:

– swimming zones in lakes and rivers and in the open sea should be marked off;

– the non-swimmer zone should be clearly marked;

– all sources of danger (water plants, reeds, bog, rocks, rubble, etc.) should be removed and the condition of the site (sand, rocky ground, gradients, abysses, etc.) should be checked and the requisite facilities and equipment, such as dressing-rooms, toilets and showers, emergency and first aid facilities, diving boards, swimming zone limits and rescue equipment should be checked to make sure that they are in order.

3. Before commencing swimming instruction the learners must be briefed on how they should behave during swimming instruction, when dressing, in the shower-rooms (thorough drying after swimming, especially of the ears and hair is particularly important), near and in the water. The danger of slipping in indoor swimming pools is great and should be stressed.

4. Discipline and good organization are a cardinal rule in swimming instruction. The intensity and success of a swimming lesson and prevention of accidents largely depend on them.

If possible a class should consist of no more than 15 learners, bigger classes are difficult to keep watch over. The instructor should know at all times how many learners were present at the beginning of a lesson and he must be able to account for all learners during and especially after the lesson. Organizational forms in and out of the water

should be well-thought out. Suitable organizational forms make it possible to conduct swimming instruction efficiently and safely (this is particularly important in diving).

The exercises and the standard of performance required should be adjusted to the pupil's age and to their performance capacity.

Beware of overexertion!

Children who have just recovered from a serious illness should be treated with special care. This also applies to people suffering from diseases of the eyes and ears.

Teacher's instructions should always be obeyed. If a pupil is told by the teacher to come out of the water as a result of breach of discipline, shivering, not feeling well, etc., the pupil should put on some dry clothes without delay lest he or she could catch cold. It should be checked to make sure that such pupils comply with these rules.

The swimming instructor should wear a swimming suit or sports clothing in order to be able to help immediately should the need arise. A bathing gown or a sweat suit and appropriate footwear should be worn as protection against cold (the teacher should take good care of his own health as well). He should be near the edge of the pool or at some other elevated point in order to be able to see and be seen by his pupils at all times. If he has to demonstrate movement patterns in water himself, the children should get out of the pool and line up in an orderly manner along the edge of the pool to watch the demonstration.

All learners should be instructed not to separate from the group without asking the teacher's or instructor's permission. If a child is found missing, it is imperative that the person in charge should consider the possibility of an accident. In such a case all pupils must be ordered by the swimming instructor in charge to get out of the water. A search party should carry out a search of the toilets, shower rooms and adjoining rooms and of the premises around the training facility. The bath superintendent should be informed immediately. Life-saving swimmers, if present, should immediately start searching in the water.

Significance of objective conditions for success of basic instruction

Successful swimming instruction depends to a considerable extent on the objective conditions, which include the state of the training facility and of the available training equipment and the air and water temperature. Often the person in charge of swimming instruction will have little if any influence on these conditions. In such cases he should carefully devise a plan of instruction that would enable him to adapt methodically and organizationally to the existing conditions.

But the teacher or instructor should not come to term with all conditions. In many instances existing training conditions can be improved through initiative or with support from such quarters as the local mayor, headmaster, pool superintendent or sports officials and the efficiency of training can be raised considerably.

1. If training instruction is given while the swimming facility is open to the public, the training area should be marked off in agreement with the pool supervisor in charge and no persons other than those belonging to the class should be permitted to enter the area.

2. All detrimental influences coming from without such as loud noise or unruly behaviour on the part of bathers (this applies particularly to public baths) should be eliminated in order to create a proper atmosphere for the swimming instruction. Otherwise the pupil will not be able to concentrate properly and will feel hampered and anxious as a result.

To reduce these difficulties to a minimum the instructor should, in cooperation with the pool supervisor and, if the need arises, with the headmaster or the local district committee for swimming, consider all relevant factors in order to work out the best possible time schedule for conducting swimming instruction. Swimming instruction sessions should be held before the bulk of the public turns up.

3. The instructor's methodical work is facilitated by swimming aids (swimming and diving hoops, reach poles and gliding boards, swimming rungs, cf. Swimming

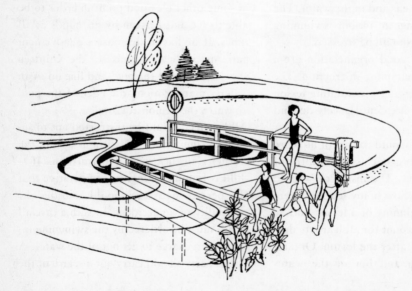

Fig. 1

aids). He should see to it that such aids are procured. Most equipment of this kind is not very expensive.

4. Efforts should be made not only to obtain swimming aids but also to erect push-off walls at every bathing place, including bathing resorts on lakes, rivers and along the Baltic coast. Such a wall can be built by boarding up the side of an existing pier facing the bathing place, only a few boards being required for this purpose (Fig. 1). It is important to make sure that there is enough room between the edge of the foot-bridge and the push-off wall for a secure hold. If there are no gangways, then provisional gangways or push-off should be built, from which the teacher can watch and instruct his pupils. In this way the bathing place gets a fixed boundary to one side, which makes for a higher measure of safety and better organization. Swimming facilities have also been built on open water with good results by using pontoons. [7]

5. The duration of a person's stay in the water depends on the water and air temperature. The principle that effective instruction cannot be conducted when the learners are cold should be borne in mind. The younger the learners, the more important it is to have higher water temperatures to achieve good results. This is due to the fact that the adaptability of their circulatory system to cold water has not yet reached the level of development of that of adults; the subcutaneous layer of fatty tissue in young children is still much thinner in relation to their body weight than in adults. The best water temperatures for children of pre-school age and for younger school children are 25 to 27 degrees.

The instructor can often tell when it is time for individual members of his class or for the whole class to get out of the water by their bluish lips, paleness, goose-pimples and insufficient concentration. It is not possible to fix a generally valid length for the period of instruction. However, empirical values show that even 5- to 6-year-olds can stay in the water for up to 60 minutes if the water temperature is around 27 degrees and if the proper method of instruction is used.

It is imperative that the children be given an opportunity to warm up by doing suitable exercises or playing games before and after swimming if the water is colder; sometimes a swimming training session can be interrupted by such exercises and games.

The question as to *how often* training sessions are to be held has been clearly answered by numerous studies. Frequent training within a definite period of time produces better results. The best results are achieved through regular daily instruction. [39]

A *duration* of 30 instruction units under favourable weather and water conditions is recommended, for instance, for children in older pre-school age brackets in order to develop in them a feeling of confidence in water and swimming ability. Three training sessions per week has brought good results. But four training sessions a week or even daily training is possible without overexerting the children. [46] Such a training complex is given in the form of a course. Holiday swimming courses play an increasingly important role in instructing children living in areas without suitable training facilities. Such courses should last for at least three weeks, and at two training sessions per day, the total length of instruction at the end of this courses is about 35 hours, which is about the time prescribed for the first instruction complex under the curriculum presently in force in our comprehensive polytechnical secondary schools. This period of instruction is sufficiently long to enable the child to learn the basic skills of diving, jumping, gliding, locomotion, breathing and to develop the co-ordinated movements involved in an alternating stroke style (back or front crawl) and in the breaststroke.

Experience has shown that a learner from the first age bracket onward should attend at least two training sessions a week in order to complete the course of instruction successfully on an extracurricular basis.

In the case of adults the duration of their period of basic instruction will depend a great deal on their degree of confidence in water and on the amount of experience they have in movement. But with them too the best results are achieved by attending a course of instruction with daily training sessions. As a rule a two- to three-week course is sufficient for adults.

4.3. Developing basic swimming skills (first stage of basic instruction)

4.3.1. Tasks and contents of first stage

A person wishing to learn how to swim should first adjust himself to the water as a new element in his experience. The body is propelled through the water in a nearly horizontal position using both the upper and the lower extremities and utilizing the physical properties of water. To learn this method of locomotion in the water the beginner must collect new movement experience, which differs completely from his or her previous experience on land.

It is very important to know the physical properties of water in order to be able to move about in it. One should not only know them, but also feel them. This is particularly important with regard to specific gravity, Archimede's principle, cohesive force of water molecules, low compressibility of water and pressure conditions in water. Getting used to moving about in water in-

volves a lengthy process of differentiation and development of reflex reactions in response to the external forces and conditions encountered in water. Such external forces are first and foremost the *force of gravity*, which one hardly feels in the water as a result of the relations of specific gravity existing in that element, *water resistance*, which, on the one hand, must be made use of in order to propel one's body through the water, and which, on the other hand, must be overcome because it impedes motion, but *moment of inertia*, which requires other muscle concentrations in the water than on land, and the *forces of friction*, which offer a much firmer support for pushing off on land than in water, while friction in the water is greater than in the air. The learner must also overcome unconditioned reflexes, notably the labyrinthine and balance reflex, which elicit contractions in the throat muscles via the vestibulary system in order to move the head into a position in which the crown of the head is at the top. He must also learn to control the eyelid reflex whose function normally is to protect the eye from harmful influence by closing the lids at the slightest excitation of the eye. But the swimmer should be able to orientate himself also under water, which means that the unconditioned reflex must yield to a conditioned reflex enabling the swimmer to keep his eyes open under water.

To feel safe and to act in the water in line with requirements one should meet the following minimum demands: One should be able to jump from a height of 1 to 3 metres into deep water without feeling any fear, dive beneath the surface, open his eyes to find his bearings, assume a swimming position (breaststroke or backstroke position) and swim in a specified direction by using one's extremities covering a distance of about 25 metres and breathing rhythmically in the process.

To be able to do all these things at the same time, one must have the following basic skills:

Swimming with open eyes under water,
jumping into deep water from a point above the water level,
gliding in prone and supine positions,
locomotion by using arms and legs,
breathing – deliberate regular inhalation and exhalation.

One can see from this list of skills that more is involved here than just "getting used to water" in the usual sense.

Swimming under water

To feel safe in water it is important that one should be able to *swim under water*. Whoever has learned to swim under water, to get his bearings under water and swim towards a specified goal, will in most cases be able to act in an appropriate manner even if he should suddenly find himself under water unexpectedly.

In addition to the labyrinthine reflexes and eyelid reflex, the human body reacts to the carbon dioxide concentration in blood, which increases the longer one holds one's breath under water and which acts as a stimulus on the respiratory centre. As a result one tries to get one's head above the water as soon as possible in order to be able to breathe.

Through proper demonstration and explanation, which should be adapted to the level of development of the learners, it should be shown that one should not press the air while swimming under water and that one should let the air out gradually. The instructor should choose coaching forms in which stimuli are applied in controlled doses enabling the learner gradually to overcome unconditioned reflexes and, by systematically increasing the stimuli, to develop conditioned reflexes, which can be voluntarily controlled, thereby enabling the pupil to stay under water longer. In the course of further training the beginner learns to move about under water, to orientate himself and to find and carry objects under water.

Usually the ability to swim under water is developed in conjunction with other fundamental swimming skills, especially with jumping into the water and with gliding after push-off or racing dive.

The beginner also experiences the buoying force of the water. It takes an effort to dive down to specified depths in order to retrieve objects or to move in water at a specified depth. In the process the beginner gathers valuable experience in counteracting buoyancy or utilizing it in swimming. There is also a close interaction between swimming under water and conscious breathing. These multiform relations between basic skills should be taken into account in deciding on the structure and system of training sessions.

Jumping into the water

Jumping into the water is an important part of instruction because it helps the beginner build up confidence in water. It promotes the formation of such valuable character traits as resolution, willpower and courage and gives the novice an opportunity to become aware of the influences exerted on his body when it suddenly enters the water from a certain height above water level. Friction, water resistance, water pressure and buoyancy act on his body in the process. The first jumping exercises are carried out feet first from low heights above water level into hip- or chest-deep water. This variant of jumping is an extension of the basic skill of jumping which a child normally acquires in his or her third year of life. In executing these jumps the beginner touches bottom with his feet and his head comes up above the water once he straightens out.

The learner feels that the water brakes the fall and prevents a hard impact.

Gradually the learner is taught to jump into increasingly deeper water reaching up to his neck, his mouth and his eyes. At this stage the learner often does not touch bottom at all or only slightly so. The buoying force of water forces him up, enabling him to keep his head above the water. The sense of buoyancy, which is developed through other exercises, is reinforced in this manner. The learner's sense of buoyancy is further consolidated by jumping into deeper water. As the learner learns to jump into deeper water he is also gradually conditioned to jump into chest- to neck-deep water, head first from steps, ladder rungs or from the gutter using the "frog leap" or "fall-in" technique. Concrete objectives, such as retrieving objects from the bottom or diving through a hoop helps learners, especially children to execute the dives. This also helps to inhibit the posture and balance reflexes and to develop the gliding position after pushing off and after the racing start (see also section on gliding).

The instructor must take the necessary steps to make sure that those practising jumping and those already in the water are not endangered, this is especially important in deeper water.

Jumping is important not only for getting used to the physical conditions of water, for forming correct habits in the water, for developing positive character traits but it also produces positive emotional influences. If the skills of jumping into the water are developed in accordance with "didactic principles", the learners will derive a great deal of enjoyment from these exercises, which can be varied time and time again to make them more exciting; there are also many informal diving forms which can be used.

Gliding

The decisive step in the transition from being a non-swimmer to being a swimmer is made when the learner learns to push himself off from the pool wall or from the ground of a lake or river and to glide through the water in a horizontal position. Having learned this the beginner can now proceed to use his extremities efficiently to propel his body in the water. "Gliding", which is one of the basic skills of swimming, is taught in stages.

First of all the learner should learn to assume a horizontal position and to balance his body in this position in the water. He experiences *static buoyancy* by practising the "outstretched float", which he is required to know how to do in prone and supine positions (Fig. 2).

In the second phase of training the learner is acquainted with *dynamic buoyancy*. He feels how the buoying force is strengthened when the body is propelled through the water by assistance from others (reach pole, partner) or by the thrust produced from his own push-off. Through this training the pupil learns the most appropriate body position for gliding through the water in outstretched prone and supine positions. In this position the learner must stretch his body from finger to toe, hold his arms stretched out, the hands are folded together flat, the head is kept between the upper arms, the legs are kept close together.

Once the learner has successfully experienced gliding through the water he can start learning the swimming movements which propel his body through the water. We should like to stress that under no circum-

Fig. 2

stances should the pupil omit learning the basic skill of gliding or fail to learn this skill properly before going on to the next stage of instruction. Gliding remains an essential exercise throughout the process of learning to swim and in subsequent athletic training: it is the basis for learning the different styles of swimming and of the different starts and turns.

Locomotion

Unlike on land, where man moves about almost exclusively with the aid of his lower extremities, *locomotion in the water* is effected by using one's *arms and legs,* the arms being even more important than legs in most swimming styles (crawl, backstroke and butterfly). Owing to the fact that the physical conditions in the water differ completely from those encountered on land, the beginner must elaborate new reflex complexes to enable him to respond to the influence of the new external forces through new forms of co-ordinated arm and leg action.

There are numerous ways of using one's extremities to propel one's body through the water. Currently four forms of locomotion predominate in swimming, known as swimming styles. They are crawl, back crawl, breaststroke and butterfly stroke. Efficiency, economy and speed were the main criteria which determined their dominant position. The pupil should learn all four swimming styles in the course of swimming instruction to get a good basic training. The sequence in which they should be learned depends largely on the specific objectives set and on the age of the learner.

Young people being instructed in the People's Army should first be taught the breaststroke, because this is the most suitable style for overcoming water obstacles in combat conditions without causing much noise and carrying one's field pack. On the other hand children of pre-school age and of early school age should start with the crawl stroke.

The reasons are:

Firstly, the alternating pull action of the arms is more beneficial for the mobility of the spinal column and for proper body posture than the simultaneous arm movement in the case of the breaststroke.

Secondly, alternating movements and transverse co-ordination (crawling, toddling, walking, climbing, running) predominate in the process of development of locomotion in babies and small children. Thus it is easier for a child to learn the alternating movements used in the crawl stroke.

Thirdly, by exercising the complementary crawl technique in prone and supine positions the pupil learns the essentials of two swimming styles and the way is paved for teaching him the butterfly stroke with dolphin kick, which has many characteristics in common with crawl.

Fourthly, the greater importance attached to the alternating stroke in competitive swimming (freestyle and backstroke account for over 70 per cent of the Olympic events) should also be mentioned in this connection.

An elementary training programme in water polo and in synchronized swimming can also be built up on the basis of alternating stroke forms of locomotion in water.

Owing to the fact that at present swimming instruction is given mainly to children (and this will probably be the case in future as well), we shall concentrate our attention on teaching with the aid of alternating stroke patterns in the first phase of instruction dealt with in the following.

Despite the fact that leg action contributes less to propelling the body in water than does arm action in most swimming styles, the principle of teaching the leg movement sequence first, followed by arm movement and then by the co-ordinated arm and leg movement has asserted itself in modern swimming instruction. The flutter kick in prone and supine positions, which is relatively easy to learn, propels the body continuously through the water. It enables the swimmer to keep his body in a streamlined position, in which the chest is somewhat higher than the abdomen. A good hydrodynamic position adjusted to the speed is important to enable the swimmer to swing his arms forward above the water and to work his legs in the water at an appropriate depth.

For this reason the beginner is first taught the kick. He should learn to use his legs and feet well enough to be able to cover a distance of 20 to 25 metres.

There are also a number of exercises designed to prepare the learner for the alternate arm stroke movements. In this connection it should be pointed out that teaching the crawl technique by way of the "dog-paddle" technique is unpractical and tends only to prolong the learning process. For this reason it is important to make sure that the learner raises his arms properly out of the water. The beginner learns this technique in its elementary form at an early stage. At the end of the first phase of instruction the beginner achieves a certain measure of co-ordination between the arm and leg movements, but at this stage he should not be expected to co-ordinate his breathing rhythm to this as well.

Breathing

Proper, effective *breathing* is important in all sports if good performance is to be achieved. This is particularly true of sports requiring a great deal of endurance. Proper breathing is even more important in swimming, because of the increased metabolic activity, of the pressure the chest is exposed to in the water while inhaling and of the re-

sistance that has to be overcome when exhaling into the water. An optimum rhythmic movement can be maintained over a prescribed distance in the cyclic sequence of movements used in a given swimming style only by using a perfect breathing technique executed automatically. That is why it is important to pay attention to a learner's breathing from the very first lesson. The integration of breathing processes into the movement pattern of individual swimming techniques is a complex process, which as a rule takes several years of systematic practice to stabilize.

Owing to the specific conditions under which a swimmer practises his sport, he should get used to *inhaling only through the mouth*. Due to the fact that the swimmer's head is constantly in the water the swimmer is likely to get water into his sinuses through the nasal cavities, which would interrupt his rhythm of movement and could result in disruption of the entire movement co-ordination.

On the other hand, *exhalation* should be through the *mouth* and *nose,* in this way any water that might enter the nose despite oral inhalation is blown out.

Controlled exhalation should be practised during basic instruction. This is done by forcefully blowing e.g. at small balls, floating plastic objects, etc., against the water and underneath the surface. Later on, this exercise is linked with controlled inhalation through the mouth.

In the course of his further training the pupil learns to link the rhythmic inhalation and exhalation to the cyclic arm and leg movements. The learner practises turning his head sideways when preparing for the crawl stroke. Already at this stage sufficient attention should be paid to co-ordinating breathing with the movement cycle.

At the end of the first phase of swimming instruction the learner should be able to make integrated use of his newly-acquired basic skills. He should be able to enter and come out of deep water without assistance. At this stage a swimmer should not be expected to meet certain standards in any given swimming technique, but he should be taught the basics for learning the different swimming styles. For children it is recommended to start with crawl and back crawl and then proceed to the dolphin or breaststroke styles. But this rule should not be applied dogmatically; the main thing to bear in mind is to make sure that the learner learns all swimming styles if possible and that he does not neglect the other fields of swimming.

4.3.2. Methods and means used in the first phase

The objectives outlined in the foregoing make it necessary for the learner to get used to the new conditions encountered in the water and to gather experience that will enable him to propel himself through the water. This process of teaching the pupil how to act and move about properly in the water is facilitated if the pupil is assisted by an experienced swimming instructor. [52] (Many people acquire swimming skills on their own. But in most instances the movement patterns acquired in this manner do not comply with the principles of efficiency and economy and they do not come up to the standard of a swimming style.)

By knowing the routine of the learning process in the three characteristic phases of elementary co-ordination, fine co-ordination and stabilization of movement (after *Meinel*) the instructor is able to organize swimming instruction in such a manner that the learner becomes consciously aware of the proper way of acting in the water by actively coming to grips with the new element.

New tasks are set in conformity with good teaching principles, taking into account the principles of instruction according to a certain plan and system, of clear and understandable presentation and of reinforcement of skills already learned.

The methods and means of instruction should be chosen in such a way as to ensure that the skills of movement and physical abilities are developed in the shortest possible time and that they become permanently assimilated.

The best way to introduce the pupil to a new movement is to demonstrate it to him. If the pupil is properly motivated he will be receptive and the demonstration will help him to form a visual idea of the movement. The demonstration should be immediately followed by practice, because the concrete idea of the movement takes shape in the course of a pupil's own execution of it in the water through the kinaesthetic motor analyser in conjunction with his optical and tactile perception. Explanatory and corrective remarks, adjusted to the pupil's level of mental development, supports this process.

The method using practical exercise helps to develop movement skills and to form co-ordinative and conditional abilities. For this reason both aspects should be taken into account in planning each instruction unit. Repetition of the exercises within a specified length of time should be properly balanced between the load and the relaxation phases and adjusted to the level of development reached. The use of certain forms of competition are the principal way of raising the level of physical abilities and of further improving the quality of movement control.

The instructor uses various means to implement the methods in practice. This shows that methods and means are directly interdependent. The method is the route by which a certain aim is to be achieved, while the means are designed to complete the process successfully and as quickly as possible.

The means in the wider sense include styles and exercise forms, routines of exercise complexes (e.g., in the case of the interval method: standard distance sections, relaxations sections, break organization) and aids which help the learner directly, such as optical or acoustic signals (they also include pacemaker systems, brake clocks, telemetric equipment, walkie-talkies and other equipment used in competitive sports training).

Use of equipment aids

Equipment aids play an important part in promoting the learning process in the entire field of athletic training.

They are an adjunct to the methods of the instructor.

Methodical aids proved themselves in practice a long time ago and they have become indispensable in instruction.

1. They support the acquisition of complete and correct ideas of movement.

2. They promote the development of movement skills.

3. They help achieve a faster rate of performance improvement.

In most cases they resemble preliminary exercises, which make it possible to learn difficult movements routines. They enable the learner to concentrate more on the exercise to be performed, and since they are especially useful in helping the inhibited child overcome fear they are an important educational factor.

They enable the teacher to add variety and excitement to instruction, to stimulate the learners interest, to raise the intensity and to achieve better performance.

Selection and use of aids

The following swimming aids have proved useful time and again for basic training:
– little plastic boats or floating animals, soap-boxes, little balls and similar floating articles
– hoops
– objects to be retrieved by diving
– gliding poles
– multi-purpose swimming rung devise
– floats

We should like to point out once again that the purpose of these aids is to support swimming instruction, and *support* does not mean that this should be the only methodical approach. It would be wrong to assign aids a central position in instruction and to confine tuition to the possibilities offered by such aids. But the aids can be very useful if used wisely. They are used for teaching swimming under water, diving, gliding, locomotion or breathing and solving individual organizational tasks. One should choose the most suitable aids.

Game and exercise equipment is used with a view to achieving certain results, such as getting the learners used to a certain *order*. For this purpose the pupils should be familiarized with the intended organizational forms and their terms while they are still on land. Another purpose is to get the learners *adjusted to water* with the aid of games adapted to the age group in question. Concentrating their attention on the game or exercise device helps them overcome their initial fear of water and makes it easier for them to get used to their new environment. In addition, the use of toys stimulates their intensely felt need for movement. In this playful process they learn to execute movements which they could not learn at all or only to a very limited extent otherwise.

Methodical aids are also used to help the learner to develop *self reliance* in water and to *learn movement routines.* The successes experienced in the process boost the learner's selfconfidence and are a source of continuous inspiration to make fresh efforts. It is amazing how much patience and endurance even children of pre-school age have in practising certain movement routines. And finally game and exercise devices are used for movement training. They are useful in teaching certain important movement components.

The *use of swimming aids* (cork belts, inflated pockets, etc.) such as *artificial buoyant aids* (worn at the body's centre of gravity) is rejected in modern swimming instruction. "Athletic movements are more than just a mere biomechanical process, they are a complex manifestation. They are purposive functions which make demands on a person, they are forms of a person's actively coming to grips with his environment". [52] The philosophy underlying our modern instruction is based on this realization. Applied to swimming this means that the necessary conditions must be created for the learning process. The novice should be familiarized with water before commencing movement exercises in order to enable him to cope with the new physical conditions and to get him accustomed to new stimuli such as cold, water pressure and more difficult breathing conditions.

To start the learning process without meeting these conditions would mean limiting success to a minimum. Getting adjusted to water by being in water and especially experiencing and feeling the upward buoying force cannot be replaced by examples, lucid explanations or industrious land exercises. The adjustment phase cannot in any case be using floatation devices or replaced by them. It is also possible to teach swimming by using floatation devices, and regrettably many swimming instructors still resort to this method. The upward buoyant force is enlarged by wearing a buoyant aid on the trunk enabling the learner to execute movements in swimming position which he learns on land. As the novice acquires more and more experience, the swimming movements become automatic and enable the learner gradually to do without the floatation devices. But these "swimmers" are not swimmers in the true sense of the word. Often they feel insecure and are unable to cope with situations arising in the water. Many of them never get rid of their fear of water and of drowning. Experience has shown that if a movement is not learned in the active process of coming to grips with one's environment then such a movement will very rarely meet requirements in practice.

In using floatation devices the learner puts his trust in these aids but not in the water. He is not given a chance to feel the buoyancy. The increased buoyancy the swimmer gets from the buoyant aid facilitate his breathing and does not force him to get used to normal breathing in water. But "swimming is breathing" – those who fail to learn to overcome the new conditions of pressure when exhaling into the water will always feel insecure, they will never feel "at home" in water. Moreover, they will not learn to balance their body in the water, a skill which one most have in order to learn a movement. Plenty of examples can be given of the importance of maintaining one's balance in water. If the novice is unable to cope with the shift in the centre of gravity in the water he will not have the necessary confidence to feel comfortable in the water in outstretched position, his movements in water will either be tense or he will not be able to execute them at all. The pupil can learn the outstretched position only through the intensive practice of the five basic skills. This often requires a great deal of patience on the part of the instructor. But if thorough instruction is sacrificed for a fast teaching pace, the learner will be unable to learn the swimming movements properly.

Artificial aids

1. Small floating articles, etc. (floating animals, toy ships, soap-boxes, balls)

These objects are normally used in the first few lessons, in which it is important to help the beginner adjust to water. They help him to overcome inhibitions and they prepare him for learning how to swim under water and how to breathe properly. Games adjusted to the learners age help them to develop their concentration and reaction, to enjoy the lessons and to add variety to the instruction.

2. Hoop

The gymnastics hoop made of aluminium tube is a multi-purpose aid. It is easy to hold, wear resistant, waterproof and it is hygienic. Coloured plastic bands can also be used in a variety of ways, but they are more prone to damage. The hoop is especially useful in facilitating the organization of instruction, especially in the early stages of tuition. The learners get used to a certain formation and order, which makes instruction not only easier but also safer. It also promotes the feeling of being part of the team among members of smaller groups. The hoop's many uses help to develop confidence in the water. The various exercises which can be performed with the hoop cover all aspects of the 1st phase of instruction ranging from the most elementary jumping and diving exercises up to gliding. The hoop gives the instructor a number of ways in which fun and variety can be added to instruction. The more exciting the task to be accomplished by the novice, the more sustained his concentration on its execution.

3. Diving objects

No limits are set to the instructor's crea-tivity here. Any object that is convenient to hold, has no sharp edges and is not too heavy for a pupil to carry in water can be used. Colours should be chosen to provide plenty of contrast at the bottom of the pool. The special value of such objects is that the children get used to keeping their eyes open under water (whole rubber rings are particularly well suited for this purpose).

4. Reaching pole

The reaching pole is an indispensable helper in the initial phase of training. The best material to use for the reaching pole are aluminium, plastic or bamboo. Wooden poles have a limited utility. They get waterlogged after a while, lose their buoyancy and finally start to rot. Lengths of 3.5 to 4.0 metres and diametres of 3 to 4 cm have proved most suitable. The ends of such an aluminium or plastic tube are sealed and a bright coat of paint should be applied. Learners should be familiarized with the pole on land in the same way as with the hoop, preferably on a meadow or lawn. All forms of organization, games and exercises that are to be done in water should be practised on land first. This saves the instructor a great deal of time explaining things to children while they are standing around in the water. If the instructor manages to capture the beginners' interest and arouse their enthusiasm on land they will be much more receptive in the water. Exercises that are a lot of fun to do on land are then done with equal enjoyment in the water. It goes without saying that minor difficulties will have to be overcome, but this technique has brought very good results. The psychological boosts children get from doing such exercises substantially help to promote instruction.

5. "Swimming rungs"–Multi-purpose apparatus (developed by Dr G. *Lewin*)

It consists of Vinidur or flexible exercise rods and Ekazell boards whose sides are 22.5 cm long (different from the dimensions of the familiar floats). The thickness of 8 cm is sufficient for drilling holes in the boards into which the exercise rods are stuck (Fig. 3). Some short connecting pieces also have to be cut with the aid of which the Ekazell boards can be joined together.

This apparatus offers the following advantages:

It is intended for instructing mainly children in kindergartens and school-children. One of the many advantages of this board, which is very stable and buoyant in water, is that the instructor can do without an assistant, which is particularly important in teaching children of kindergarten age.

The board is relatively inexpensive to make. Sixteen boards of the width mentioned can be obtained from a standard Ekazell board (light synthetic material).

The parts can be joined together or taken apart as required. The components are very light, so that even children can help carry and assemble the board in the required form. Little storage space is required.

The following apparatus can be assembled from the component parts (Fig. 4):

(a) swimming rungs,

(b) a reaching pole, although a pole made from a single piece is better than one made of several exercise rods, cf. Figs. 6 and 11,

(c) the square,

(d) the diving bridge,

(e) the merry-go-round.

Float

Little Ekazell floats (30 × 25.5 × 4 cm) have replaced the heavy, cumbersome wooden boards. They feature good buoyancy and are convenient to handle, the material is light, resistant to wear, waterproof, and free from splinters. They are available in all sporting-goods shops.

Apart from its use for various games—in lieu of the pole, the gutter or the swimming rung—this apparatus is also suitable for teaching the proper leg movements. At the same time it makes considerably higher demands on the child than other aids. Unlike the pole, which the beginner can hold on to firmly, the child is forced to learn to make do with the relatively unstable board in the water. He has to rely more on his own strength and skill.

4.3.3. Methodical routines

"The principle of graspability used in teaching means that we should take into account our pupils' individual as well as collective,

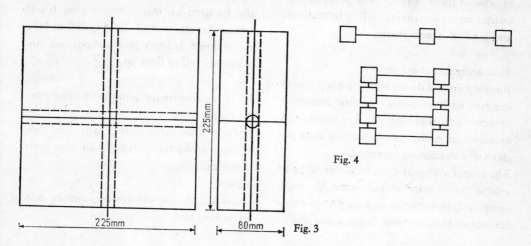

225mm

225mm

80mm

Fig. 3

Fig. 4

age-related, physiological and psychological idiosyncrasies in such a way that the subject matter at all times corresponds to their abilities and their development." (34) This teaching principle is based on the logical order of instruction, in which the student proceeds from the elementary to the complex, from the known to the unknown, etc. The methodical routines described in the following should be seen from this point of view. They should serve the instructor as a guideline and help him to be creative in the broadest sense of the word. They do not relieve him of the responsibility to scrupulously examine his teaching situation, to choose the right subject matter and to decide on the right and best methodical approach.

In the following are contained brief instructions with regard to the sequence of the individual forms of exercise in the different complexes involved in developing fundamental swimming skills. "Organization" here connotes not only the formation and the fixed exercise routine but also the use of methodical aids, presented in an outline form. All objectives mentioned subsequently have been tried out on six-year-olds (1st objective 10th exercise unit; 2nd objective 20th exercise unit; 3rd objective 30th exercise unit). The learners should be expected to achieve these objectives at progressively shorter intervals corresponding to their age and level of development.

Swimming under water
Jumping up and down with the hoop, jumping into shallow water, the first breathing exercises and a number of other elementary exercises are preliminaries leading up to underwater swimming exercises.

The aim of systematic training should be to enable the learner to submerge his body completely in water, to feel the pressure difference and to overcome it gradually and to open his eyes under water in order to find his bearings. The instructor should make sure that the learner opens his eyes only *after submerging* his head, because if he does so beforehand he will experience an unpleasant sensation when his open eyes contact the surface of the water.

The process of learning to swim under water should be started in shallow water. The learner starts by touching the water with his face for short periods; gradually the complexity of the exercises is increased.

a) Simple submersion with and without the use of hands for stabilization
– Organization:
All apparatus mentioned are used; exercises can be executed in a circle, with a partner or individually.
– Note:
The instructor should see to it that the learner inhales properly before submerging; by and by the head should be fully submerged; the duration of submersion should be extended and the learner should exhale under water;
the aim should be to enable the learner to swim under water without aids or assistance from a partner.
– Games and exercises:
Ring-a-rosy, Oranges and Lemons (Fig. 5), diving underneath the reaching pole (hoops, ropes, swimming rungs or diving bridge can also be used for this purpose) (Fig. 6), alternate breathing and diving, diving lane, move down ladders in hang position and allow oneself to float up.

b) Swimming under water with open eyes
– Organization:
Learners should practise with the help of diving objects, partners can also assist in the exercises.
– Note:
Exercises should always be coupled with a concrete task.

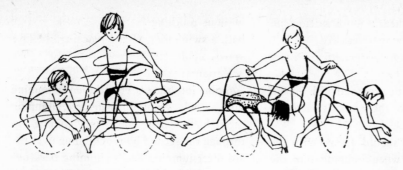

Fig. 5

– Forms of exercise:

Watching one another under water, "making faces" under water, "talking" to one another, counting fingers, identifying objects in one's partner's hand, counting tiles, retrieving objects out of the water (in conjunction with moving under water and carrying objects).

c) Diving head first

– Organization:

Using diving objects.

– Note:

Preparatory exercises should be practised before diving into deep water. The instructor should also show the learners how they should hold their extremities.

– Forms of exercise:

Preliminary exercise: Handstand position (should be done in shallow water, the instructor should demonstrate the technique), dolphin jumps, head first dives from edge of pool from sitting position with feet resting on the gutter (make sure the water is sufficiently deep).

d) Performance standards for diving as part of basic swimming instruction programme

1st objective

The learner should be able to submerge his head completely under water and dive a certain distance (under the diving bridge, cf. Fig. 6).

2nd objective

The learner should be able to keep his eyes open under water, he should retrieve two to three rings or plates.

3rd objective

The learner should be confident when diving into deep water (the dive should be executed from a jump).

Jumping into Water

Beginners should be accustomed to jumping into the water from the first swimming lesson onwards in view of the fact that jumping considerably helps to strengthen the child's confidence when in water. Most novices take to this exercise with enthusiasm. The instructor should make good use of the children's willingness to do this exercise, because it helps the learner to develop his breathing and diving skills. Jumping into deep water enables the beginner to feel the upward force of buoyancy, to reinforce this feeling and to enhance his confidence. The first jumps should be taken into hip-deep water. Jumps into chest- and shoulder-deep water can follow in quick succession. Subsequently learners can jump into deeper water.

Fig. 6

The following sequence of instruction has brought good results in practice:

a) Jumps into shallow water with assistance

– Organization:

The assistance can be provided with the aid of a pole or direct by the learner's partner.

– Note:

The learner's toes should always grip the edge of the pool when jumping into the water in order to prevent slipping. It is important to pay attention to knee flexion when jumping into shallow water.

– Forms of exercise:

The learner should hold on to the pole (partner) first with both and later on with one hand, jumping for the pole held in the water, broad jumping (pole or partner should be further off the edge of the pool). These exercises need be used only with children who are afraid.

b) Jumping into shallow water

These jumps are executed into chest- to shoulder-deep water without assistance.

– Organization:

The learners can jump individually, in pairs, as groups and in chains; numerous variations are possible by using hoops, reaching pole and swimming rungs.

– Note: same as in next exercise (c)

– Forms of exercise:

The learner should jump into the hoop

Fig. 7

without touching it (Fig. 7); over a large ball, a swimming rung, a reaching pole, towards a pole, etc.

– Variants:

Jumping into the water and then swimming under a pole, swimming rung, etc.; jumping through the first hoop and coming up through the second hoop; climbing over the aid after jumping and swimming back under water, etc.

c) Jumping into water of shoulder depth and deeper

– Organization:

A reaching pole should be kept ready to assist learners in deeper water if the need arises.

– Note:

The learner should be encouraged to open his eyes under water. The instructor should brief the learner on how he should move in the water and use his arms and legs effectively.

It is important that the instructor should wear swimming trunks.

– Forms of exercise:

Jumps outstretched, squat, pike, straddle dives with a twist, tuck dives, back dives, jumps with partners, obstacle jumps, jumps followed by transition to swimming position.

d) Head first dives

– Organization:

Individual dives, group and chain dives.

– Note:

Care should be taken when exercising in shallow water. Learner's toes should grip the edge of the pool-deck, head is held between the arms, which should be lowered somewhat, then the learner should jump off with a powerful thrust of his feet. He should jump off horizontally to the surface of the water if the water is shallow. The instructor should indicate where the entry is to be made. Transition to swimming position should be exercised as often as possible.

– Forms of exercise:
Jumping off from a sitting position from the edge of the pool, placing feet on the gutter or on the starting bar, later on diving exercises should be practised from the starting position *or* fall-in dives from tuck position, etc., (especially if the edge of the pool is very high. Otherwise beginners should be taught the normal racing dive from the start).

e) Standard diving performance expected during basic swimming instruction
1st objective
Forward feet-first jump into water of shoulder or chin depth.
2nd objective
Forward dive from 1 metre into deep water.
3rd objective
Head-first front dive from 1 metre into deep water or feet-forward dive from 3 metres into deep water.

Gliding
The first experience of "swimming" represents a decisive phase in the systematic development. Special attention should be paid to it because success or failure in the learner's further swimming career will depend largely on the success or failure of this phase.
The reaching pole is particularly well suited for exercises in preparation for gliding in the prone and supine positions.

a) Exercises in preparation for gliding in the prone and supine positions
– Organization:
The reaching pole or the swimming rung should be used or the learner should be assisted by a partner.
– Note:
Prone position, outstretched position, head held between outstretched arms, air should be exhaled into the water. Supine position, hips are kept high, head on the water (Fig. 8).
– Forms of exercise:
The learner holds on to the pole while being pulled (Fig. 9). Moving in a circle = merry-go-round (suitable only for gliding in supine position).

b) Outstretched prone and supine floats
– Organization:
The children should be positioned in such a way as to make sure that they do not get into each other's way. Partners can be assigned if necessary for the first exercises who are to help learners recover.
– Note:
The learner falls into the prone or supine position from straddle position, arms stretched out laterally. Prone position: head between arms, face in the water.
Supine position: head on the water, hips kept high.
– Recovery:
Recovery from the prone position is by pressing one's arms vigorously downwards,

Fig. 8   Fig. 9

legs are drawn up and the trunk is brought into the vertical position.

Recovery from the supine position: The torso is brought into the vertical position by drawing up one's legs and effectively using one's arms.

c) *Porpoise glide by pushing off from the bottom of the pool*

– Note:

The learner starts by gliding to something he can hold on to which is within reach, for instance from the edge of the pool to the reaching pole and back. The learner can be supported by a glide board.

d) *Gliding by pushing off from the edge of the pool*

– Organization:

The learner should be assisted by a partner if there is no edge to push off from or reaching pole.

– Note:

The beginner should start by pushing off with one leg. Later on he can use both legs. Recovery should be assisted at first, subsequent recovery without assistance.

– Forms of exercise:

Learners should be motivated to improve their performance by holding contests to see who can glide longest, who can glide up to the tip of the pole, who can glide underneath the pole and the diving bridge without touching them, etc.

e) *Gliding standards for basic swimming instruction*

1st objective

Pushing off and gliding in prone and supine positions.

2nd objective

Improving the gliding positions and lengthening gliding duration in prone and supine positions (glide diving underneath the diving bridge).

3rd objective

Extending the gliding distance in prone and supine positions (through contests).

Locomotion in water

A child responds in a perfectly natural manner the first time he is allowed to hold onto a pole or onto the edge of the pool and to let his feet touch water: He starts thrashing the water with his feet. This activity corresponds to the child's urge to move. The instructor makes use of this urge by letting the child carry out tasks designed to help the child gather experience and to develop his swimming skills.

Owing to the fact that in the first phase of the learning process the child's movements are still very inefficient and that a great deal of concentration and persistent practice is needed to reinforce the beginner's unsteady movements, appropriate aids are recommended for practising certain movements.

The learner should assume a streamlined position in the water to ensure good results in practising swimming movements.

Attention should be paid from the very beginning to co-ordinated leg movement and breathing; air should be exhaled into the water.

a) *Front crawl leg movement*

– Organization:

Swimming rungs, reaching pole or floats should be used as aids.

– Note:

Legs should be stretched out at all times, but they should be kept loose.

– Movement tasks:

Vigorous splashing, fast splashing, diminished splashing, executing movements under water, exhaling air into the water at regular intervals all the while.

b) *Back crawl leg movement*

– Organization:

Same as above.

– Note:

Knees should not be raised above water level when splashing.

– Movement tasks:

Due to the fact that leg movement in back crawl is almost identical with the leg action used in front crawl, the movement tasks are the same.

Arm movement should also be developed and subsequently co-ordinated with the leg movement.

c) Arm movement in front and back crawl

– Organization:

The learner can move his legs slightly to stabilize the position of his body.

– Note:

The hands should push vigorously before starting overwater recovery. Hands should continue their push down to the thighs, in the overwater recovery phase the arms are kept loose and relaxed.

– Forms of exercise:

Preparatory exercises carried out on land with a view to improving shoulder joint flexibility: Windmill rotation forward and backward. The movements of the arms and hands should be controlled consciously when walking forward and backward. At first the arm action is performed without co-ordination with breathing, later on arm action and breathing are linked.

d) Complex movement pattern in front and back crawl strokes

– Note:

Leg action starts after the push-off, followed by arm movement; movement co-ordination, especially in the case of crawl stroke, is performed without linking with breathing.

The elementary form of crawl learned during the first phase of instruction forms the basis for further refinement.

e) Standard of locomotion in the water in basic swimming instruction

1st objective

Preparation of flutter kick and alternating arm stroke in prone and supine positions.

2nd objective

Flutter kick in prone position using a glid-ing board; in supine position without the aid of a gliding board; locomotion by means of leg and arm movements.

3rd objective

Improvement of the leg and arm movement pattern; locomotion over a certain distance by means of complex movement.

Breathing

Breathing exercises are initiated by having the pupils move objects such as little toy animals, soap-boxes or little balls by blowing at them. The object here is to get the learner used to intensive breathing, which comprises short, deep inhalation and slow, forceful exhalation into the water. The instructor should demonstrate the breathing pattern.

a) Deep air inhalation followed by slow exhalation

– Organization:

Little toy animals, soap-boxes, little balls.

– Forms of exercise

Blowing away objects. The exercises should be varied by having the pupils blow the objects up to a goal line, through a passage formed by hoops, etc.

b) Blowing a "hole" in the water

– Organization:

Hoops, reaching pole

– Notes:

The mouth is kept just above the water surface, the emphasis is on forceful exhalation.

c) Bubbling

– Organization:

Hoops, reaching pole, multi-purpose apparatus–edge of pool, circle, partner (Fig. 10).

Fig. 10

– Notes:

The mouth is kept in the water. Who can bubble loudest? Who can bubble and splash most vigorously? Children should be reminded not to rub their eyes when they take their heads out of the water.

d) Deliberate exhalation into the water

– Organization:

All aids, especially the board, can be used.

– Note:

The face should be fully immersed when exhaling. The instructor should make certain that the pupils inhale and exhale rhythmically, first five, then ten times in a row. The mouth should be open and ready for inhaling as it is raised above the water surface; not even "the last rest" should be exhaled above the water.

– Forms of exercise:

Inhaling and exhaling in standing position, walking forward and in conjunction with locomotion, e.g., leg movement in prone position.

e) Side breathing

– Organization:

Mainly with the aid of reaching pole, board, swimming rung, edge of the pool deck or support from the partner.

– Note:

Preparatory exercise for the crawl stroke: The head is turned to one side for inhalation in such a way that one ear is submerged, then the head is turned in the other direction after inhaling. The head should not be raised in the process (Fig. 11). The instructor makes sure that the learners exhale vigorously into the water.

Fig. 11

– Forms of exercise:

The exercises should be performed bilaterally and linked with the arm or leg movement and with the complex movement.

f) Breathing-in-water standard for basic swimming instruction

1st objective

Rhythmic inhalation above and exhaling into the water, the breathing cycle being repeated ten times.

2nd objective

Inhalation and exhalation while raising and lowering the head and inhalation and exhalation while turning the head in both directions linked with locomotion in the water.

3rd objective

Inhalation and exhalation in conjunction with the combined movement in prone and supine positions (elementary co-ordination).

4.3.4.   Use of all acquired basic swimming skills

The basic skills of swimming under water, jumping into the water, gliding, locomotion through the cyclic action of the arms and legs and controlled breathing are taught simultaneously and systematically. There are a variety of ways in which they can be combined with each other. There are many things in common, e.g., between jumping into the water and diving, gliding on the surface and under water, gliding in the prone and supine positions and the corresponding forms of locomotion as well as between breathing, diving and locomotion, etc. The quality and quantity of instruction is measured by the learner's degree of mastery of the complex movement.

Some examples:

Head first front dive from 1-metre springboard;

deep dive and exhalation into the water;

surfacing and orientating oneself in relation to a given object;

swimming to said object, which is about 10 metres away, and breathing regularly in the process;

carrying said object to the edge of the pool using one's feet for propelling one's body through the water.

Using this method children of pre-school age were expected to execute this series of movements after 30 units of instruction and almost all of them passed the test.

4.3.5.   Special factors to be taken into account in carrying out the first stage of instruction in deep water

Owing to the fact that numerous swimming pools are being built which are 1.80 metres deep or deeper at all points, the need to modify the 1st stage of basic swimming instruction is being increasingly felt. Field studies conducted in Leipzig [32], Neubrandenburg and elsewhere have shown that buoyant aids worn on the trunk can be dispensed with also for instruction in deep water. This holds true also for group instruction (school swimming instruction, preschool swimming classes, extracurricular swimming training).

But the methodical routines and the choice and use of aids become more important under conditions of deep water instruction.

On methodical routines

The teaching of basic skills in underwater swimming should be given priority if swimming instruction is given in deep water, especially in the early phase of instruction.

With the help of suitable aids the beginner should first practise complete feet-first vertical immersion, holding on the gutter or other suitable objects at first. Soon he will

realize that the water's buoyant force does not allow him to sink any lower so it will not take much effort to persuade him to let go of the gutter and, by pushing himself off, to dive to a greater depth and allow himself to be raised to the surface by buoyancy. These exercises should be combined with all exercises which encourage the beginner to open his or her eyes under water. Maximum importance should be attached to a beginner being able to orientate himself under water from the very start.

Exercises designed to let the novice experience static buoyancy should be started immediately after, and in the further course of instruction in conjunction with, the diving exercises. At first the best way to execute these in the form of the *"extended float"* in prone position, the beginner holding on to the gutter. Holding the arms slightly spread to the sides and the legs spread out help the beginner in this phase to develop the skill of balancing his body in the water. He will soon be able to let go of the gutter or the object and to float freely on the surface. The process of experiencing buoyancy is reinforced by the *"turtle float"* exercise, in which the learner's body is rolled up into a compact bundle and in which part of the pupil's back protrudes above the surface of the water once its position is stabilized following a little initial forward and backward rocking (the exercise should be demonstrated first).

Once the learner has become aware of the static buoying force he can start with his first jumping exercises by practising the *feet-first-jump*. The learner's confidence should be kept up at all times by using a pole (see section on jumping into the water). These jumping exercises also serve to help the pupil feel the static buoyancy.

Head-first jumps are introduced in much the same way as the jumps into shallow water described earlier, except that additional precautions should be taken by using such aids as the pole, lane markers, safety zones (see Fig. 12), etc., to ensure the learners' safety at all times. The dive from a sitting position is a good way to introduce the *front glide*. This exercise too should at first be arranged in such a way that the learner can get a firm hold of an object at the end of the glide. Once the learner has gained the necessary measure of confidence he can start practising free glide forms from a standing dive and by pushing off from the pool wall. Experience has shown that it is best to start with the extended float and with the *back glide* in deep water only after the beginner has acquired a good command of these exercises in a prone position. It is particularly important to have him consciously experience the kinaesthetic sensation associated with the complete extension of his body, because a certain measure of insecurity can easily cause the learner to flex his hip joint, thereby assuming a "cradle" position in the water. Supporting exercises can also be performed on land: raising oneself, with the help of the instructor or the partner, from a stiff lying position to stand upright the learner maintaining his outstretched posture by tensioning his muscles.

The following preliminary exercises are recommended before practising *locomotion*: Having the pupil move hand over hand along the gutter or a similar object offering a firm hold with a view to letting him experience the resistance of water; doing the flutter kick while sitting on the edge of the pool deck; executing the flutter kick in a prone position while holding on to the gutter or another object providing a firm hold; practising the flutter kick lying in the water in a supine position supporting one's neck on a lane rope or a pole.

Numerous other exercises can be performed with the aid of the swimming rung. The rung can also be used in combination with the gutter or with the lane rope.

Not all the *breathing exercises* described for shallow water can be practised in deep water, because some of them can be performed only when standing in water of hip or neck depth. But then the learner can be assigned exercises which he can perform on his own in a bath-tub or wash-basin and which can complement and help him master the technique, which he can improve with the help of the gutter or other aids.

(2) On choice and use of artificial aids

The reader will have gathered from the remarks concerning the methodical routines that the success of basic swimming instruction in deep water hinges on the wise use of aids. The "gutter" as an aid deserves to be mentioned first. It gives the beginner the security he needs in the first few lessons to learn the fundamental swimming skills.

But owing to the fact that the large area of a 25 by 12.5 metres swimming pool could not be used economically by beginner groups if the gutter were the only aid offering a firm hold, *Lewin* has developed in Neubrandenburg what are known here as "safety zones" (Fig. 12). They consist of aluminium pipes about 40 mm in diametre sealed at the ends and joined together by Ekazell blocks (450 mm × 450 mm) in the same way as the swimming rungs mentioned earlier. They are used to mark out parts of a swimming pool for use as exercise areas, their size being adjustable to the learners' level of proficiency. "Safety zones" make it possible not only to use various forms of organization and for the teacher to keep better track of his class but also give more pupils a chance to practise all the forms of exercise that in the past could be done only with the aid of the gutter or lane ropes (moving in a hanging position with hands only, alternate floating, leg movement in

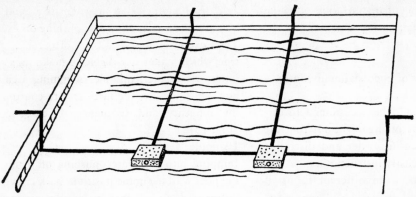

Fig. 12

prone and supine positions, breath control exercises, etc.).

Lane ropes, which are used to divide up pools into longitudinal or transverse lanes, are also very useful as aids. As soon as the learner begins consciously to feel static and dynamic buoyancy he can use the lane rope to hold on to or as a goal in glide exercises, locomotion exercises and diving exercises. Another very important aid is the *"reaching pole"* (aluminium, plastic or bamboo, about 2.5 to 3 metres in length). The teacher supports pupils in their first attempts at jumping into the water with the aid of this pole. The pupil can grab hold of the pole after diving or later on after surfacing; goal markers can also be used in the initial phase, by drawing back the rope the learner can be encouraged to dive greater distances. Diving exercises are performed by placing one end of the pole on the pool floor and holding it in a vertical position (the pole can also be secured in this position if necessary); learners practise by "climbing" up and down the pole. Coloured markings spaced half a metre apart can be painted on the pole to help learners judge the depth (this encourages them to go deeper and to open their eyes under water).

Solid rubber rings (cf. aids and their uses), which can be suspended on ropes from safety zone bars or fastened to swimming rungs, can also be used for diving practice and as a means of encouraging the learner to open his or her eyes under water. The depth at which the rings are suspended can be varied by altering the rope length. By using this aid the learner can be systematically accustomed to greater depths and to greater degrees of difficulty until he is able to retrieve the rings from the bottom of the pool. All other aids described in the section on swimming instruction in shallow water are also used in deep-water swimming instruction, the importance of the role played by the different types of aid varies from case to case. The most versatile and for this reason the most important artificial aids are the *swimming rungs* and the *floats*.

To conclude the chapter on the special features of the first phase of basic swimming instruction in deep water it should be stressed that the teacher has a greater measure of responsibility for his pupils than in shallow-water instruction. This should not deter the teacher from teaching the basic skills in accordance with the recommendations set forth in the foregoing, but it should encourage him methodically to plan his instruction, to choose the most promising forms of organization of exercises and to use the aids in the most expedient manner.

4.3.6. Forms of organization of swimming instruction

Basic standards of good swimming instruction
1. Learners should be accustomed to certain strict forms of organization from the very start (to ensure order and discipline and thus to intensify instruction).
2. Transition between different forms of organization and between different parts of a lesson should be fluid (they should be safe and orderly and there should be no less of time).
3. Pupils should be kept moving to prevent them from getting cold too early (the pace of exercise can be speeded up to keep the pupils warm).
4. The instructor should pick a good vantage point to be able to survey his group properly.
5. Acoustic cues or sign language should be used during instruction. (The instructor should seek ways of improving communication with his pupils and avoid overstraining his voice.)

Forms of organization in shallow water
Intended mainly for beginners:
Row, alley, circle—with all forms the instructor can decide whether the pupil should hold hands with members of the group or partners or not. Beginners should be positioned in such a way that they can stand securely and that they can at all times get a firm hold of the edge of the deck, of the rope or other object used to mark off the swimming area, or of artificial aids such as hoops, reaching pole, multi-purpose device or partner. With growing confidence the beginner learns to get by without these aids.
Lining up the pupils along the edge of the pool deck or along other pool bounds and letting them swim or glide to the opposite side or to another goal in groups is a good way for beginners to practise pushing off.
The "exercise lane" is a form of organization which makes it possible to make maximum use of the available swimming area and which enables the instructor to control the intensity and frequency of exercise (Fig. 13).
Example:
Jumping into the water—pushing off from the pool wall in supine position—back crawl flutter kick up to first mark—dive under rope (1st time)—back crawl complex movement up to 2nd mark—dive under line (2nd sign)—back to the edge using back crawl flutter kick—climb out
report for assigment of 2nd task—repeat exercise.
These and similar forms of exercise are designed to give children a chance to move about in water, a thing they are fond of doing anyway, and to develop their endurance.

Organizational forms for deep and shallow water
Suitable for basic swimming instruction and training:
Swimming across the lane (Fig. 14); exercising in groups (Figs. 15 and 16), "flow line" exercise (Fig. 17) (T = instructor).
The instructor splits up the class into groups of learners of equal performance level in order to prevent those who are still unable to do this exercise properly from getting in the way of those who have already mastered it. But the instructor should keep trying to get the weaker learners to improve their performance so as to enable them to take part in normal group exercises.
If the class is very large and the exercise unit limited, then it is recommended to have the learners swim in one direction individually, in twos or in groups (Fig. 18). Once the learner has swum one lane he gets out

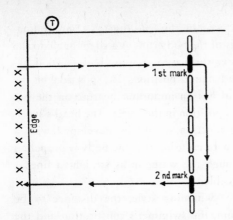

Fig. 13

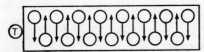

Fig. 14

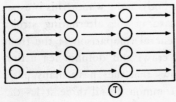

Fig. 15

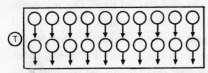

Fig. 16

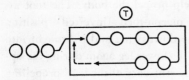

Fig. 17

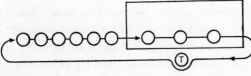

Fig. 18

of the water and walks back to the starting point again. This technique is also used in interval training and in spurts (Figs. 14 and 18).

4.4. Second phase

The main aim of the second phase of instruction was outlined in the introduction to the section on basic swimming instruction: It is to teach swimming style techniques, including starts and turns. Swimming styles are the strokes which are used in swimming events held at present in accordance with FINA rules and regulations: breaststroke, backstroke (using the back crawl technique), free-style (using the front crawl technique) and butterfly with the dolphin kick. There are also numerous variants of these swimming techniques which are used for such specific purposes as transporting objects, rescuing people in distress, overcoming obstacles, etc. They are used as "general means of training in water".

To achieve greater versatility two or more swimming styles are taught in the second phase of basic swimming instruction, depending on how much time is available for this phase and on the level of performance of the learners. In compulsory school swimming instruction, which consists of two complexes covered in a total of about 60 lessons, most of the pupils learn the elementary co-ordination of three swimming techniques: back crawl, front crawl and breaststroke. But if for some reason only one instruction complex consisting of about 35 lessons is available, then most of the pupils manage to master the elementary co-ordination of only two swimming strokes, e.g., back crawl and breaststroke.

If time is available for instruction on an

extracurricular basis the learners can be taught the butterfly stroke. The following views on the teaching approach should be seen in this light and applied in practice. Scientific advances in the fields of biomechanics, hydrodynamics, sports physiology and sports psychology have not only revolutionized training methods, but they have contributed to the evolution of the different techniques of swimming and of starts and turns. The breaststroke is a good example of this development. The early forms of "breaststroke" with their long glide phases after each movement cycle have evolved to become a "simultaneous stroke technique" in which the cycles of movement are executed almost without intervals.

The efficiency of movements depends on the laws of physics, on the athlete's anatomical makeup and on the specific movements of his arms under and over the water.

To get a better general picture we shall first analyse the *common features* of the techniques of the *freestyle* (crawl), *back crawl, butterfly* (dolphin) and *breaststroke* styles.

We shall use the front crawl stroke as a basis for studying these common features. It is important to bear in mind the characteristics of movement of this swimming style.

This will be followed by an analysis of the specific technical questions involved in the other three swimming styles.

4.4.1.   Crawl

On the body's position in water
The swimmer should lie in a relaxed prone or supine stretched out position in the water. The shoulder line should be raised slightly above the water surface, the pelvis should be deep enough below the surface to permit convenient leg action beneath the surface. In this position the longitudinal axis of the body runs at a slight angle to the water surface to give the body a good hydrodynamic position. The position of the head has an important bearing on the body's position in the water. The head's steering function should be developed with a view to ensuring that the body is propelled through the water in as straight a line as possible.

The swimming style, the distance to be swum, the swimmer's constitution and the speed a swimmer develops should be taken into account in deciding on which is the best body position.

Leg movement
The leg action gives the swimmer an upward drive and forward propulsion and balances the body in the water (this is especially the case in the alternating stroke styles). A general comparison of the front crawl, back crawl and dolphin leg action patterns shows that they have many basic features in common. In all three styles the movement commences at the trunk and continues sequentially along the thighs, knees, lower legs, ankles and toes. The leg action is in the vertical plane and the kick amplitude varies between 30 and 50 cm, depending on the constitution of the swimmer, the beat rhythm and the frequency.

Both the upswing and the downswing of the leg help propel the body. The foot assumes a pigeon-toed (inverted) position during the downswing and is brought into line with the lower leg again during the upswing. The efficiency of the legs' propelling action depends, among other things, on the speed of the swing reversal, on the extension of the foot joint and on how relaxed the feet are kept. The leg movement in the crawl techniques are largely analogous. Let us examine the front crawl leg swing to get a clearer notion of the leg action.

Movement of one leg

The swimmer moves his thigh *downward.* Water pressure on the shin causes the leg to bend at the knee. At the lower point of reversal, as the upward swing is commenced from the hip joint, the swimmer completes the kick by a whipping action of the foot which ends in an extended position of the leg. Reversing the swing the thigh is moved *upward* and the lower leg follows while the pressure exerted by the water on the calf causes the knee joint to be extended. At the upper point of reversal, when the downswing has already been started again, the action carries the foot toward the surface for the final whip-like kick, which can end with the heel breaking the surface. Then the leg is flexed again.

Movement of both legs

The legs are continuously swung in alternating up-and-down kicks driving the body forward by pushing the water backward. The point at which the legs meet should roughly coincide with the longitudinal axis of the body so that the thrust is pointed at the body's centre of gravity. The reverse movement pattern should be used with the back crawl technique.

Arm movement

The movement of the arms plays a vital role in achieving maximum propulsion in front and back crawl styles and in the butterfly stroke. In all three strokes there are distinct underwater and overwater phases of the arm movement. In the breaststroke there is no overwater recovery phase and the underwater phase is short compared with other strokes.

The thrust produced by the arm action is governed mainly by the principle of the lever. The swimmer's arm can be seen as a one-armed lever, the shoulder joint being the fulcrum. The entire arm acts as the weight arm, while the force arm is the part of the arm from the shoulder joint up to the muscle origin of the upper arm. The length of the force arm is almost a fixed quantity, while the load acting on the load arm can be shifted closer to the fulcrum by flexing the elbow joint, which is tantamount to shortening the load arm.

By virtue of the lever principle (load $\times$ load arm $=$ force $\times$ force arm) the swimmer can alter his individual force-load ratio. Through strength training he can increase the force of the force arm and he can reduce the load by flexing his arm. The latter technical alternative enables the swimmer to increase his stroke rate without increasing the amount of force. In addition, the efficiency of the force applied is increased as a result of the fact that the length of the period during which the force is applied in a direction parallel to that of the direction of propulsion is prolonged by flexing the arm.

Just as in the case of the leg movements, a comparison of the arm movements executed in the different swimming styles shows that they have several features in common.

The thrust produced by the pull and push phase of the arm movement through the water is produced by the palms and by the inside surfaces of the arms. The fingers are kept closed during the pull and push phases. The hands are slightly cupped and "planed" in such a way that they are almost constantly at right angles to the direction of thrust. During the power phase in the crawl and butterfly strokes the arms move under the body almost parallel to the direction of propulsion, thus ensuring an optimum thrust. In the back crawl and breaststroke styles the arm movement is executed sidewise from and above the shoulder line, the hand describing a more or less distinct semicircular path. Even propulsion is produced by the alternating arm movements executed in the front and back crawl strokes; this is not so in the case of the breaststroke and butterfly techniques, in which simultaneous thrusts are produced through simultaneous arm movements. To achieve optimum efficiency of the arm stroke all phases of the underwater arm movement should be fluid and executed as straight as possible in the direction opposite to the direction of propulsion, which means that optimum propulsion is achieved through steady acceleration and controlled force application from the point of entry up to the most effective phase of the arm movement, which depends on the stroke in question.

The only fundamental difference between the arms movement patterns used in butterfly and crawl techniques is that the arm movement in the former is simultaneous and alternating in the latter technique. For this reason we can take the crawl technique to illustrate the arm action used in both techniques.

Movement of one arm

During the *underwater phase* the palm of the hand should be kept as nearly as possible at right angles to the direction of the thrust. The hand secures a purchase on the water and the arm pulls and than pushes the water in a relatively straight line under the body toward the hip. The hand precedes the elbow all the while and the arm is flexed at the elbow joint at an angle depending on the individual swimmer's force load ratio. The arm's movement is accelerated under water up to the last phase. Towards the end of the underwater push phase the arm is almost completely extended. The arm recovery phase over the water is initiated by raising the elbow out of the water. After the hand has been raised out of the water as well, the arm is swung out as far as possible to the front to what might be

called the starting position. (Strictly speaking there are no starting positions in cyclic movement patterns. We have picked the term "starting position" arbitrarily to help describe certain movement patterns in swimming. It should be construed to mean the arm's entry phase.) During the recovery phase the hand should move close to the surface of the water and the elbow should be kept high. The arms' muscles should be relaxed to the utmost. The swimmer should try to reduce his body's frontal resistance surface to a minimum during the recovery phase.

Movement of both arms

The arms keep driving the swimmer's body through the water by means of their rhythmically alternating strokes (Fig. 19). Owing to the fact that the density of the water is higher than that of the air, it takes more time for the arm to move through the for-

Fig. 19

mer than through the latter. A peculiar technique of co-ordinating the arms' movements is used to compensate for this difference. For instance, at the point at which the left arm has just made its entry in line with and forward of the shoulder, the right arm completes the pull phase and commences the push phase of its drive. While the left arm is executing the pull phase, the right arm completes the push phase and goes on to starting position. As it makes its entry in front of the right shoulder the left arm completes the pull and commences the push phase, etc. (Fig. 19).

Breathing

What all four strokes have in common is that the swimmer's body is almost wholly immersed in the water and exposed to its pressure and heat drain from all sides. Another thing that makes the situation more difficult are the unusual breathing conditions, and a mastery of the breathing technique is vital for achieving good swimming performance. The breathing depth, breathing rate and breathing rhythm are the chief components of the breathing technique. The *breathing rhythm* is linked to the movement co-ordination. It should be integrated into the movement's timing in such a manner that it does not impede the propulsive efficiency of the movement and that it enables the swimmer to breathe.

The *breathing technique* most frequently used is the one in which the movement cycle is co-ordinated with a breathing rhythm consisting of the inhalation and exhalation phases. Alternating lateral inhalation is normally used with the alternating stroke techniques. After inhaling (which in front crawl can be done when the right arm leaves the water, in back crawl when the right arm is recovered) three underwater arm movements are executed before inhaling again (which in front crawl is done when

the left arm leaves the water, in back crawl when the left arm is recovered). The alternating bilateral and unilateral breathing techniques can be used optionally, depending on the exercise task (three-, four-, five-stroke breathing, etc., can be used). Air is inhaled quickly through the mouth *only,* and it is exhaled forcefully and deeply through the mouth *and* the nose. In all strokes except back crawl the air is exhaled *into* the water. Let us examine the *technique of breathing used in the front crawl stroke* in its relation to the arm movement.

The air is exhaled into the water while one of the arms executes its underwater drive. Exhalation should be completed by the time the hand completes its push phase at the thigh. The head—not the shoulders—should be turned to the side of the arm completing the power phase and the inhalation started when that arm is raised from the water for recovery. If the swimming speed is sufficiently high a bow wave is formed in front of the head, in the wake of which there is a little furrow or through which the swimmer can inhale without having to raise his head. The face is turned into the water again during the recovery phase. The inhalation and the turning of the head should bo done relatively fast.

Complex movement

In all strokes the athlete's physiological idiosyncrasies should be taken into account in co-ordinating the leg and arm movements and breathing. These movements should be co-ordinated in such a manner that the legs and the arms give optimum propulsion to the body. The movement of the head that is required for breathing and arm and leg movements should have the least possible detrimental influence on the body's position in the water and on its straight propulsion.

The six-beat kick is used in most cases with the crawl strokes, i.e., six leg strokes (three upswings and three downswings) to each complete arm movement cycle. But good results have also been obtained with the four- and two-beat kicks.

In the case of the *dolphin stroke*, two dolphin kicks for each complete arm movement are held to be most rational at present. In the *breaststroke* the arm and leg movements are in a one-to-one ratio and form an integral cycle.

4.4.2. Back crawl

It can be assumed that the back crawl style has been known since antiquity, although there is no documentary evidence to confirm this or to show just how the stroke was executed.

The back crawl techniques used in more recent times are the popular backstroke and the old English backstroke. The back crawl technique has proved to be the most economical one in the supine position.

In the following we shall describe this style and the technique that has proved most efficient in practice to date. Deviations from this technique are most apparent in the arm movement. Some swimmers keep their arms almost straight, other tend more and more to bend them at the elbow. The arms of the latter groups describe a flat S-shaped curve during the power phase, thus enabling them more efficiently to propel their body through the water. The shortened leverage of the arm also helps to increase the swimmer's stroking rate.

Body position

The swimmers should lie stretched out on his back in the water. He should bring his chin slightly towards the throat so that his ears are just below the surface.

Leg action

The descriptions given of the leg movements in preceding sections apply also to the back-stroke style.

Arm movement

Just as in front crawl, the arm movement cycle in backstroke consists of the overwater recovery phase and of the underwater power phase. In its initial position the swimmers' arm lies almost extended in the water parallel to the long axis of the body. The hand enters the water and the underwater phase starts. The arm is nearly extended at the end of this phase. Throughout the underwater phase the arm is moved about 15 to 30 cm under the water surface, the angle formed between the forearm and the hand being varied continually in such a way that the palm is kept at right angles to the direction of thrust as long as possible. The hand should precede the elbow throughout the power phase. In this stroke too the arm is moved in such a manner that the highest speed is reached at the beginning of the push phase and retained till the end of the power phase. The arm is raised from the water (this is executed in conjunction with raising the shoul-

Fig. 20

der) and swung back to the initial position in as relaxed a manner as possible. The hand is twisted in such a way that it can obtain a purchase on the water as soon as possible after entry.

The movements of the two arms alternate, so that while one arm is executing the power phase, the other arm recovers to the starting position and begins immediately by getting a firm hold on the water.

Breathing

Thanks to the fact that the swimmer's mouth and nose are above the surface most of the time, less difficulty is usually experienced in mastering the breathing technique with this stroke than with others. Breathing is co-ordinated with the arm movement rhythm: The swimmer inhales through the mouth during the recovery phase of one arm and exhales through the mouth and nose during the push phase.

Complex movement

The characteristics of complex movement described for crawl apply also to the back-stroke technique with due adjustments (Fig. 20).

4.4.3.   Butterfly stroke
          (with dolphin kick)

The oldest drawing of a swimming person on record (4000 B.C.) and some drawings from antiquity suggest that movements resembling the modern dolphin kick were already in use then. These swimming techniques and those used with other swimming styles were later forgotten.

The dolphin kick was rediscovered when attempts were made to raise the efficiency of the breaststroke. The dolphin kick was linked with simultaneous overwater arm recovery. This co-ordination has proved it-self in practice and the speed achieved with the butterfly stroke with dolphin kick approached that of the crawl stroke.

Body position

The body's position in the water is less rigid in the butterfly stroke as a result of the body's undulating movements than in the other swimming styles. As a result of this movement the angle of the longitudinal axis of the body to the water surface is also reduced. But the angle should still be big enough for the legs not to break the surface of the water.

Leg action (dolphin kick)

Flexibility of the spine is an important condition for the successful use of the dolphin kick technique. Since in the dolphin kick it is the trunk *and* the legs that produce the thrust it is misleading to speak of the leg action. As the name suggests, in executing the dolphin kick the swimmer imitates the movement of the dolphin's tail, which moves up and down in the vertical plane. The swimmer propels his body continuously through steady up and down leg action, keeping his legs close together. Once the swimmer has mastered the technique, hardly any of his movements will retard his progress through the water.

The dolphin kick commences at the lower thoracic vertebra and the undulating action continues on down the lumbar vertebra, the pelvis, the thighs, the lower legs, the feet and ends at the toes. During the *downward movement* the pelvis is pressed downward, followed by the thighs, lower legs and feet. During the downward beat of the legs the swimmer first allows the water pressure on the shins to flex his legs at the knee joints, followed by a whiplike straightening of the legs, at the end of the downward movement. While the legs are still executing the downward kick, the next *upward movement* is initiated at the hips. This movement is

Fig. 21

followed by the legs, which are extended during the upward beat. The knee joint is flexed slightly in the last part of the up-swing, because the lower legs and feet are still completing the upswing phase while the next downward movement initiated at the hips has already reached the thighs. The next movement cycle is started. The feet are turned inward during the downward kick in order to enable the swimmer to kick with the greatest possible foot surface (cf. crawl stroke). They are straightened in line with the lower legs again and kept close together during the upward swing.

Arm movement

The characteristics of the arm movement technique (cf. p. 65 et seq.), which have general validity, apply analogously to the butterfly stroke as well. The physiologically limited shoulder joint flexibility and the swimmer's efforts to keep his body as flat as possible in the water are the reasons why the arms are nearly extended in their simultaneous overwater recovery.

Breathing

Breathing is co-ordinated with the combined movement rhythm in such a manner that it interferes as little as possible with the latter and that it still provides the swimmer's organism with an adequate supply of oxygen. Whether the swimmer executes one or two arm strokes to one breathing cycle will depend on the distance to be swum and on the swimmer's condition. The following is a description of the co-ordination of the breathing cycle with one complete arm stroke: The swimmer begins exhaling during the power phase and ends the exhalation approximately when his arms are at right angles to the long axis of the body. He inhales during the push part of the underwater power phase by raising his head a little, thrusting his chin forward to the water surface and curling his lips outward. He ends the inhalation phase when he raises his arms from the water. He lowers his face again during the overwater recovery phase of the arms.

Complex movement

Different variants of co-ordination of the arm movement with the dolphin kick have envolved in the process of development of the butterfly stroke. At present most top international athletes use two dolphin kicks to one complete arm stroke, which we shall describe in greater detail here. Some swimmers carry out one dolphin kick to one arm stroke, and there are variations between these two techniques.

In the case of two dolphin kicks to one complete arm stroke cycle the first dolphin kick is introduced, i.e., the legs execute the downward kick, when the arms commence the pull phase. At the end of the power phase of the arms the legs have just completed the downward kick and start moving upward; the swimmer inhales during this phase. The arms are recovered overwater and the next downward kick initiates the second dolphin movement. The second dolphin movement ends with the arm entry and with the hands obtaining a hold on the water and the next cycle is started (two-beat timing, cf. Fig. 21).

4.4.4.　　Breaststroke

Documentary evidence indicates that the breaststroke was also used in antiquity.
The pattern of movement of the arms and legs, the breathing and their co-ordinated timing have gone through many changes in the course of the evolution of the breaststroke before it has reached its present level of development. In the following description we shall take into account recent trends of development of this technique.

Body position
The body should be kept in a streamlined position in the breaststroke as well in order to ensure effective leg action in the water. The body's angle relative to the surface of the water (planing angle) depends on the leg action pattern. The more the legs are flexed at the knees, the greater the planing angle. The other technical characteristics correspond to those already described.

Leg action
Starting from the extended position the swimmer flexes his legs at the hip and knee joints until the heels are brought up to a position above the knees. The knees are spread only about a hand's breadth, the heels are almost touching. Thus during this initial phase, which retards the swimmer's forward movement, the swimmer's legs are in his body's slipstream.
Immediately after executing this movement the knees are turned inward and the toes dorsiflexed for an effective backward

thrust. The feet drive almost directly backward, the angle of the soles being adjusted throughout the thrust in such a way as to provide maximum resistance.
The transition between the two phases of movement, i.e., the leg recovery and the fast and powerful lower leg action, should be executed smoothly.

Arm movement
The drive phase starts from the outstretched position in which the arms pull simultaneously outward in a lateral stroke. The hands are turned so that the palms face outward and slightly cupped to give the swimmer a good hold on the water and to en-

Fig. 22

71

able him to make effective use of the backward resistance for maximum thrust.

The swimmer progressively accelerates the arm movement during the pull phase adjusting the angle of his hands and forearms in such a manner as to ensure maximum backward resistance. The horizontal thrust of the vertically held hands should predominate if maximum propulsion is to be achieved. Just before the arms reach the shoulder line, the hands and forearms are moved inward until they are close together under the chin; the elbows should not be drawn back in the process. The arms are recovered in a smooth forward movement which completes the movement cycle. The next power phase starts after the arms have reached a fully extended position.

Breathing

In breaststroke the swimmer usually breathes once to every complete movement cycle. Thanks to the fact that he keeps his arms and his trunk in the water at all times he gets enough buoyancy to keep his head steadier than in butterfly stroke; this also facilitates breathing.

The swimmer exhales into the water during the pull phase. In the next phase, in which the arms are pressed inward and down, the upper part of the body is raised somewhat until the mouth is just above the surface of the water and the swimmer inhales quickly and deeply. Inhalation during this phase is facilitated thanks to the fact there is a certain measure of relief of pressure on the chest; the legs have been dorsiflexed and are ready to start their backward thrust. It is advisable for the swimmer to hold his breath for a brief instant while he recovers his arms and while his legs execute the propelling backward thrust.

Complex movement

One complete arm stroke and leg movement form one combined movement cycle in breaststroke. The legs are flexed while the arms are moved inward. The propelling whipping action of the lower legs is executed while the arms are being recovered. The swimmer initiates the next movement cycle as soon as his body reaches the fully extended position. A brief glide in the extended position is necessary, but it's length depends on the individual swimmer's constitution (streamlined body built, propulsive action of his kick) (Fig. 22).

4.4.5.   Medley swimming

The *medley* distances swum are 100 metres, 200 metres and 400 metres the choice depending on the standard of performance and on the age group of the contestants. In a medley event the swimmer must swim four equal distances without interruption using the following strokes and in the following sequence: butterfly, backstroke, breaststroke and crawl. Only those athletes who have outstanding abilities in adjusting to new movements can become good medley swimmers. Mastery of the techniques of all four swimming strokes and the associated turns is the prime pre-requisite. Advances being made in the individual strokes should be made use of in medley swimming as well.

4.4.6.   Relay swimming

In a medley relay each of four swimmers of a team swims an equal part of a total distance specified (usually 4×100 metres) in succession using the following strokes and in the following sequence: backstroke, breaststroke, butterfly stroke and crawl.

In other relay events, such as the men's and women's 4 × 100-metres freestyle and the 4 × 200-metres men's events, which form part of the Olympic events, each swimmer swims part of the total distance using the specified stroke.

4.4.7.   Racing dive

There is hardly any difference between the racing dive techniques used in the prone strokes. In all three strokes (crawl, butterfly, breaststroke) the swimmer should try to react very fast and to push off forcefully in order to make a good start in the race.

Starting position
The swimmer stands behind the starting block and waits for the signal (or he stands on the back edge of the block). On hearing the command for the swimmers to take their marks the swimmer assumes the starting position whose purpose is to tension the muscles used in the racing dive. In this position the swimmer concentrates on the starting signal, his toes gripping the front edge of the downward sloping starting block and keeping his feet 10 to 20 cm apart. His knees and hips are flexed just enough to give his trunk a horizontal position without tiring the swimmer. Tensioning the appropriate muscles only slightly the athlete holds his arms laterally or slightly raised to the front. He keeps his head slightly raised and his eyes on the spot of expected entry.
In the case of the *grip start* the trunk is bent far enough downward to enable the swimmer to "grip" the front surface of the starting block, to give him a good starting position and to enable him to use this surface for additional thrust.

Takeoff and flight phase
What the racing dive has in common with all other forms of locomotion by jumping is that the body's trajectory is determined by the force of the push-off and by the direction of the jump. This fact stresses the importance of the take-off. It should be executed forcefully, and the takeoff thrust should be in as direct an alignment with the body's centre of gravity as possible. The takeoff is introduced either by winding up the arms or by pushing off from the block with one's hands. Depending on the starting position, the arms are moved more or less backward and up and swung smoothly forward again. A good starting position is ensured for the muscles involved by the winding up of the arms, which *Meinel* referred to as the "preparatory phase of the main phase". (52) The winding of the arms initiates the stretching and then the forward fall of the body. This phase is of decisive importance for the correct thrust transmission to the body's centre of gravity and for the optimum takeoff angle. The takeoff drive is produced by flexing the hip, knee and foot joints followed by the quick and vigorous uncoiling and stretching of the feet, trunk and arms.
The takeoff angle depends mainly on the height of the block above the surface of the water and on the racing dive technique. The body's centre of gravity should describe an optimum parabola, since the aim is to push the body as far away from the starting block as possible, to keep it in the most streamlined form to minimize resistance and to achieve a shallow dive. The parabolic trajectory is determined mainly by the takeoff angle. The higher the starting platform is above the surface of the water, the smaller should be the takeoff angle.
During the flight phase the body is kept extended from the fingertips to the toe tips, the head is lowered between the outstretched

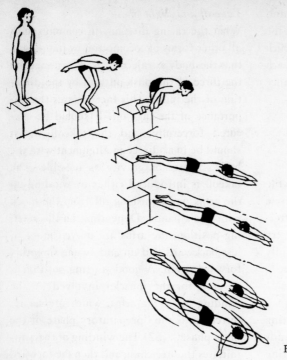

Fig. 23

arms, the palms of the hands are parallel to the water surface with the index fingers touching each other. The body enters the water in this streamlined shape, thus completing the last phase of the racing dive or start (Fig. 23).

Entry and commencement of swimming movement

The swimmer "slips" into the water at an angle of about 20 to 25 °. This angle is not identical with the entry angle of the body's centre of gravity. The latter angle is the angle formed between the surface of the water and the tangent of the parabola at the point of entry of the body's centre of gravity. It is 30 to 35 °. The body glides beneath the surface of the water in a fully outstretched position; the initial speed imparted to the body by the racing start is on the average two and a half times greater than the highest speed attainable through swimming. But resistance of the water soon slows down the body's gliding speed. By adjusting the position of his head and arms in an appropriate manner the swimmer steers his body to the surface in a flat curve and, in the case of crawl, backstroke and butterfly, when his gliding speed has diminished, he first starts with his leg action. In the case of breaststroke the swimmer is allowed one complete movement cycle under water. He takes advantage of this opportunity by following up the glide phase with an underwater stroke (Fig. 24). He does this by executing a pull and push movement with his arms from the outstretched position laterally along his body down to the thighs. He then recovers his arms by moving them close to and underneath his body and stretching them in front of him. During the arm recovery he executes the leg action normally used in breaststroke. The next movement cycle has to be carried out on the surface.

It is advisable for the swimmer to start

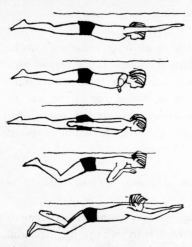

Fig. 24

breathing only after completing one or two complete surface strokes in order to prevent braking his body's glide phase by suddenly raising his head.

4.4.8.   Backstroke start

All laws of biomechanics and dynamics that apply to the racing start apply analogously to the backstroke start. In principle this start too is a "jump" by which the swimmer tries to throw his body as far back as possible above the surface of the water. Existing rules impose greater restrictions on the backstroke start than on the racing dive. The swimmer's legs and arms are at the starting wall or at the backstroke starting bar. During the introductory phase the swimmer can coil his body slightly to tension the muscles that are involved in the start. The rules also leave little room for technical variation. The only part of the start the swimmer is allowed to vary according to his own discretion is the movement pattern involved in whipping back his arms on pushing off (cf. takeoff and flight phase).

Starting position

On hearing the starter's command the swimmer gets down into the water and assumes the prescribed starting position. He takes hold of the handgrip or gutter and places the balls of his feet against the pool wall, making certain that his feet are completely below the surface of the water. He can place his feet against the wall either at the same level or one slightly below the other. The latter position provides greater stability when pushing off from the pool wall, especially if the wall is slippery.

Waiting for the starting signal the swimmer pulls his body up close to the wall in a crouch; his eyes are focused on the wall.

Takeoff and flight phase

On hearing the starting signal the swimmer lets go of the bar or gutter and whips back his arms sideways from his body or over his head (the former technique results in a shallow trajectory and glide curve, the latter in a higher trajectory and deeper glide curve) followed by a quick and vigorous takeoff whose purpose is to push the body out far over the water. Through appropriate head and arm control he slightly arches his back for better entry. He inhales during the takeoff phase.

Entry and commencement of swimming movements

The backstroker's flat trajectory makes for a flat entry angle. Everything else said about the racing start also holds true for the backstroke start. The swimmer straightens his slightly arched back once his arms and head have made the entry, he lowers his head somewhat towards his chest, glides in an outstretched position just below the surface and steers his body in a flat curve to the surface once its speed has diminished in order to commence the active leg and then arm movements (Fig. 25).

Fig. 25

4.4.9.   Relay start

In a relay race the racing start of the first swimmer is similar to that of an individual competitor, but the swimmers that follow can win time by taking advantage of the possibilities offered by the rules of competition, which state only that the hands or feet of the relieving swimmer can leave the starting block or backstroke starting bar or handgrip only once the arriving swimmer has touched. This means that the winding movement and the shifting of the centre of gravity can take place before that. This is the main reason why better times are clocked by relay swimmers than by individual competitors swimming the same distances, provided that the relays of the former are well timed.

What the incoming swimmer should remember

The incoming swimmer's touch should be made in a clearly visible manner either above or at the surface of the water. It should be made smoothly and without hesitation; the arriving swimmer should try to avoid making an intermediate stroke before making the touch. In the case of backstroke relays the relay team should agree beforehand on which side of the lane the incoming swimmers are to make their touch to give the relieving swimmer enough room for his start.

What the relieving swimmer should remember

When the incoming swimmer has about 10 to 15 metres left to swim to the pool wall, the relieving relay swimmer steps onto the starting block or, in the case of backstroke, descends into the water. Mentally he keeps pace with the movements of the team-mate he is about to relieve, and while his teammate is approaching the pool wall he prepares for the takeoff by vigorously winding up (this applies of course only to racing starts from starting blocks). By anticipating the touch he is able to jump the instant his team-mate makes it. These instructions apply analogously to the backstroke relay, which means that the relieving swimmer should pull himself up close to the backstroke handgrip and should let go and jump the instant the arriving swimmer touches the wall.

Relays should be practised intensively in preparing for relay races because they often have a decisive influence on the outcome of a meet.

If a relay is made too early the swimmer can swim back to the wall and start anew in order to prevent being disqualified.

4.4.10.   Turning technique

We have already mentioned earlier that turns play a decisive role in determining the outcome of a race. Well-executed turns are characterized by a clean touch, lightning turn, vigorous push-off and fluid transition to swimming movements.

Upright and flat turns used in crawl, butterfly and breaststroke

In the case of the upright turns, the swimmer assumes an almost upright position during the turn keeping his head above the water. In this position the swimmer can inhale without any difficulty. Thanks to the fact that the turn is relatively easy to learn and that the swimmer's mouth is kept above the water for inhalation during the turn, this technique is preferred in basic swimming instruction. Its drawback is that due to the fact that the swimmer executes the turn in an almost erect position is not very fast (Fig. 26).

In the case of the flat turns, the swimmer's upper body and head remain in an almost horizontal position on the surface of the water during the turn; the swimmer can inhale. The swimmer turns his head and torso in the opposite direction, keeping both level with the surface of the water. He does not straighten out his body in an erect po-

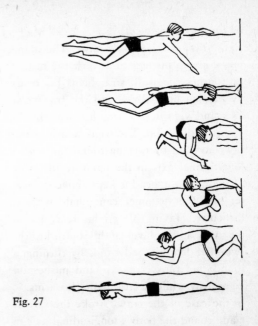

Fig. 27

sition, as a result of which the upper part of his body which is level with the surface produces greater resistance. Inhalation is more difficult, as a result of which the turn is more difficult to learn. Properly executed, the flat turn is slightly faster than the upright turn (Fig. 27).

a) Approach

When approaching the wall the swimmer estimates with which hand he is going to touch the wall and prepares for the corresponding direction of turn. The breaststroker must keep his arm *in the water* at all times, while the butterfly swimmer swings his arms forward *over the water* to the wall (he can also glide to the wall with outstretched arms if the distance to the wall is too short for another stroke). Breaststrokers and butterfliers must touch the wall with both hands simultaneously and at the same level. The swimmer must stay in the prone position until both his hands have made contact. The crawl swimmer, on the other hand, is required to touch the pool wall only with one hand; he is also not required to stay in the prone position.

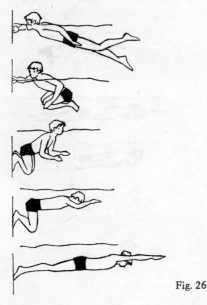

Fig. 26

b) Turning movements

In the case of the *upright turns:* The swimmer coils up his legs to a squat the instant he touches the wall, straightens his trunk by turning his body round the transverse axis and vigorously turns his head in the opposite direction. The trunk and hips follow the head by turning round the body's longitudinal axis in the opposite direction of the pool, the head is kept above the water and the swimmer can inhale without difficulty. Having placed his feet against the wall at the level of his buttocks, the swimmer lets his body sink by turning it round the transverse axis and pushes off vigorously while stretching out his arms.

In the case of the crawl stroke the turn is made round the body's longitudinal axis in the direction of the "open" side, i.e., away from the hand touching the wall. The swimmer's free arm pushes the water towards the pool wall thereby supporting the twist drive produced by the turning of the hips.

Flat turns: flat turns differ from upright turns in that the swimmer does not straighten out his body to an upright position. He keeps his trunk and head in a position flat on the surface of the water and turns his face away from the direction of the turn. He inhales through the furrow that is formed behind the bow wave in front of his head. The turns are executed mainly around the dorsoventral axis.

c) Push-off and transition to swimming movements

After executing these movements the swimmer immediately extends his arms to the front and pushes off vigorously from the wall in the opposite direction keeping his head between his outstretched arms. In the butterfly and breaststroke styles the swimmer must resume the prone position once his feet leave the pool wall.

Fig. 28

Fig. 29

The transition from the glide to the swimming movements is the same as in the case of the racing start and all suggestions given for the latter apply to the former as well (Figs. 26 to 29).

Forward tumble turn used in crawl

The swimmer dives down with his upper body. This movement is initiated with the aid of the arms or with one arm and with the head, the latter reaching the deepest level. With this turning technique the swimmer can inhale before instand of during the turn.

Thanks to the efficient movement pattern the forward movement is smoothly converted into the turning movement. The swimmer forcefully throws his legs over towards the wall thereby speeding up the turn. The efficiency of this turning technique makes the tumble turn the fastest of all.

a) Approach

The swimmer should *approach* the wall at maximum speed. The orientation is effected the same way as in erect and flat turns, the only difference being that with the tumble turn the swimmer inhales during the last arm movement, then he pushes his head down, while throwing his arms and legs over water against the wall to support the turning movement.

b) Turning movements

The sequence of movements involved in changing the direction starts already in the approach phase. Two variants of executing the turn have evolved. In the variant shown in Fig. 30 one arm remains in front of the shoulder after the recovery phase and, together with the other arm–immediately after its extension–, pulls the body forward and down. In the second variant one arm remains at the thigh following the push phase, while the recovered arm pulls the

body in the direction of the turn. The swimmer bends his head downward in order to steer the body in the direction of the turn. The rotation round the transverse axis is immediately linked up with the rotation round the longitudinal and dorsoventral axes. The swimmer coils up his legs to a squat, throws them over towards the wall and places his feet against the wall about 40 cm under the surface of the water. At this point the body is in a lateral squatting position in the water.

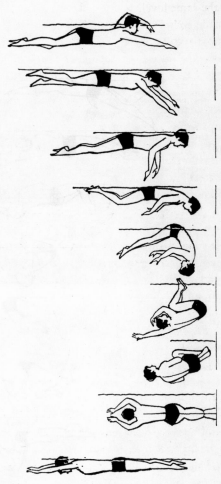

Fig. 30

79

c) Push-off and transition to swimming movement

Just as in the case of the upright and flat turns, the turn is immediately followed by the forward extension of the arms and the body is given a powerful thrust by the push-off. During the glide phase the swimmer levels off completely into the prone position by twisting his body round the long axis of the body. Due to the minor significance of the tumble turns in breaststroke and butterfly they are not described separately. Essentially their execution is the same as that of the forward tumble turns used in crawl, the only difference being that in the former both hands have to touch the pool wall at the same level.

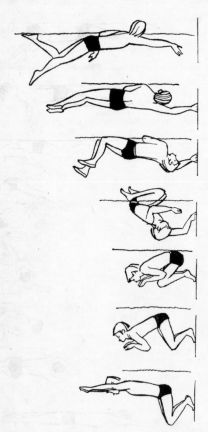

Fig. 31   Backward tumble turn used in crawl

Backstroke turns
a) Approach

The swimmer estimates the number of strokes he has to make before making the turn by slightly dorsi-flexing his neck. He estimates with which hand he will reach the wall first, which will determine with which hand he will initiate the turn. During this orientation phase the swimmer's leg action should be particularly vigorous; however, the swimmer must remain in the supine position in this phase.

b) Turning movements

In the case of the upright turn the swimmer reaches the wall with an extended arm, reaches out to the gutter and grips it from the top or he puts his palm on the flat wall. He then immediately turns round his touch arm almost into a prone position, quickly draws up his legs to a squat and moves them underneath his body towards the wall. During this movement he straightens his trunk to an upright position and inhales. With his free hand he supports the body's rotation round its longitudinal axis and the process of shifting his trunk to an erect position. After his feet have touched the pool wall the swimmer tilts his body in the opposite direction by turning round the transverse axis of the body, dives and stretches his arms overhead (Fig. 32).

In the case of the *flat* turn the swimmer touches the wall over his head with a flexed arm. He puts the hand on the wall just beneath the surface of the water, the fingers pointing in the direction of the twist. Having done this the swimmer immediately coils up his legs to a squat in the direction of the touch arm and quickly throws them sideways towards the wall over the water. The spin is executed about the imaginary dorso-ventral axis with the swimmer remaining in the supine position. He can inhale during the first part of the turn. He

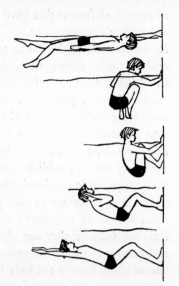

Fig. 32

stretches out his arms in the opposite direction after his feet have found a secure foothold on the pool wall and pushes off.

When executing the *deep* turn the swimmer flings his touch arm towards the wall, takes a deep breath tucks in his chin and puts the palm of his hand on the wall about 30 cm beneath the surface, arching his body slightly. He then tucks his legs and flings

them in a slanted curve above the water towards the wall. The turning movement is supported by pushing against the touch wall with the touch hand and against the water with the free hand. The following turning movements are carried out sequentially: round the transverse axis, round the longitudinal axis and round the dorsoventral axis. The swimmer places his feet approximately where his touch hand was before, he turns his body into the supine position and extends his arms in the direction of the opposite pool wall (Fig. 34).

c) Push-off and commencement of swimming movement

In a fluid series of movements the swimmer extends his hip and knee joints and vigorously pushes himself off from the pool wall. At the instant of the final push-off the swimmer must once again assume the supine position.

The transition to the swimming movement after turning corresponds in every respect to the transition to the swimming movement after the backstroke start.

Fig. 33

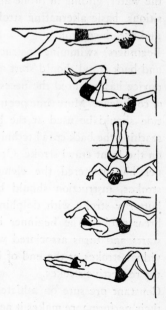

Fig. 34

Turns used in relay swimming

Efficient turns play an important role also in relay swimming. When changing the stroke the rule is that the touch should be made according to the rules governing the preceding stroke, while the push-off should be made in compliance with the rules set down for the stroke to be swum.

In the first change from butterfly to backstroke the swimmer can use an upright or a tumble turn, this also applies to the second change from backstroke to breaststroke; in the third change from breaststroke to crawl the swimmer is free to choose between the upright and the flat turn. A tumble turn is also permitted, but it is seldom used in practice.

4.5. Teaching swimming as a sport

The trainee should have a mastery of such elementary skills as diving, jumping into the water, gliding in prone and supine positions, basic alternating stroke swimming and breath control.

Beginners' swimming instruction in front and back crawl should start as soon as the novice has acquired the necessary measure of confidence. More time per unit of instruction should be used at the beginning for teaching the back crawl technique and later on the front crawl stroke. Once the beginner has mastered the elementary crawl strokes, instruction should be started in butterfly stroke with dolphin kick and in breaststroke. The beginner is taught the starts and turns associated with the individual strokes at the end of instruction in the respective strokes.

Constant pressure on athletes to improve their performance makes it necessary to try to perfect all factors that have a bearing of the athlete's performance.

In the training of the young generation of athletes this means that the emphasis should be on political, ideological and psychic factors, physical abilities and on movement skills, which find their expression in terms of optimum technique. To achieve a higher quality of locomotion in the water and to establish a sound foundation for possible top level athletic performance it is necessary to take into account these factors in organizing workouts and training, because they are closely interrelated and therefore the improvement of any one of these factors not only brings about improvements in other factors but also conditions them.

Despite the necessary unity of all these factors priority should be given to the essential factors in the training of young athletes, notably to the technical and co-ordination factors. The systematic and continuous development of a young athlete's condition should go hand in hand with these performance factors taking into account the educational objectives to be achieved in the process of training and exercise.

The young athlete should not only learn the specific movements and skills involved in his or her athletic field, which is the main objective pursued in basic training, but he or she must also develop the endurance, stamina, speed, joint flexibility, co-ordination, motor learning ability as well as his or her abilities of linking up the different movement patterns, of regulation and orientation in order to be able to practise the technique in question. The beginner should also acquire knowledge and be acquainted with advances in the fields of technique, theory and rules of competition and organization of swimming instruction in the theoretical part of his training. The teacher, coach or instructor will be able to achieve maximum results in a minimum of time only if he concentrates his attention on the development of his student's physical abilities, on teaching and helping them perfect the necessary movement skills and if he does not neglect the theoretical side of instruction. All three sides should be seen as forming a unit in swimming instruction at beginner's level and they should form an integral part of the process of bringing up and educating young people.

4.5.1. Methods of developing physical abilities and movement skills

Before starting with the regular and systematic development of the beginner's condition in the water he should be able to swim a distance of about 25 metres using the front or back crawl leg kick and he should have mastered the elementary form of the complex movement pattern, i.e., in this phase the process of learning should be given precedence over the development of condition. Leg movements for the crawl stroke are taught with the aid of the methodical routines described in the next section.

The simple and complex movements are then developed along with the athlete's condition (particularly his general endurance). One should start using training methods in swimming instruction already at beginners' level in order to meet these requirements in practice. The "interval training method" and its special form of "series interval training" are suitable for use in the initial phases; later on, the "endurance training method" should be used to raise the athlete's level of general endurance.

In the series interval training method used in coaching beginners a given distance is broken up into component distances of 25 metres or more, depending on the standard of performance of the class, which make up a "series". Short rest periods are "built in" between the component distances of the series and at the end of the series the trainee is allowed to take a longer break. The number of series to one training unit will also depend on the performance capacity of the class.

The athletes should cover the individual component distances at an average speed. (In this context average speed should be construed to mean a speed of 80 to 90 per cent of the maximum speed achievable in the component distance using the stroke in question). If properly scheduled, this type of training, which again should be based on the class' standard of performance, helps to develop the swimmers' general endurance and especially their stamina for swimming short distances at high speeds. The component distances should be gradually lengthened in order to achieve functional adaptation of the swimmer's cardiovascular system. In this way the swimmer is prepared for the endurance training method. But the transition to the latter method should be made only once the swimmers have improved their technique to the point where the component distances can be lengthened.

The rest periods–dispersed between the series in the series interval method–are designed to give the swimmers a chance to rest, at the same time they can be used to teach them new movement elements. The coach should take into account two important aspects. On the one hand the swimmer should get enough rest to be able to carry out the next stage of exercise, on the other hand new component movements should be introduced and their elementary execution learned. The intensity (speed) should be reduced to an appropriate level, i.e., below 70 per cent of the maximum intensity.

To get a better notion of the series interval method let us consider the following example of training a group of children (Chart 5).

The group's standard of performance is a decisive factor in using the endurance training method. Swimming distances of 200 metres is tantamount to endurance training for instance in the case of 6 to 7 year-olds.

Once the trainees have achieved a sufficient measure of refinement in swimming short component distances the distances should be lengthened. This results in greater stress on the swimmer. He is forced to carry out all movements economically in order to overcome the water resistance in the most efficient manner and on the other hand to utilize the resistance in the most efficient manner for propulsion. This method is designed to refine the technique and to develop such physical abilities as general endurance. Wrong movements should be constantly corrected.

Chart 5 An example illustrating the series interval method

Distance		Rest at end of component distance or series
Warm up		
200 metres	Back crawl complex movement	3 minutes
Main part	Crawl leg action	30 seconds
1st series	Butterfly stroke and	5 minutes
2×50 metres	dolphin kick	
1st series rest		
2nd series		
4×25 metres	Crawl complex movement with alternate lateral breathing	15 seconds
2nd series rest	Dolphin movement in prone position with push-off (up to 5 metres)	5 minutes
3rd series		
2×50 metres	Crawl arm movement	30 seconds
3rd series rest	Dolphin movement in supine position with push-off (up to 5 metres)	5 minutes
4th series		
4×25 metres	Crawl movement with alternate lateral breathing	15 seconds
4th series rest	Repeat of the dolphin movement in supine position	5 minutes
5th series		
2 × 100 metres	Back crawl complex movement	30 seconds
5th series rest	Repeat of the dolphin movement in prone position	5 minutes
Final part	Dolphin tag	5 minutes

4.5.2. Methodical routines for teaching the strokes

The technical elements of the different swimming strokes are taught in the following sequence: leg movement, arm movement, combined movement; breathing is linked up with the individual movement patterns and with the combined movement (cf. ch. 4.3.1.), which together form the complex movement.

The mode of instruction is based on the psychological, physiological and motor level of development of the learners, on the phases of motor learning (after *Meinel*) and on the facilities available.

Swimming instruction of any age group always begin with a demonstration. It is followed by emulation and oral instruction and, if need be, the movement is demonstrated on land to give the learner a better visual idea of it. Swimming exercises are first carried out with human assistance in water of hip to breast depth, wise use being made of artificial swimming aids. If no

84

shallow swimming facilities are available the exercises should be performed at the gutter or in the safety zone formed with the aid of the swimming rungs described earlier.

Once the learners are able to swim a distance of 8 to 10 metres using a movement they have just learned in its elementary form they can begin with the next part of the exercise. The newly-acquired movement is improved by swimming short component distances using that movement. The sum of the component distances is the total distance planned for the instruction distance.

The following are the reasons why the short component distance is advisable:

1. The movement pattern can be maintained.

2. The breathing difficulties a beginner experiences have little detrimental influence on the combined movement pattern.

3. The speed of movement remains nearly constant.

4. Frequent repetition reinforces the skill with which a movement is performed.

5. The rest periods between the individual component distances can be short and yet they are long enough for the swimmer to recover after the brief period of work.

6. Brief instructions can be given during the rest periods. The component distances should be lengthened systematically in order further to reinforce the movement learned and to improve the swimmers' endurance. The learners should start with the aid of simple movements and later on proceed to combined movements.

The common features of all swimming strokes are illustrated on the basis of the *crawl stroke*. This is followed by showing the learners special exercises designed to help them learn the other strokes.

Teaching the crawl leg movement

A short demonstration should be given *on land* of the leg movement to help the learners get a better notion of the leg movement pattern. The person demonstrating the movement should stand in such a manner that the supporting leg is somewhat elevated (on a step, edge of the pool deck, etc.) so that the joint of the other foot can be extended. It is advisable to carry out this exercise in water of knee depth, the supporting foot should also stand in an elevated position.

All other exercises should be carried out in the water. If water of knee depth is available the exercises can be carried out in the *body press* (push–up) position. The arms should yield to the thrust produced by the leg action by being placed one in front of the other as if one were walking on one's hands.

If the exercises are conducted *at the pool wall* the learner gets hold of the gutter or of the handgrip with one hand using the ordinary gasp and supports himself with the other hand which he presses against the wall 30 to 40 cm below the surface of the water, the fingers pointing to the bottom of the pool. He should keep his arms stretched out in order to keep his body in a horizontal position. At first the learner raises his head to be able to breathe freely, later on he lowers his head and inhales on the side of the supporting arm and exhales in the direction of the pool bottom. Once in a while the arms should be alternated.

At the beginning the leg movement is performed with nearly extended legs.

If *human support* is used, the person exercising should lie outstretched keeping his body in a streamlined position and his arms extended in the swimming direction. His partner stands in front of the learner and places his hands below those of the latter; he should make sure that they are on the surface of the water. The partner should yield to the thrust produced by the swimmer's leg action by walking backward, but he should not pull him.

The learner should not exercise too long on land, at the pool wall, in the body-press position or with human support. As soon as he is able to perform the movement in its elementary form he should practise it after *pushing off and gliding*. It is advisable to have him use a float in order to enable him to concentrate fully on his leg movement. The float, made of plastics such as Ekazell, should be held on the sides with the arms extended, the float should not be pushed under the water. The learner should start with the leg movement after pushing off and gliding, he should not hollow the small of his back. He should raise his head just high enough so that his mouth is above the surface so as to be able to breathe freely. Once the learner has swum a distance of about 25 metres using the leg movement he should start practising lateral breathing used in the crawl stroke linking it up with the leg action. He should keep his face in the water up to the hairline. The swimmer uses four leg beats to an inhalation and two beats to an inhalation. He then puts his face in the water again and begins exhaling again. The learner counts his leg beats (1 to 6). Inhalation on either side should be learned and practised by turning the head.

The following exercises are recommended for short distances for the purpose of refining the leg movement and strengthening the leg musculature:

1. Pushing off and gliding followed by leg action. Arms are held outstretched in front of the body.
2. Repeat of exercise 1, except that arms are overlapped in front of the head.
3. Repeat of exercise 1, except that arms are held along the sides of the body.

4. Repeat of exercise 1, except that the hands are folded on the back.

Since no arm support is used in exercises 2 to 4, the leg movement must be executed more powerfully.

Technical and methodical suggestions:
These suggestions apply to exercising front and back crawl leg movements:

1. The swimmer should maintain a streamlined position keeping his shoulders on the surface of the water. One should avoid hollowing the small of one's back.
2. The kick is initiated at the hips.
3. During the ventral beat the swimmer flexes his legs slightly in the knee joint and pigeon-toes his feet. The ventral beat should be executed with special force.
4. In executing the dorsal beat the swimmer keeps his legs extended and straightens his feet in line with his lower legs.
5. He should find his individual optimum leg swing amplitude of between 30 and 50 cm and stick to it.

The crawl arm movement
The learner obtains his initial notion of the arm movement pattern from a demonstration, a description, by trying the movement in the water and by practising the movement for a short time on land (in order to get a visual idea of the movement pattern). This initial notion is then perfected through systematic exercises in the water.

The learner starts out by standing with one foot in front of the other and with his body bend forward and arms stretched in front in water of hip or chest depth. It is important that the learner keep his trunk in a position as if he were swimming and his shoulders on the surface. The learner starts by alternately swinging his arms forward using the technique that had been demonstrated to him. Breathing is not taken into account at this stage. Once the pupil has learned the movement pattern in its elementary form he repeats it, linking it up with breathing. He should practise inhaling on either side. The next exercise is carried out by having the learner's partner position himself between the spread legs of the learner and support him on the surface of the water by holding him by his legs just above the knees. The partner can also stand behind the learner and support him by his ankles, which are kept together. He should not raise his legs out of the water because this would disturb the learner's streamlined position. The helper yields to the drive produced by the arm movement by walking forward. Artificial swimming aids such as inflatable rubber rings or small floats can also be used for supporting the swimmer's legs. In exercises with human assistance and with artificial aids the learner should first practise the arm movements without linking them up with breathing, later on he should co-ordinate the timing of his movements with breathing.

During the next stage of skill development the pupil practises the arm movement without support; this is done best by pushing off from the pool wall. He should balance his body by swinging his legs gently up and down. Just as in the case of the preceding forms of exercise the learner co-ordinates his breathing with the arm movement. Once the learner achieves a clearly perceptible amount of drive through his arm movements, he should begin co-ordinating the arm swing with the leg action and exercise the combined movement.

Notes on technique and method:

1. The learner should maintain a streamlined body position when practising the arm movement.
2. The hand should trail the elbow throughout the power phase ("high elbow" position, cf. Technical and methodical suggestions).

3. The movement should be accelerated throughout the pull phase and it should reach its peak in the last third of the underwater power phase.
4. The learner should not avoid the water resistance during the power phase by swaying.
5. The drive or power phase should not be broken off too early. The learner should try to achieve an optimally long, horizontal drive path.
6. The learner should try to achieve maximum relaxation of his arm during the overwater recovery phase. The elbow is kept pointing upwards.
7. The transition from one movement phase to the next should be fluid.
8. The hand should not reach across the longitudinal axis of the body when making the entry; the entry should be made in front of the shoulder. The learner should keep his eyes open in the water in order to check the correct arm movement.

Teaching the combined crawl movement

Most learners do not find it difficult to co-ordinate their arm and leg movements. Many beginners start combining the arm movement rhythmically with the leg action as they start learning the arm movement. But some learners will find it necessary to use the exercises described in the following in order to co-ordinate their arm and leg movements.

The push-off and glide are followed first by the leg movement, with the arms being held stretched out to the front and the head, slightly raised, between the arms. The arm movement is linked with the leg movement four to five metres after the push-off. During the six leg beats one arm must execute one complete movement cycle consisting of the power phase and the recovery phase. The correct rhythmic co-ordination of the arm and leg movements can be supported by acoustic signals or keeping a mental count of the leg beats.

It is also possible to co-ordinate only one arm with the leg beat in order to enable the person practising better to concentrate on the arm-leg movement co-ordination, in which case the other arm is held stretched out to the front (it can also be supported by a little Ekazell float). Breathing is then integrated into the stroke pattern in such a way that the head is always turned to the side of the active arm when inhaling.

A good breathing technique is indispensable in sustained swimming performance, that is why special importance should be attached to it in that part of the training in which the learner is taught to integrate his arm and leg movements into combined movements.

After the push-off and after starting the combined movement, the pupil first starts concentrating on the "breathing arm". He should cover a short distance using the complex movement, exhaling, inhaling and exhaling again in the process.

The technique of first teaching the learner to link up one breathing cycle with two complete movement cycles has proved to be effective in preventing undue disrupting influence on the breathing rhythm; in the subsequent training phase the learner is readjusted to one breath cycle for each stroke cycle. It is advisable to have the learner practise inhaling on both sides from the very start. The swimming distance shoudl also be lengthened systematically.

Notes on technique and method:

1. After the push-off and glide the learner should first start with the leg movement followed by the arm movement.

2. Attention should be paid to maintaining an effective leg movement throughout the complex movement.

3. The body should be kept extended and the shoulders horizontal to the surface of the water.

4. Air should be exhaled *into the water* and the exhalation should be timed in such a way that it is completed when the "breath arm" completes the power phase. Only the head, not the shoulders, should be turned to the side when inhaling.

5. Inhalation should be practised on both sides.

6. The swimming distance should be gradually lengthened in order to prevent the development of faulty complex co-ordination.

7. The point of transition from the glide to the active use of the leg and arm movement, which should be fixed on an individual basis, should be practised frequently until the swimmer has mastered the timing.

Special features of backstroke swimming
a) Leg movement

Learners should start exercising with *human support*. The learners should stand in a circle holding hands in such a way that their arms are stretched out. Every second learner lies in the water in a supine position, his feet pointing to the centre of the circle. In this position the learners are told to start beating their legs up and down alternately keeping their feet extended and loose. They should make certain that only their toes break the surface of the water.

After changing partners several times the learners are told to turn their feet inward in the foot joint during the upward beat.

After these exercises instruction should centre on the leg movement after the push-off and glide.

The following forms of exercise have brought good results:

1. Push-off and glide assisted by leg action, paddling action of the arms on either side of the body helps the swimmer float in the water.

2. Exercises described in item 1 above are performed, the arms are kept motionless beside the body.

3. Exercises as described in item 1, hands are clasped beneath the buttocks, hips held high.

4. Exercises as in item 1, arms held stretched out on the surface of the water, hands gripping above the hips.

5. Exercises as in item 1, one arm held overhead in the water, the other is placed against the thigh (the arms are alternated).

Notes on technique and method:
In addition to the points to bear in mind in connection with crawl swimming, the novice learning the backstroke technique should

1. constantly match his feet,

2. make certain that his body is kept stretched out and not "broken" at the hip joint,

3. keep his knees under the water in all phases of the kick, but he should also try to achieve a quick and powerful upswing.

b) Arm movement
In a brief introductory drill the learners practise the hand movement by rotating their arms in a windmill fashion on land. They then stand with their backs against a wall or lie down on their backs on the ground and modify the windmill arm movement in such a manner that they move their arms sideways along the body. It should be made certain from the very start that the swimmer's arms never stop even for a brief moment at the thighs, in overhead position or in the slanting arms-up position. This exercise can also be performed very effectively in shallow water about 15 to 20 cm deep.

All other forms of exercise can be derived from the methodical routine for crawl arm movement.

Notes on technique and method:
The points mentioned in connection with crawl swimming also apply analogously to backstroke swimming. In addition the learner should remember that

1. the elbow joint should be flexed progressively from the point of entry until the hand reaches the shoulder line and from that point on extended quickly and forcefully,

2. the "high elbow" position used in the crawl stroke is applied analogously to the backstroke and is maintained during the power phase until the last third of the underwater movement, the movement of the hand being accelerated until the elbow joint is fully extended,

3. the arm movement is executed 15 to 30 cm under the surface of the water,

4. the arms should be as relaxed as possible during recovery.

c) Complex movement
The exercise forms described for crawl swimming should be analogously applied to the backstroke. Thanks to the fact that the swimmer's mouth and nose are above the surface of the water almost all the time it is relatively easy for him to integrate breathing into the complex movement. It is advisable to link up breathing with the movement of one arm, inhaling during the recovery phase, exhaling during the push phase.

Special features of the butterfly stroke (with dolphin kick)
a) The dolphin kick
The swimmer must master the front and back crawl kick before starting to learn the dolphin kick. Dexterity of the torso is very important in executing the dolphin movement. This dexterity can be developed through specially designed gymnastic exercises and through swing exercises on the

rings, horizontal bar and asymmetrical parallel bars (undershoot). Preliminary exercises in the water should also be selected in such a manner that they also help to develop nimbleness along the thoracic and lumbar sections of the spinal column and to help the swimmer become consciously aware of the flow of movement from the torso to the legs.

The learner is introduced to the dolphin movement when he first begins to practise *dolphin leaps* during crawl swimming instruction. "Dolphin leaps" are practised in water of hip to chest depth. The learner makes a powerful leap up and forward, swinging his arms forward and then going into a dive with his arms and then his head, which he holds between them, entering the water first. During the leap the body describes a flat arc above the surface of the water. Immediately after the dive the arms and the head steer the body to the surface again as a result of which a pronounced hollow is formed in the small of the swimmer's back. The swimmer then coils up his legs close to his body and places his feet on the bottom in preparation for the next dolphin leap.

To avoid hitting the bottom of the pool with the head when practising in shallow water the swimmer should touch the bottom of the pool with his hands and push off to the top. Continuous repetition of such dolphin leaps helps the swimmer acquire the dolphin leg kick. The swimmer swings his arms forward over the water when practising these leaps.

In the next phase of acquiring the dolphin kick the swimmer should learn to swing his legs in a whip-like fashion after pushing off from the bottom of the pool; the swing should start from the torso. Backward and sideways dolphin leaps can be executed in a similar manner.

Dolphin tag should be added to the programme to give it more variety once the learners have mastered the dolphin leap technique. This simple form of tag should be played in water of hip to chest depth, the players being allowed neither to run nor to swim; they should move forward, backward or sideways only by using the dolphin leap technique. To add enjoyment to training, dolphin tag will also be used in the swimming training programme described in the following.

Demonstration of the movement pattern is a very important means of helping the learner to acquire other skills required for the dolphin movement. The demonstration helps the learner to see how the movement impulse starts from the torso and how it flows down to the thighs, lower legs and feet. Visually going through the movement pattern makes it easier for the learner to graps the movement structure and to improve his own rendition of it. His learning of the movement pattern is also facilitated by his acquiring manifold movement experience in the course of performing the dolphin movement.

Good results have been achieved by starting the dolphin movement from a position in which the learner stands erect against the wall. The pressure his legs are exposed to in the water is equal from all sides, and thanks to the fact that he has a secure hold with his arms he can control his movement pattern. With his arms extended forward the learner holds on to the gutter, handgrip, swimming rung or some similar object and watches his movements, making certain that the ventral movement starts with a conscious forward movement of the hips.

By letting go of the object he is holding on to for brief periods he can check the action of the dolphin movement.

This is followed by exercises in prone, lateral and supine positions. In the initial phase human support can be used as in crawl swimming; later on the learner begins with the dolphin movement after the push-off and the glide. The gliding float is also used in the supine and prone positions.

If the dolphin kick is practised in the *supine position* following the push-off, the movement is supported by paddling movements of the hands on either side of the body to help stabilize its position. Attention should be paid to pushing the hips upwards and to the whip-like kick with the lower legs. The swimmer's shoulders should not move too much up and down. The learner can breathe unobstructed.

When exercising in the *lateral position* (right or left), the lower arm is stretched out forward, while the other supports the body's lateral position by paddling movements behind the back or in front of the chest. In this exercise the learner can watch his movements and make sure that he forcefully pushes his hips forward.

The dolphin movement in *prone position* is practised below and on the surface, the former should always start with pushing off and gliding, the arms are stretched out to the front at first. Once the body loses some of its drive, the swimmer pulls his arms through laterally down to the thighs without interrupting the dolphin movement. (The swimmer should slowly exhale into the water in the process.)

On the surface the learner should start practising the dolphin movement after pushing off and gliding first without breathing. When it is time to link up rhythmic breathing with the movement it is advisable to use a gliding float at the beginning.

Good results have been achieved in the initial phase of integrating breathing by having the learner inhale and exhale once to every four dolphin kicks. This gives him more time to concentrate on breathing. He should time his breathing in such a way that exhalation ends with an upswing of the legs so as to link up the inhalation with a downswing. This principle applies, also when breathing is linked with two dolphin beats. It is advisable to start a few swimming exercises by using the crawl leg movement after pushing off and gliding in order to achieve a quick and whip-like movement rhythm. After about 3 metres the learner continues swimming using the same quick leg movement, except that he performs the swings of the legs simultaneously.

Notes on technique and method:
1. In all forms of exercise one should make certain that the movement impulse starts from the trunk and that the ventral hip movement is stressed.
2. The swing amplitude (distance between the highest and the lowest foot position) should be about 30 to 40 cm. In the initial phase of instruction it is advisable to use a lower swing amplitude in order to preserve a smooth flow of movement.
3. If the swing amplitude is still too high for the beginner, the use of a few vigorous crawl kicks after pushing off and gliding followed by a quick transition to the dolphin movement has proved effective.
4. There should be no breaks between the individual movement cycles, and it is particularly important to make sure that there is no break at the end of the downswing.
5. The head and the shoulders should be as steady as possible during the dolphin movement.

b) Arm movement
The methodical routine described for the crawl arm movement should be used in its adapted form when learning the butterfly arm movement.

Notes on technique and method:

1. The swimmer should apply progressively more force during the power phase, maximum effort being made in the last third of the power phase. The last part of the propulsive movement should be stressed in order to achieve the right force application pattern in the dynamic structure of the movements.

2. At the end of the power phase the swimmer pushes his hands laterally away from his body. He should end the power phase before the hands reach the thighs. The elbows are slightly bent when the swimmer commences the over-water recovery.

3. He begins inhaling during the last third of the underwater power phase, his body lying flat in the water.

4. He should keep his arms relaxed during recovery. To enable the swimmer to swing his arms forward without touching the water during the recovery phase he should be instructed to swing his arms forward quickly while keeping elbow high and his head and shoulders on the surface.

c) Complex movement

It is not easy at the beginning to co-ordinate the dolphin kick and the arm movements and the learner must practise a great deal before he can do it properly. Beginners should start learning the complex movement only when they are able to cover a distance of about 20 metres using the dolphin movement alone.

First a few dolphin kicks are performed after pushing off and gliding a short distance, the arms being held stretched out to the front.

The pull commences when the legs start a downward beat. At the beginning the swimmer covers a short distance without inhaling again. During this period he should exhale the air slowly through his mouth and nose into the water. It is advisable to use acoustic signals or to count ("one and two, and one and two") to co-ordinate the arm and leg movements and in this manner to help the learner acquire the rhythm of the complex movement pattern.

To disrupt the movement rhythm as little as possible the learner should be instructed first to inhale and exhale once to every four movement cycles, later on once to every two cycles. Linking one movement cycle to one breathing cycle often makes the process of learning this stroke more difficult.

Notes on technique and method:

1. After the push-off and glide the swimmer should first start with the dolphin movement and then with the butterfly stroke.

2. There should not be any breaks in the succession of dolphin movements during the complex movement.

3. To make it easier for the learner to time his breathing it is important for him to bear in mind that he should complete the exhalation by the time he reaches the middle of the power phase movement during which he exhales (e. g. when breathing once to two stroke cycles he should finish exhaling by the middle of the second power phase movement) in order to be able to inhale properly in the next movement.

Special features of the breaststroke

Once the pupils have learned the first three strokes it is not difficult for them to learn the breaststroke. All forms of exercise described for the other swimming styles should be applied analogously in the methodical teaching of the breaststroke.

a) Leg movement
Notes on technique and method:

1. The swimmer's body lies stretched out in a streamlined position during the leg movement, his head steady.

2. His leg movement should be continuous, fluid and without jerks. His heels should be kept close together and at the beginning his knees should also be kept together, his lower legs moving to his buttocks during the recovery phase of the leg movement; but the buttocks should not be raised in the process. In the last phase of the leg recovery the knees may be opened slightly, the feet should be flexed.

3. To make certain that there is a smooth transition between the initial phase and the main phase of the leg movement it is advisable to help the swimmer regulate his effort by calling out the cadence (e.g., "and press–and press"), the emphasis being laid on "press".

4. In those cases where pupils have particular difficulty in learning the breaststroke leg movement or where faulty execution (unequal leg recovery, "scissors") is noticed, the following procedure has proved effective: The learner lies in prone position on a bench, the end of the bench being situated below the mid-length of the learner's thighs. He flexes his knees and retracts his legs so that his heels almost touch his buttocks and then extends them again to the starting position. He keeps his knees and heels close together, flexes his feet towards the shins and points his toes outwards. A partner holds his hands against the learner's soles to make the latter conscious of the "sole pressure" when he stretches his legs. Later this exercise is repeated in the water until the learner feels the water pressure against his soles and the resulting thrust. At first the exercises should be performed in shallow water, the arms being used for *"walking"* forward on the hands. The exercises can also be performed with *human support*. Once the pupil has learned to move a few metres forward in this manner he should practise on land again. The movement described above is then fol-lowed by slightly opening the heels after retracting the legs. The learner now executes a sort of back "straddle kick" with his lower legs. To enable the learner to concentrate on the proper foot position it is advisable to put a rubber band, which should yield somewhat, around his legs above the knees. The swimming instructor should still check to make sure that the learner's heels are close together during leg recovery and that the feet are flexed towards the shins at all times.

Once the learners have acquired a firm grasp of this breaststroke leg movement pattern they should start parting their knees slightly at the beginning of the backward thrust and extending their feet at the end of the straddle kick. This improves the efficiency of the propulsive movement in the water.

b) *Arm movement*
Notes on technique and method:
1. The arm movement is practised in shallow water in kneeling position and in standing position one foot placed in front of the other.
2. The instructor helps the learner time the dynamics of the effort pattern with the aid of acoustic signals in a manner similar to that described for the leg movement.
3. The arms should be fully extended after each movement cycle.
4. Unlike the other strokes, breathing in the case of the breaststroke should be integrated into the movement pattern already in the preliminary arm exercise phase.

c) *Complex movement*
Notes on technique and method:
1. The legs are used at the beginning of the link between the arm and leg movement when the arm movement is completed. The instructor calls out "arms"–"legs", "pull"–"push", etc., to signal the learner

when he is to apply the maximum amount of effort.

2. Subsequently in the course of the exercise the acoustic signal cadence is modified in such a manner that it corresponds to the technically correct movement pattern (after the push-off and glide the learner first starts with the arm movement and at the end of the pull he starts with the leg movement).

3. At the end of the leg movement the arms should remain extended for a brief instant (glide phase) so as to enable the learner to concentrate fully on the next movement cycle.

The glide phase is systematically diminished as the learner's proficiency improves, until at the end it disappears almost altogether.

4. For the learner to maintain a steady position in the water he should hold his head as steady as possible, i.e., he should not turn or incline it to either side.

Special features of medley swimming

The significance of medley swimming has grown especially thanks to the fact that it plays an important role as a means of special training in perfecting co-ordination and improving the swimmer's condition, i.e., in developing all-round faculties, and it is included in the Olympic events programme as a 400 metres women's and men's event. Medley swimmers should practise the different strokes involved in special complexes. Experience has shown that it is not advisable to start with all four swimming styles, but to begin by connecting two strokes (including the associated turn), adding the third and subsequently the fourth stroke to the training programme.

The following combinations are recommended for training purposes: butterfly–backstroke, backstroke–breaststroke, breaststroke–crawl.

This applies analogously to the athlete who begins practising swimming as a sport. Once he has learnt a new stroke he should link it to the stroke he had learnt before that and practise the two as part of the complete medley series.

4.5.3. Methodical routines for learning the start

The swimmer's jumping strength must have reached the average level of development and he must have mastered the technique of commencing the different swimming movements after gliding in prone and supine positions before he can start learning the racing starts.

The racing start

The swimmer should first practise the simple popular forms of jumping into the water before starting to learn the head-first starting dive. Easy head-first diving in shallow water, rolls, handsprings–with human support if necessary–dolphin leaps, etc., are part of the preparatory exercises. Training according to the system is conducted at the next higher stage of preparation, this is followed by the development of the forward head-first jump (cf. "Jumping into the water", Chart 18).

A relatively large number of learners, especially children of early or middle school age, learn the elementary co-ordination of the racing start practically at the first attempt if the start is properly demonstrated to them. They can start learning the refined form of the start without going through the preliminary methodical steps leading up to it.

In any case it is worthwhile to try to have the learners acquire the racing start technique "at the first try".

The glide phase is directly connected with

the trajectory and the entry angle. That is why the learner should be assigned concrete tasks such as gliding a certain distance after takeoff, or the pupils should be made to compete to see who can glide farthest or who can cover a fixed distance in the shortest time. A feeling for the jump, the flight phase, entry and the glide phase is reinforced by such exercises. In the final phase the learners practise the racing start in conjunction with a signal to get them used to the actual contest situation.

Notes on technique and method:
1. The water should be sufficiently deep for the initial phase of practising the racing start.
2. Forward fall-in dive exercises from standing position should be carried out in several variations from the pool deck and from the starting block.
3. To achieve a good takeoff the learner should prepare for it by winding up several times.
4. The learner's trajectory can be corrected by holding a pole at a certain height in front of the point of takeoff or by marking the point of desired entry.
5. In all racing start exercises the body should be stretched out.
6. The transition from the glide to the active swimming movement should be practised often in order to develop in the learner a feeling for the right moment to start the active use of his arms and legs.

The backstroke start
The beginner often finds it difficult to dive backwards head first. He can overcome this difficulty by learning the importance of the head's steering function during the flight phase, at entry and during the glide (by explaining and demonstrating this function).
The swimmer first practises throwing back

his body over the surface of the water in such a manner that after takeoff a deep hollow is formed in the small of his back, even if he dives deeper as a result. His feet need a good foothold for the thrust, there should also be a proper handgrip which he can hold on to. If these facilities are not available at the pool in question they should be built or improvised in the form of handgrips on starting blocks or ladders, ropes, poles, etc. To prevent slipping, learners should be permitted to put their feet in the gutter at the beginning. This can also facilitate the transition from the extended body posture to hollowing the small of the back.
In the second phase of the exercise the trajectory is gradually flattened to enable the swimmer to enter at the best possible angle.

Notes on technique and method for the backstroke start:
1. In preparing for a vigorous takeoff the swimmer should wind up several times in the starting position.
2. The transition in the body posture from the takeoff to commencing the swimming movements should be practised repeatedly. The backward dolphin leap is recommended as a supplementary exercise for this purpose.
3. The backstroke start should also be practised under simulated race conditions.

4.5.4.   Methodical routines for learning the turns

The ability to execute turns efficiently and quickly depends on the swimmer's reactions, his springiness (thrust) and his linking and orientation capacity. For this reason, *all forms of exercise on land* that help to develop these abilities can be used. New turning techniques should be demonstrated and explained to the learners before they start practising them. It is also advisable to illustrate the movement pattern of a turn with the aid of films or picture series.

Preliminary exercises should be performed *in the water* before the learners are asked to execute the actual turns. The purpose of these exercises is to make the swimmer consciously aware of the turning movements involved in performing a particular turn and to enable him to retain his orientation throughout all the phases of a turn. During these exercises the emphasis should be on twists about the long axis and somersaults about the transverse and dorsoventral axes of the body. It is important that the swimmer should tuck in his legs quickly and that he should use his head, his free arm, his shoulders and above all his hips. The following exercises have proved useful:

1. Continuous twisting about the long axis, the trunk is held upright in the water, legs tucked, the arms support the twist.

2. As in item 1, except that the arms are crossed in front of the chest, as a result of which the hips must be used more vigorously to support the twist.

3. As in item 1, except that the swimmer should perform a halftwist (180 degrees) instantly at call. The swimmer should practise with and without the assistance of his arms.

4. Twisting from supine position through the vigorous use of hips and hands in the water.

5. Repeated turning about the dorsoventral axis of the body. The swimmer lies in supine position, legs tucked, chin slightly tucked in, arms and hands push against the water to produce rotation in the desired direction.

6. As in item 5, except that the 180-degree turns are performed at call instantly.

7. As in item 6, except that the turns are made from supine outstretched position, legs

should be tucked in at lightning speed, the lower legs describe a semi-circle over the surface in the process.

8. Shoulder circle, forward and backward (turning about the transverse axis).

The swimmer then learns *turning and twisting from swimming position in the water without touching the pool wall.* The swimmer executes turns and twists about the different body axes as described above, performing the turns that are used with the different strokes. But in this phase of instruction attention is focused on turning in the water without touching the pool wall. The purpose of this exercise is to have the swimmer acquire the different body twists and turns involved with the different turning techniques. Turning in the water without touching the wall is practised as the swimmer approaches the wall and just before he touches it. After the swimmer has performed the turn he should touch the pool wall with his feet and push off in the opposite direction. It is important that the swimmer should stretch his body completely after pushing off.

The swimmer then performs preparatory exercises for developing high and flat turns *as he glides toward the pool wall.* These exercises help him develop optimum timing for commencing the turn sequence.

The swimmers stand 1.5 to 2 metres from the pool wall in water of hip depth with their trunks bent toward the wall. One or both arms are stretched out toward the wall, depending on the turn to be performed. The swimmer vigorously push themselves off with their legs from the pool floor, glide toward the wall and practise the turn and the subsequent transition to the particular stroke. In the next phase of instruction the swimmer approaches the wall from different distances and practises the different turning and twisting movements in either direction involved in the different turns.

Preliminary exercises designed to precede the *flat back turn* should be performed on smooth, wet tiles on land. In these exercises the swimmer lies on his back on the tiled floor with one hand touching the wall behind his head. He tucks his legs in the direction of the hand touching the wall and at the same time pushes himself off the wall with the hand touching it, turning about the dorsoventral axis by 180 degrees in the process. He feels for the wall with his feet, stretches his arms back over his head and pushes himself off the wall. This exercise can also be performed in shallow water (15 to 20 cm deep).

It is not advisable to resolve the movement sequence into its components when learning the low turns, because a high approach speed is needed for correct execution. Turning movements about the three body axes described previously in deep water away from the wall and intensive pushing off and transition exercises are recommended among other exercises.

Notes on technique and method for teaching the turns:

1. The swimmer should learn consciously to perform the different twisting and turning movements involved in the different turns.

2. The approach speed should be at its peak the swimmer commences the turn sequence.

3. Proper hand position is important when making the touch. It is one of the decisive factors determining the speed of the turn and the initial phase of the turn.

4. A good push-off can be made and time won only if the swimmer's feet touch the wall 30 to 40 cm below the surface of the water.

5. The transition from the turning movement sequence to the swimming movements should be practised just as often as the tran-

sition from the racing start to the swimming movements.

6. It is important for the swimmers to learn and practise the turns to either side.

7. Swimming across the pool and practising the turns is a good method of refining the turning technique, because the distance across the pool is shorter, allowing the swimmer to execute more turns per unit distance swum than swimming lengthwise, and to rest more frequently between the distances swum.

To conclude, we should like to say that advances that are constantly being made in the application of physical, physiological and psychological laws and the evolution of educational methods result in constant improvements being made in the training methods, which, in turn, will lead to further improvements in swimmers' performance.

4.6. Basic training in swimming as a sport

4.6.1. Characterization and purpose of basic training

Basic training, the first and fundamental phase of training, follows immediately after *basic instruction* and in some cases it is given in conjunction with the last phase of basic instruction.

Due to the fact that performances of international note in swimming can be and are being achieved already by athletes in their early teens, basic training, preceded by basic instruction, should be started at an early stage. Experience gathered to date shows that the best age at which basic training should be started is 8 to 10 years (variations are determined by the type of basic instruction, biological maturity, sex and other individual factors). The duration of basic training in swimming is generally 4 to 6 years, but it is subject to many different factors. The purpose of basic training is to prepare athletes for athletic achievement of the highest standard. Relatively good performance must be achieved in basic instruction before going on to basic training with a view to reaching international performance level. But aspirations for record performance should never be the primary objective of basic training, they should be secondary to the main objective, which is *optimum* preparation for advanced training and for *future* record performance. The principle of unity of education and upbringing is realized in basic training by paying equal attention to the development of physical abilities and swimming skills, to the formation of valuable character traits and to teaching basic theoretical knowledge in the field of sports in planning and carrying out the training programme.

The methods and means used should create the conditions necessary for systematically, continuously and harmoniously strengthening young people's desire and readiness to strive for higher performance. A smooth transition to advanced training characterized by its considerably more taxing regimen and by the beginning of specialization can be made only this basis.

4.6.2. Tasks of basic training

Education and theoretical training in the field of sports

The training process forms a unity of education and training. The success achieved in training–expressed in terms of results achieved in tests and competitions–is the result of education and training, which includes theoretical and tactical training in the field of sports.

Educating all-round socialist personalities with a firm class stance who are in a position to achieve a high standard of performance is the socailist objective pursued by physical training instructors and coaches in shaping the educational programme.

The socialist objective is the determining factor in elaborating educational plans, laying down educational measures and in choosing ways and means. Fundamental theoretical and tactical knowledge should be presented to the young athletes in a simple manner adapted to their level of intellectual development. This can be done in part during training and in competitions. But special group meetings should also be held at which certain theoretical questions pertaining to training and competition are dealt with.

The following themes constitute the principal content of the necessary theoretical training in the field of sports:

– The techniques used in the different strokes, starts, turns and relays.

– Some rules of competition (techniques in compliance with rules of competition, age groups, qualification, provisions covering the protection of young people, laws and disciplinary rules, tasks of judges, etc.).

– Selected areas of the theory of training (physical abilities needing special development in the swimmer; methods and means used for this purpose; rules of behaviour before, during and after competitions, etc.).

– Hygiene and health protection.

– Problems involved in the planning training.

– Competition tactics.

– The physical properties of water in relation to techniques used in the different strokes.

– Problems of sports policy.

Effective co-ordination with the school and

young pioneers' organization is important in dealing with problems pertaining to sports theory and sports policy.

Comprehensive basic physical instruction
We must regard comprehensive basic physical instruction, as an objective of basic training, from two aspects. The first and obvious aspect of versatility is that the young swimmers should be given comprehensive training in the field of swimming based on an all-round development of their physical abilities. This means that they must be trained in all four strokes until they reach a certain minimum standard of technical proficiency and that a certain standard of performance in short-distance swimming (speed) and long-distance swimming (endurance) must be aspired for.

The second aspect is that the swimmer should acquire a large stock of movement experience and technical skills, which can be made use of later on in advanced training. Viewed from this aspect the use of other sports and exercises in training young swimmers becomes more than just adding variety to the training programme. If ball games, rowing, skiing or other sports are to be used meaningfully and effectively in subsequent advanced training, then the requisite technical skills must be developed in basic training. These two aspects of comprehensive basic physical instruction have a positive bearing on the all-round development of an athlete's condition and co-ordination, which he needs to achieve the high standard of performance aimed at.

Development of condition, co-ordination and flexibility
The development of all physical abilities constitutes a unity in the training process. One main task of basic training, which is the development of physical abilities, can be resolved in relation to the structure of the performance-determining factors involved in swimming as a sport. The following aspects are involved in *conditioning*:
● endurance (general endurance and endurance in specific events)
● strength (maximum strength, stamina, springiness) and
● speed,
which must be developed.

The following abilities are important for the swimmer in developing skills involving *co-ordination*, i.e., skills conditioned primarily by processes of co-ordinating movement (cf. Schnabel, G.: "Die koordinativen Fähigkeiten und das Problem der Gewandtheit", appearing in Theorie und Praxis der Körperkultur, No. 22 (1973), 3, pp. 263 to 269; and Team of Authors: "Training von A bis Z", A Glossary of Terms for Theory and Practice of Training, Sportverlag, Berlin 1978, p. 48).
● motor learning ability
● ability to adapt and adjust oneself
● ability to link up movements
● ability to steer one's movements
● ability to regulate one's movements
● ability to execute movements rhythmically
● ability to differentiate and
● ability to orientate oneself.
Together they determine an individual's agility and feeling for water.

Another physical ability that is important for the swimmer to develop and perfect is *flexibility*.

Great flexibility of the joints of a swimmer's skeletal and muscular systems along with his condition and co-ordination are an important pre-requisite for developing optimum swimming techniques. The development of the physical abilities mentioned above in general and of specific parts thereof in the process of training is an important task of basic training.

Refining the swimming techniques, starts and turns

The techniques employed in the strokes, starts and turns are developed in basic training to a high degree of perfection.

The object of the training process is to keep developing the swimmer's physical abilities and perfecting his techniques. Refining the swimming techniques to a high degree of perfection and up to the point where the swimmer develops his individual style (in advanced training) is a continuous process, which is never quite concluded. Technical perfection becomes particularly important when the swimmer starts specializing in a certain stroke or distance. Such aspects as the evolution of an optimum cycle, length of pull, stroke rate, tempo pattern in the course of a competition, etc., gain an importance in this phase of training.

For the sake of completeness we shall only mention that innovations in swimming techniques (such as the elimination of touching the wall with the hand in the freestyle turn or development of the grip start in the past) should be taken into account in training young swimmers.

The basic principle that should be borne in mind in refining a young swimmer's technique should be to enable him to comply with the objective criteria of effective swimming, starting and turning techniques and to adapt them in an optimum manner to his individual constitution and abilities.

Preparing for competitions

Competitions during the basic training phase can be seen as tests of efficiency of an athlete's training. They are very important for the young swimmer emotionally and they are highlights in his athletic development. These are among the reasons why it is so important to start preparing the athlete for competition in the basic stage of training.

The organization of training before the competition should be considered first in preparing the athletes for competition. The athletes are systematically prepared for competition over a period of several days up to several weeks, depending on the importance of the competition. The main aspects of this systematic preparation are:

● a certain reduction of the overall workload,

● adapting the training to the events and distances to be swum in the competition.

An effective warm-up programme and the tactics for the individual events should be worked out and discussed with the athlete.

The purpose of theoretical training in sports is to teach the athletes what to do before, during and after a competition and how to do it. The main points to remember in this respect are proper sleeping habits (if need be the athletes should rest but not sleep between individual events), proper eating habits (light food at least 1 to 2 hours before the competition, the athlete should not drink too much), appropriate clothing (to keep the athlete warm, he should put on dry clothing after swimming, etc.), the purpose and scope of warming up and warming down in the water.

One of the objects of basic training is to prepare the swimmer for competition and to develop proper habits in such competition. This object is of great importance in the young athlete's future athletic development.

4.6.3. Means and methods of developing and refining special technical and physical abilities

4.6.3.1. Means and methods of developing and refining physical abilities

The view that "swimming can be learned only by swimming" prevailed a few decades ago. It implied that only those who swim a great deal and do not "waste" any of their time available for training "on unimportant things" achieve a high level of performance.

This notion is obsolete. Although the number of kilometres swum by an athlete in training is an important factor in developing high swimming performance, swimming alone is not enough to achieve high and outstanding performance.

We have already mentioned that basic training in swimming is started at an early school age. The fact that exceedingly narrow specialization in one sport or event is by no means good for top performance holds true particularly in the case of children. The entire motor system, the musculature, the different systems, including the central and vegetative nervous systems, are constantly developing in the course of ontogeny. Balanced development can be achieved only through physical training which is designed to exercise all parts of the child's body and to produce stimuli for the development of all systems. Such training includes the development of all physical abilities. It will always be necessary to take all relevant factors into account in trying to perfect an athlete's performance. Situations might arise, however, in which this or that factor will take precedence over others at certain levels of development or phases of training or in connection with certain objectives.

4.6.3.1.1. Objectives and scope of all-round general physical conditioning

Although swimming is a sport in which nearly all muscle groups and organ systems are involved, it is still true that certain physical abilities can be developed and perfected faster and better through selected exercise complexes from different landbased sports than through aquatic training alone. In addition, the interest in and enjoyment of swimming can be preserved by remembering that children like play and variety and by organizing the training programme accordingly. Training sessions with children should always be organized in such a manner that they participate with enthusiasm and that each training session is an experience! This does not mean that no high demands are to be made on their performance, on the contrary, children should be systematically confronted with tasks and problems of increasing difficulty in order to stimulate their enthusiasm in coming to grips with them and mastering them.

The sense of achievement a young swimmer gets from accomplishing a task successfully helps to strengthen his will and promotes his training work. The direct influence of psychological factors on physical development is seen here. Although the principle of versatility should be fully complied with the developing the swimmer's physical capacities through basic training, one should bear in mind that the ultimate objective is to prepare the swimmer for top *swimming performance.* Endurance, strength, speed, agility, flexibility and explosive strength springiness should be developed in specific proportion to each other. (Endurance, strength and speed are considered from the psychological point of view in the section dealing with the special features of swimming from the point of view of sports medicine.)

Swimming is one of the endurance sports, which means that a swimmer must be able to swim a certain distance at high speed. To be able to do this he must be able to maintain the optimum rhythm of the cyclic swimming movements over the entire distance to be swum, which means that he must acquire the endurance abilities of short-, medium- and long-term endurance and of stamina and speed endurance through specific training. Agility springiness and dexterity are also important in performing starts and turns, which are an integral part of a swimming competition. All these abilities should be developed on a broad basis. That is why in the basic phase of training the accent is on the development of basic skills. All-round basic physical conditioning in which the swimmers' *conditioning* and co-ordination are developed and refined with the aid of a variety of effective means and methods lays the groundwork on which specific swimming abilities and performance can be developed in an optimum manner. If this groundwork is absent, i.e., if this foundation has not been laid and if the athlete does not constantly try to perfect this basis, to make further progress through all-round physical conditioning, then this will have a most undesirable influence some day on some phase of performance development. In other words if a swimmer does not get adequate all-round basic physical conditioning or no physical conditioning at all this will become a factor at some stage which can limit his ability to develop a specific swimming performance and make it impossible for him to achieve better results in competitive swimming.

All-round basic physical conditioning should be seen as an immanent part of a swimmer's overall training programme. All-round basic physical conditioning is particularly important in the first three to five years of an athlete's training. A broad basis of physical abilities, which offers optimum conditions for developing high swimming abilities and for achieving a high standard of performance in swimming, should be developed in the 9- to 14-year olds using a variety of means and methods of training not only in the water but also on land. For this reason it is essential that boys and girls should use part of the time available for training (regardless of how limited it might be) for developing their all-round physical abilities, for engaging in general, all-round basic physical conditioning.

The emphasis laid on the importance of all-round basic physical conditioning in the case of younger and weaker trainees does not mean that this aspect of training is to be dropped once a certain standard of development is reached. This aspect of training should remain an integral part of the training programme also in the case of older and better swimmers. Efforts should constantly be made throughout the training process, from the initial phase of instruction until the swimmer reaches the top performance class, to keep raising the general and all-round level of basic physical conditioning in order to keep improving the basis on which the athlete's swimming skills are built up.

Although the fact that general all-round basic physical conditioning as an immanent part of training is stressed, this does not mean that certain aspects should not be given priority over others.

In the course of the overall process of training, which lasts several years, the amount of time devoted to developing an athlete's all-round physical abilities with the aid of various means and methods of training will diminish and the amount of time spent developing and polishing specific swimming skills will increase. Differentiation between boys and girls and between the different strokes and events (competition swimming distances) is also possible and advisable. But a certain amount of time will be devoted to the development of a swimmer's all-round physical abilities throughout the process of training.

This applies in principle to the entire period of training and to each individual year of training: All-round basic physical conditioning always forms part of the overall training and it is always one of the tasks of the training process. But the emphasis should and will tend to shift to specific aspects of training even in the course of a training year. More time will be devoted to developing and refining basic physical conditioning with the aid of general means and methods in the first part of a training year than towards the end of the year highlighted by the competition season, and more time will be devoted to this aspect of training at the beginning of each period than towards the end, when the emphasis will shift to the development of specific swimming skills.

The object of all-round physical conditioning is to develop all important and necessary physical capacities using general means and methods (as opposed to specific swimming methods). All-round basic physical conditioning takes place mainly with in the framework of land-based training. The athlete's abilities connected with condition and co-ordination are developed and refined with the aid of manifold means and methods as a supplement to and condition for the development and refinement of specific swimming skills. The following are the main physical abilities which are to be developed and polished within the framework of all-round basic physical conditioning:

- general endurance
- strength (maximum strength, stamina, springiness, and especially take-off strength)
- agility
- flexibility.

These abilities are developed and perfected using general means. The methods, too, generally correspond to the means used, but they can also be adapted systematically and specifically with regard to the load duration, amount of resistance, movement frequency, number of repetitions, etc., to the conditions of swimming or they can be modified to meet the special recquirements of swimming. A wide variety of means can be used.

Running, skiing, cycling, rowing and canoeing are among the sports suited for developing endurance.

Apparatus work, obstacle gymnastics, dumbell workouts, gymnastics apparatus work and other gymnastics with and without partner assistance, special harness exercises and jumping exercises are among the sports and exercises that are suited for developing the athlete's strength.

Games, apparatus work, combative sports and special exercises help to develop the athlete's agility, while his joint flexibility can be improved mainly through special gymnastic exercises.

It goes without saying that swimming training, i. e., aquatic training also has all-round aspects and there are means and methods of supporting basic physical conditioning through such training. If the object is, for instance, to develop a swimmer's technique in all strokes up to the highest possible pitch, to develop general endurance for relay swimming events or to improve his co-ordination by having him practise combined arm and leg movements involved in different strokes, then this too forms part of the tasks involved in all-round basic physical conditioning.

The basic principle governing the use of means and methods in all-round basic physical conditioning in the course of a training year and in a training period should be progressively to shift the focus from general means and methods to means and methods adapted to the special conditions and requirements of swimming.

4.6.3.1.2. On development and perfection of abilities connected with conditioning

Development of general endurance

By endurance or general endurance we mean the body's resistance to fatigue during prolonged athletic exercises (cf. Harre, D. et al.: "Trainingslehre", 8th ed., Sportverlag, Berlin, 1979).

For the swimmer this means being able to swim long distances at relatively high speeds during which his body efficiently uses its aerobic metabolic energy.

General endurance training is designed progressively to improve the efficiency of the metabolic processes involved in any athletic effort. This is achieved mainly through functional adaptation of the cardiovascular and nervous systems. The level of the muscular endurance performance is also raised in the process. The improved general endurance achieved through general endurance training enables the swimmer to swim longer and longer distances at increasingly higher speeds with economically functioning, balanced metabolism. A high level of general endurance also enables the athlete to depart from the economic metabolic balance for a time (increasing speed during training or competition, intermediate spurt and then to continue swimming at the initial speed at an economic rate of metabolism. The development and improvement of general endurance is of great importance for swimmers. Swimming is an endurance sport in which general endurance or the level of general endurance ability is the most important condition for achieving a high standard of performance in competition despite the relatively important role played by stamina in achieving such performance.

In basic training the emphasis is on the development of general endurance. But basic training continues to play an important role in the overall training process also in high-performance training, in which the development of specific endurance becomes increasingly important.

The amount of time swimmers devote to general endurance training correspond to its varying scale of importance, which is determined by age, level of performance, the distance and stroke in which they are to compete and by the pattern of training during the training year.

The proportion of time spent for speed training in a specific stroke and distance increases with increasing training age and performance level, although the importance of general endurance training does not diminish.

There are also slight difference in the significance of general endurance training dependent on the stroke and distance to be swum in competition, which results in a corresponding share of time being spent for such training. General endurance is obviously more important for a 1,500-metres swimmer than for a 100-metres specialist, although general endurance is the essential basis for achieving the desired standard of performance in the 100-metres event as well.

The performance-determining components or the individual necessary physical abilities can never be developed independently of each other and one after the other. However, it is understandable that more emphasis must be put on some aspects than on others. Thus, although attention must be paid on general endurance throughout the course of a training year, more time should be devoted to it in the initial periods of training and at the beginning of a training period than later on. The emphasis should shift from general endurance to specific endurance and speed only after the athlete has undergone the requisite amount of general endurance training.

The means and methods used in developing general endurance through aquatic training are many and varied. In principle general endurance can be developed by using all relevant means, i. e., all swimming styles and simple movements, and by swimming with the aid of foot flippers or hand flippers. But in practical training work preference is given to freestyle, backstroke and medley swimming in developing and improving general endurance. Due to the higher force components involved in the butterfly and breaststroke movements these styles are less suited for developing general endurance than other training means even in athletes specializing in these strokes.

The time spent practising with foot and hand flippers in doing simple or complex movements should not take up more than 10 per cent of the total time spent for general endurance training. The training distance is the decisive factor. Exercises in which individual distances are swum at very high speeds using foot and hand flippers help to develop stamina rather than general endurance.

The following methods are used in general endurance training:

– endurance training methods (including disjointed repeats),
– series interval training,
– repetition,
– competition and test matches.

The amount of training done in using the *endurance training method* (continuous method) can be defined by the distance (1000 to 5000 metres) or by the time (20 to 60 minutes). In the course of this distance or time the strokes, alternating simple swimming movements, alternating simple and complex movements, distances swum using each, etc., can be varied. This variation of training components is designed not only to give variety to training but also to prevent the athlete from forming stereotype movements by getting used to a single stroke (e. g. freestyle) in endurance training over long distances, because once the swimmer develops such a stereotype he will not be able to break it.

This is one reason why the disjointed repeat method is being increasingly used for developing general endurance.

Total distances of different lengths are swum, specific sections of which are covered at specified speeds. If we take a total distance of 1000 metres, the swimmer can swim the component 100-metre distances at alternating fast and slow speeds. The 1400-metres distance can be covered in three 400-metres sections swum at normal speed interspersed with two 200-metres sections swum at high speed. Between the endurance method and disjointed training method lies the progression swimming method, which is used not only within the framework of the series interval method. With this method a total distance is divided into sections, which are then swum at progressively faster speeds. For instance a total freestyle distance of 800 metres is swum in sections of 50 metres, the first 50 metres being swum at slow speed and the succeeding 50-metre sections at progressively higher speeds, the last 50 metres being covered in the shortest time at maximum speed if possible. The disjointed training method ist characterised by great variability with regard to the length of the individual sections into which a total distance can be divided and to the speed at which the "fast" and the "slow" sections can be swum. This makes it possible for the coach to apply different training stimuli and to work out the most effective variant of developing his athlete's general endurance.

In using the *series interval training method*

for developing general endurance a total distance is divided into sections which are swum at sub-maximum speeds, the athlete's metabolism functioning between the aerobic and anaerobic ranges. Rest periods between the individual sections and the individual series should not be long enough to permit full recovery.

The following are a few typical examples of series interval training used for developing general endurance: 3 × 4 × 200 metres freestyle with rest periods of 30 seconds between the sections and rest periods of 2 minutes between the series, or 8 × 200 metres medley with rest periods of 40 seconds between the sections.

It is very important to adjust the lengths of rest periods between the sections and series to the speed fixed for swimming them in series interval training. In any case care should be taken not to overtax the athlete through exceedingly long or frequent periods of anaerobic metabolic activity, for this would be counterproductive to developing his general endurance. The essence of series interval training is the systematic variation of the total distance to be swum, sections, number of repetitions, swimming speed and length of rest periods in the course of the training process with a view to achieving basic endurance. This calls for a high level of knowledge and a great deal of empathy on the part of the coach if the training is to be crowned with success.

The repetition method, whose purpose is to develop and improve an athlete's general endurance, involves swimming several long distances at maximum or sub-maximum speed, the rest periods between the individual sections being long enough for adequate recovery. A typical example is the 3 × 1500 metres freestyle with a rest period of 10 to 20 minutes between sections. The speed should be such as to enable the athlete to swim all three sections at the

same speed. The time for the individual 1500-metre sections should be 30 to 90 seconds below the athlete's best speed, depending on the athlete's general endurance. The sections for athletes of younger training age are shortened corresponding to their level of performance.

The competition and checking method in developing and improving athlete's general endurance consists mostly of test meets and competitions over long distances (800 and 1500 metres). After a comprehensive warm-up swimming the swimmers can be asked once a week or once every two weeks to swim the same distance (800, 1500 or 2000 metres) at top speed in test meets or "against the clock". Such tests help to check the athletes' level of general endurance and they are a source of training stimuli which help to develop and improve the athletes' general endurance.

Summing up we can say that all methods mentioned in the foregoing can be used for developing an athlete's general endurance. But the main methods used in general endurance training are interval training and endurance training or disjointed training. The interval training method is suited for the first part of the basic training of younger children thanks to the fact that they recover quickly after physical stress that is relatively high but short in duration. Good results have been obtained with numerous repetitions of short distances and short rest periods. In order gradually to raise the requirement standards the coach keeps increasing one of the components (speed, number of repeats, building up series, enlarging the number of series, lengthening the sections, shortening the rest periods between the individual sections or series) each time. The use of the interval training method is also very effective for monitoring progress in the course of the general endurance training of children. The interaction of an athlete's skills of condition and skills of co-ordinating can be clearly seen here. On the one hand physiological stimuli that tend to adapt the organic systems to progressively higher requirements are produced through frequent repetitions and relatively short rest periods, on the other hand the dynamic and motor stereotype of the swimming technique in question is improved and reinforced. This in turn results in an economy of effort as a result of which the standard of training requirement should be raised again. Endurance training is also used at all stages of the systematic training process. A swimmer can cover a section of the total distance at a onsiderable speed during interval training thanks to the fact that the section is relatively short and that it is immediately followed by a rest period, while in endurance training the swimmer is required to swim at "intermediate" or "sub-maximum" speed. (We do not state at what speed relative to the competition speed the swimmer should swim as is sometimes done in competitive training, because in the initial stages of basic training there is no more or less constant competition speed that can be given for reference purposes. This speed is developed towards the end of basic training.)

In endurance training a relatively long distance is swum without a break or a rest period at as even a speed as possible or at increasing speed, while in disjointed training the athlete varies his speed according to a fixed pattern.

Sections of 400 metres can mean endurance training, but this depends on the level of development of the children in training.

The section length is systematically increased with the swimmer's developing abilities.

General endurance training can be monitored by checking the pulse rate. In interval training the fresh stimulus should be applied before the pulse rate reaches its resting value. If the resting pulse rate is about 80 beats per minute and if a pulse rate of 160 to 180 beats por minute was measured immediately after the athlete has swum a section, he should start swimming the next section once his pulse rate drops down to about 120 beats per minute. Checking the pulse rate is an expedient and simple method of monitoring the efficacy of training stimuli and of properly timing the rest periods.

The aim of developing and improving general endurance is also pursued in land training. The main forms of exercise for this purpose are track and field (especially cross-country), skiing and games, but other sports such as cycling, rowing, canoeing and other endurance sports are also suitable. Cross-country skiing, rowing and caneoing have brought particularly good results in the training of swimmers. The connection of these sports to swimming is particularly close due to the considerable amount of stamina and arm and shoulder muscle activity involved, and for this reason they are very effective in achieving the specific training results aimed at.

In principle the methods used for developing general endurance on land are the same as in water training. But here too the emphasis is on endurance training or disjointed training method.

Typical training examples are cross-country running lasting up to one hour, cross-country skiing up to two hours and intensive ball games (basketball, soccer, handball) lasting at least 30 minutes.

In land training too the workload (duration of workout, mean speed, number of repeats, etc.) is raised gradually and systematically in order to vary the stimuli applied and to raise their effectiveness in developing the athletes' basic endurance.

The coach will want to have yardstick by which to measure the level of development of his athletes' basic endurance at regular intervals in order to monitor their progress. Apart from relatively involved physiological tests and measurements such as the measurement of maximum oxygen intake, which reflects the quality of an athlete's basic endurance, good results have been obtained in practical basic training work with standard exercise sets, such as

6 × 100 metres with 1 minute's rest periods in between

8 × 200 metres with 2 minutes' rest periods or

2 × 400 metres with a 5 minutes' rest period.

The coach can assess the progress made by his athletes in developing their basic endurance by monitoring their performance in carrying out such exercise sets and he can draw conclusions as to the further course to be taken in the general endurance training programme.

Development of specific competitive endurance

In this context the term specific competitive endurance means an athlete's endurance under the concrete competitive conditions involved in the specific swimming event.

A distinction is made between short-, medium- and longterm endurance, dependent on the competitive distance swum. Through specific competitive endurance training an athlete develops his ability to make optimum and maximum use of all of his energy generating systems for achieving the best possible performance in a specific competitive distance. This applies especially to the development and improvement of using anaerobically generated energy in the competition.

The ultimate result of specific competitive endurance training or of raising the specific competitive endurance is that the swimmer continuously improves his performance in his special competition distance by improving all factors involved in the performance and especially by more effectively utilizing anaerobic energy generation. The development of specific competitive endurance on the basis of a good general endurance becomes more important with increasing training age and growing performance.

The development and improvement of specific competitive endurance is of minor significance during basic training. But the development of endurance qualities can and is aimed at and adapted to achieving short-, middle- or lang-term endurance (depending on the athlete's abilities) already at this stage of training. In the case of a swimmer showing obvious abilities in the sprint range, endurance training within the scope of basic training should be organized along different lines than in the case of a swimmer showing promise in long distance swimming.

The time devoted to and the significance of specific competitive endurance training also vary in the course of a training year. More emphasis is put on the development and improvement of specific competitive endurance towards the end of the individual periods of a training year before the main competitive events taking place in the different periods and especially towards the end of the last period of the training year in preparation for the main competitive event of the training year. A wide variety of means can be used for developing specific competitive endurance. All strokes and swimming techniques as well as simple movements of arms and legs can be used in such training. But specific competitive endurance training, starting at the basic training stage, involves mainly swimming in the specific stroke in which the athlete is to compete and using complex movements.

The interval training method is used almost exclusively in developing athletes' specific competitive endurance.

– Either the sections correspond to the competition distance, the swimming speed being initially slower than the competition speed and is then gradually increased to competition speed in the course of training;

– or the sections are shorter than the competition distance, the training speed corresponding to the competition speed and the sections being gradually lengthened or the rest periods shortened.

This basic principle also includes the variant of breaking up the competition distance into equal multiples or unequal stretches and shortening the rest periods in the course of the training process to about 10 seconds.

Another methodical variant used in endurance training, which is designed to develop basic endurance and specific competitive endurance, is the progression swimming technique. The basic principle involved in endurance training is to simulate the conditions of competition and to develop the abilities associated with all the components and factors such as speed, duration of strain, competitive technique (pull path, effort, stroke rate) having a bearing on an athlete's performance in competition.

Special attention should be paid to the development of balanced effort, speed and rate of movement during specific competitive endurance training. It can be observed time and time again that the thing all world record performances have in common is a high measure of uniformity, which is expressed particularly by a high measure of equality of the times in which parts of the total distance are swum. The ability to swim evenly, economically and efficiently should be developed in specific competitive endurance training.

However, this need for economical balance in competition does not mean that athletes should swim at an even pace in training as well. Although the athlete should learn to swim evenly in training, it is particularly important in developing specific competitive endurance frequently to break away from the even pace during training in order to apply fresh stimuli. This is the purpose of progression swimming within the framework of specific competitive endurance training.

Typical training exercises for developing and improving specific competitive endurance for a 200-metres freestyle swimmer, for instance, are:

2×200 metres at maximum speed with a 5-minute rest

4×100 metres at maximum speed with a 3-minute rest

2×100 metres or 150 metres plus 50 metres with 30 seconds of rest.

A large measure of variety is possible in this training. It is particularly important to time the rest periods in such a manner as to achieve a swimming speed at which specific competitive strain can be simulated. If the rest periods are too short, repetitions too frequent or sections too long, the training assumes the form of general endurance training rather than specific competitive endurance training.

Chart 6 illustrates the use of the interval training method for the purpose of developing long-, medium- and short-distance endurance.

The development or supporting the development of specific competitive endurance plays a role in land training only in two respects:

– the duration of certain land workouts designed for developing endurance can be adjusted to the duration of the competitive event in question;

– the duration of work, the amount of resistance of the apparatus and the rate of

Chart 6 An example illustrating the use of the interval training principle in basic swimming training for developing different kinds of specific competitive endurance

Variables	Long-distance endurance	Middle-distance endurance	Short-distance endurance
Length of distance	400 metres	50–100–50 metres	25 metres
No. of repeats	5	8	20 (5×4)
Intensity	medium	sub-maximum	maximum
Rests between distances	45 s	60 s	90 s
Rests between series	–	120 s	180 s
Type of rests between distances	passive	passive	passive
Type of rests between series	–	active (25 metres using other strokes)	active (50 metres using other strokes)

movement involved in stamina training can be adjusted to the competitive event in question. But such controlled supplementation of specific competitive endurance training on land, especially in the case of basic training, will tend to be the exception rather than the rule. The bulk of the training performed with a view to developing and improving specific competitive endurance will be carried out in the water. Obviously the best method of checking the level of development of an athlete's specific competitive endurance is through swimming competitions. Due to the fact that having an athlete swim the competition distance to test his level of performance without the associated competitive conditions does not always and with every athlete enable the coach to make a reliable assessment of the level of development of that athlete's specific competitive endurance, the practice of splitting up the competitive distance in practical training under standard conditions, e.g., a 200-metres swimmer can swim 150 metres plus 50 metres with a 10 seconds rest period, has brought good results in training. Adding the times needed for swimming the two stretches the coach gets a good idea of the swimmer's specific competitive endurance and of how he is likely to perform in competition.

In exceptional cases it is also possible to determine by means of physiological tests the amount of energy generated anaerobically or the degree of energy utilization and on this basis to draw conclusions concerning the quality of the athlete's specific competitive endurance. But in basic training the tests described and similar tests are sufficient for assessing an athlete's specific competitive endurance and for regulating the further course of training.

Developing speed
Speed is in this context an athlete's ability to swim at the highest possible velocity (cf. Gundlach, H.: "Zur Trainierbarkeit der Kraft- und Schnelligkeitsfähigkeiten im Prozeß der körperlichen Vervollkommnung" in "Theorie und Praxis der Körperkultur" No. 17 [1968] supplement part II, p. 167). Speed as an ability should not be confused with speed strength, which is only one of the conditions of speed.

In swimming, speed is the ability to swim short distances of up to 25 metres at increasingly greater speeds. Thus, speed is an important basis for short-term endurance.

The flexibility of nervous processes is raised, the available strength is used more effectively, the muscles' elasticity and ability to recover are improved and explosive strength increased through training designed to develop speed. The quality of the swimming technique and the function and effectiveness of the biochemical mechanisms on which speed performance is based are also improved through this type of training.

The psychic aspect of speed training is that it improves the swimmer's willpower. The relations between the strength and rational technique on the one hand and speed on the other are particularly close in swimming as a sport. For this reason developing strength and optimizing the swimming technique should always be seen in relation to speed training. The main importance of speed in basic training lies in acquiring and increasing a swimmer's "basic speed". Ultimately this basic speed is an important condition for achieving good performance in all distances. If basic speed is not systematically and continuously raised, then the stagnation in the development of this ability will sooner or later become a limiting factor even in attempts to improve performance over 800 or 1500 metres. This does not alter the fact that speed training is more important for the "sprinter" (the 100- and 200-metres swimmer) than for the distance swimmer.

Attention should be paid to the development of basic speed throughout the training year, but special importance should be attached to it towards the end of each training period and especially towards the end of the last period before the main competition season of the year.

The development of basic speed is an important aspect of basic training, because improved speed is an expression of improved co-ordination, technique and strength.

All strokes can be used initially for improving speed during basic training. Priority should be given to the stroke in which the swimmer shows most promise only in the last phase of the part of basic training devoted to developing speed.

The main methods of developing basic swimming speed are interval and repeat training.

The length of the section in the case of children who have just started their basic training should be about 10 metres; towards the end of basic training it should be gradually increased to 20 to 25 metres.

It is very important that the rest periods between sections swum in speed training are long enough to enable the swimmers to achieve a maximum measure of recovery (resting pulse rate). In each training unit the exercises designed to develop speed should be performed at the beginning or in the first third of the unit, because stimuli designed to develop speed are effective only if they are applied to an organism that is relatively rested.

Fast swimming of short distances starting at the starting signal (reaction training) and linking up with turns is advisable. (The turn can be made either at the beginning of the sprint distance, in the middle or at the end.) These forms of training are particularly suited for raising an athlete's basic speed and for simulating competitive conditions. The use of short-distance progression swimming and of hand flippers is also effective for breaking through movement stereotypes, which inhibit the development of basic speed ("speed barrier").

Typical training examples designed for developing basic swimming speed are:

– 6 × 25 metres with racing start; maximum speed; 5 minutes rest between the sections;

– 6 × 15 to 25 metres progression swimming after pushing off; 5 minutes rest (swimming back slowly to the pool wall, followed by passive recovery); the swimmer should stop practising progression swimming each time he feels that he can no longer swim any faster;

– 400 metres at intermediate speed, at the beginning of 50 metres of which the athlete should swim 10 to 15 metres at maximum speed.

Land training can contribute only indirectly to developing swimming speed. In this connection we should like to remind the reader what we said earlier about the relations existing between strength, springiness, flexibility, elasticity, ability to recover and speed.

All land exercises that help develop and improve these abilities are suitable from this point of view. Such exercises can be gymnastics with balls, bars, bats, light dumbells, harness exercises at low resistance but at high rate of movement in short periods of time, sprints, progressive runs and similar forms of exercise. It is important to bear in mind that these exercises should always be performed with loosening up and recovery exercises in order to raise their effectiveness.

As in swimming training the main methods involved in using the exercises mentioned in the foregoing are the interval training and the repeat methods.

15- to 25-metres sprints performed from the racing start or from the push-off can be used for checking an athlete's progress in developing speed. The time clocked by the swimmer in such sprints is a reliable indicator of his level of development.

Development of abilities connected with strength

Distinction is made between the following abilities connected with strength:
– maximum strength
– stamina
– springiness

Maximum strength is the highest amount of strength an athlete's nervous and muscular systems can master through voluntary muscular contraction, while stamina is the body's resistance to fatigue during sustained effort. Springiness on the other hand, is the ability of the nervous and muscular systems to overcome resistance at high concentration speed (cf. Harre, D. et al.: Trainingslehre. 8th ed., Sportverlag, Berlin, 1977). Stamina is a particularly important factor in swimming as an endurance sport. Stamina is closely related to an athlete's maximum strength.

It is essential for the swimmer to try to develop his movement speed in order to be able to improve his starting and turning speed.

In practical training work one often hears the words "general" and "specific" training. In the basic training phase of swimming the main purpose of strength training is to develop an athlete's so-called general strength, which restricts the choice of exercises and methods that can be used.

Strength training is part of the training of a swimmer of any age or performance class. But certain differentiation and variation of emphasis does exist. The share of the total training time devoted to strength training, for instance, diminishes with increasing training age or with improving performance, while that part of the time devoted to specific strength training in which specific exercises and methods are used increases.

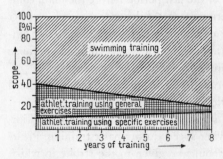

Chart 7   Share of time devoted to swimming training, athletic training using general exercises and athletic exercises using specific exercises in the course of several years of training

While it is possible to differentiate the intensity and scope of strength training used in swimming even according to sex (more strength training for boys), such differentiation is expedient and necessary in any case for the different competitive events. It is obvious, for instance, that the strength characteristics of a 100-metres butterfly swimmer should be different from those of a 1500-metres freestyle swimmer. Realizing this it is only natural that the share of time devoted to the different aspects of strength training and the pattern of the strength training programme should be adjusted accordingly.

Strength training is normally concentrated at the beginning of each training year and at the beginning of each training period. Towards the end of each period and during the last period of a training year the emphasis is on the development of specific abilities connected with strength and on their conversion into specific competitive endurance and into speed or into swimming performance.

We have already mentioned that the emphasis in basic training is on developing general abilities based on strength. But in this connection too we should point out once again the close connection between the quality of these strength abilities and the improvement of the swimming technique. Some standards of optimum technique simply cannot be achieved if an athlete does not meet certain strength requirements.

Swimmer's strength training is conducted mostly as part of land training. Strength abilities can be developed more effectively with the aid of various means and methods of land training than with the aid of aquatic training. Exercise complexes are selected in such a manner that as many muscle groups as possible are worked and developed. It should be borne in mind that

exercise forms designed to help develop an athlete's maximum strength should be used with particular care.

The skeletal and muscular systems is not yet very developed in the child and loads with considerable resistance can be dangerous. In addition one should take into account the fact that the ultimate objective of comprehensive strength development is to provide a basis for stamina which is required in swimming. From this point of view good results have been obtained with exercises using optimum resistances or loads (adjusted to individual force-load relations) and a relatively high number of repeats. The upper limit of the loads or resistances used for maximum strength development are approximately equivalent to the athlete's body weight, while the lower limit in land training should always be higher than the force exerted by the extremities during the drive phase when the athlete is swimming.

The resistances that have to be overcome in executing the swimming movements and the amounts of force that have to be exerted by the arms and legs per movement cycle in swimming are shown in Chart 8. But the exercises used for developing maximum strength and stamina on land are weight-lifting, apparatus work, pole and rope climbing, pulling and pushing one's body over gym benches and ladders, strength gymnastics with and without partner assistance, expander and impander training and harness training of different kinds.

The amount of load chosen within certain optimum limits determines by and large whether the exercises will help promote the development of maximum strength or of stamina. In any case it is not advisable for swimmers to try to develop maximum strength using means and methods that are used by weight-lifters and throwers.

Studies have shown that maximum strength

Chart 8 Water resistance in relation to swimming speed (V) and body section in kg (after Juřina, K.: "Training problems of crawl swimming from the point of view of strength". From: Teoria a praxe tělevých. (Czech.) 11 (1963) 12, pp. 558–564

V (m/s)	Corresp. 100-m time	Maximum body section (dm²)							
		5	6	7	8	9	10	11	12
1.1	1 : 30.9	2.95	3.15	3.29	3.66	3.78	3.96	4.15	4.40
1.2	1 : 23.3	3.40	3.61	3.79	4.10	4.32	4.55	4.78	5.01
1.3	1 : 16.9	3.87	4.13	4.30	4.66	4.91	5.18	5.40	5.69
1.4	1 : 11.4	4.39	4.70	4.90	5.27	5.54	5.81	6.10	6.40
1.5	1 : 06.6	4.96	5.25	5.59	5.90	6.20	6.52	6.85	7.20
1.6	1 : 02.5	5.60	5.95	6.30	6.61	6.97	7.33	7.74	8.08
1.7	0 : 58.8	6.29	6.96	7.04	7.36	7.80	8.20	8.65	9.00
1.8	0 : 55.5	7.00	7.45	7.82	8.18	8.68	9.10	9.61	10.01
1.9	0 : 52.6	7.76	8.25	8.69	9.05	9.57	10.10	10.62	11.10
2.0	0 : 50.0	8.61	9.15	9.95	10.02	10.55	11.18	11.76	12.30

developed in this manner does not help to achieve high swimming performance. For this reason the actual purpose of strength training for swimmers is to develop stamina, which is closely related to swimming performance and which can be converted directly into higher swimming speeds through the proper technique.

The method used in strength training with general aids and the interval training method is based on what we call the circuit or station training technique which has a strictly systematized form.

Heavy loads or resistance, small numbers of repeats and long rest periods are used if the emphasis is on developing maximum strength. Low resistances, numerous repeats and short rest periods between the individual exercises are intended mainly for developing stamina.

Chart 9 illustrates an example of a workout circuit used for the general development

Chart 9 Exercise circuit for developing stamina (one-minute exercise and one-minute for each station)

1. Strengthening the muscles used in jumping, squat jumps with bounces in between

2. Strengthening the stomach muscles by means of wall-bar exercises; back hanging, leg raises to half lever position

3. Strengthening arm and shoulder muscles by rubber cord exercises; supine position: pulling the rope from arms upward position to hips

8. Strengthening the back and hip extensor muscles. Prone position (box), legs hanging down: repeated raising of extended legs

4. Strengthening the back muscles; prone position, legs astride, feet underneath the wall-bar, hands placed behind the head, trunk curls alternate elbow touching opposite knee

7. Strengthening shoulder and arm muscles and muscles used in jumping through horizontal bar exercises; repeated jumping and pressing with the horizontal bar at shoulder level

6. Strengthening the stomach muscles; supine position, feet underneath wall-bars, hands clasped behind the head, trunk curls with maximum forward bending

5. Strengthening arm and shoulder muscles through stretch cord exercises; supine position: pulling cord with both hands from arms upward position down to the sides of the hips

NOTE: Such an exercise circuit repeated several times after warm up in conjunction with flexibility and limbering up exercises forms the major part of a strength-developing training unit on land.

of stamina. Strength training with the aid of harness equipment, whose resistance can be varied has a more specific character than dumbell training or circuit or station training technique involving numerous stations designed to exercise various muscles. Regardless of whether simulator training devices, stripping ropes, harness training devices, roller slide sliding on inclined planes or other pulley weight systems and friction resistance equipment are used in the training, series interval training is used almost exclusively as the training method here.

Great importance should be attached in stamina training using friction resistance equipment not only to the variables involved in the interval training method (duration of the individual exercises, length of rest periods between the individual exercises and between the series) but also to the resistances to which the devices are adjusted and to the movement rate. (Movement frequency is the number of movement cycles an athlete performs per unit time. It is normally expressed in cycles per minute [c/min].) By varying the movement rate and the resistance setting the coach can apply just the right amount of stimulus to achieve maximum effectiveness in developing an athlete's stamina, which is so important in swimming.

The principle of gradually shifting from relatively high resistance (about 80 per cent of an athlete's maximum strength) and 5 to 15 repeats per minute to lower resistances (down to about 25 per cent of the maximum strength) and increasingly higher movement rates (about 60 c/min) in the course of a training section is employed. This means that in long-term training in which spring exercisers are used the number of springs should be gradually reduced, in the case of rubber ropes the extension should be reduced, in the case of roller slides the angle of inclination should be gradually re-

duced. But in any case, the resistance should remain higher than the resistance a swimmer will experience even at maximum swimming speed. The duration of individual exercises on pulley weights and friction resistance exercisers can be closely adjusted to the duration of the swimming event concerned (the resistance being adjusted accordingly). 100-metres swimmers, for instance, should work out 60 to 90 seconds, 200-metres swimmers 2 : 30 minutes, etc.

A typical example of stamina training on a pulley weight or friction exerciser would be a 4 × 4 × 90 seconds' workout with both hands (simulation of the butterfly arm movement) with a resistance of about 40 per cent of the maximum strength and a rest period (passive rest, possibly with a few limbering-up and relaxation exercises) of 2 minutes between the individual exercises and 5 minutes between the series. This training example, which includes a warm-up before the intensive and very strenuous main part of the exercise followed by a game involving running, constitutes a complete training unit for developing and improving stamina. But such training units should be an exception rather than the rule in basic training. The emphasis in this phase of swimming training is on the development and improvement of general abilities associated with strength, so that pulley weight or friction exerciser workouts designed for specific strength endurance (stamina) of the arm and leg muscles are used mainly as stations within a workout circuit, as one of many exercises.

All forms of exercise are suited for developing springiness, which is important for the swimmer in executing starts and turns. They include long-jump from standing position and double-footed take-off, and one-legged jumps with and without the use of arms, jumping onto and off a vaulting table,

115

squatstretch jumping and other jumping exercises (e.g., hopping and squatting, straddle or legs astride) and rope skipping. A wide variety of methods can be used depending on the exercises involved. In principle, strength workouts should be interspersed with limbering-up and relaxation exercises. In this manner cramping is avoided, recovery is promoted and the resilience of the muscles involved is raised. Although the strength training of swimmers is carried out mostly on land, there are also stamina-developing exercises that can be done in the water.

Such exercises can consist of simple movements over short distances at high speeds, using flippers and floats.

In this case too the main method used is interval training. An example of exercises to develop stamina through water training is swimming $4 \times 3 \times 50$ metres with one-minute rest periods between the sections, the individual 50-metres sections being swum in the following sequence using maximum strength: butterfly arm movement with hand flippers, butterfly arm movement, butterfly complex movement.

Thanks to the fact that the exercises are constantly varied in this type of training, the formation of undesirable motor stereotypes is prevented and at the same time the athlete's sensomotor abilities, which enable him to translate his newly-acquired stamina into swimming performance through the swimming technique, are trained.

During the basic training phase the use of foot and hand flippers is advisable and useful in aquatic training, but in the initial period they should be used exclusively for the purpose of achieving variety in training. But generally such specific aids should be used in subsequent phases of training in order to be able to apply fresh and effective training stimuli in more advanced stages of training as well.

The main way of developing and improving an athlete's strength and related abilities is through strength training on land, this is especially true of the basic training phase.

Various methods can be used for checking the progress an athlete makes in developing his strength. One good way of measuring maximum arm strength is with the aid of a calibrated dynamometer, the athlete holding his pulling arm approximately at right angles to his trunk in lying position. It is important that the arm position should correspond as closely as possible to the power phase movement when swimming and that such errors as the elbow preceding the hand during the pull phase should be avoided. Any training device suitable for stamina training and whose resistance can be exactly adjusted can be used for checking the level of development of an athlete's stamina. The ability to do more repeats, the resistance remaining unchanged, or to overcome greater resistance, the number of repeats remaining the same, is an expression of an athlete's progress in improving his stamina.

Good results have been achieved in checking athletes' stamina in practical training work by setting a certain time limit on the work period (which corresponds to the time it takes to swim the distance and stroke in competition) and to have the athletes work with a resistance that lies between 50 and 70 per cent of the maximum strength. The resistance is reduced if the athlete is unable to achieve a movement rate of 30 cycles per minute or more; it is raised if he exceeds a movement rate of 60 c/min. Such a test not only shows the level of development of an athlete's stamina but it also enables the coach to draw conclusions as to what future course should be taken in strength training with regard to the resistance and movement rates to be used.

The easiest way of measuring the level of

development of an athlete's springiness which is useful in certain swimming movements is by measuring an athlete's long-jump from standing position taking off with both legs. Other methods that can be used for this purpose are the stretch jump test with or without the use of arms, in which a tape measure attached to a fixed point on the ground is pulled out by the athlete as he jumps, or the same jump, with the athlete marking off the highest point he can reach with a chalk. Both methods make it possible to measure an athlete's actual increase in springiness in centimetres without technical components (as in the case of the long-jump from standing position) playing a role.

Warming up, interval compensation swimming and compensation swimming

We should like to mention a few things to bear in mind about the significance and purpose of warming up, interval compensation swimming and compensation swimming in connection with the development and improvement of an athlete's condition and related abilities especially in aquatic training. The body as a whole should be prepared in an optimum manner for any physical task, be it a competition or a training unit. Warming up in the water is used for this purpose.

All organs are 'tuned' and adjusted to the subsequent load through warming up in the water before competition or at the beginning of a training unit. This enables the athlete to achieve maximum performance in competition and optimum efficiency during the training unit that follows.

The scope and contents of a warm-up in the water depend largely on the level of development of a swimmer.

The warm-up is considerably less extensive in basic training than in competitive training. As a rule a warm-up should last between 10 and 25 minutes. In this period the swimmer covers a distance of 400 to 2000 metres, depending on his level of performance.

Most of the warming up is done at medium rate, complex and simple movements being used.

Progressive overload swimming and some sprints towards the end of the warm-up promote the body's readiness for the effort that is to follow.

The scope and contents of the warm-up programme also depend to a certain extent on such factors as the time of day when the training unit is performed, water temperature, contents of the training unit, type of competition, etc. The warm-up should be organized in such a way that the workload is organized in an optimum manner, taking into account the existing conditions. A short period of limbering-up and stretching exercises at the edge of the pool deck is advisable. Even some press-ups, stand-ups and side straddle hop or strength exercises can be used.

In exceptional cases (if no warm-up pool is available during competition) a series of gymnastic exercises containing limbering-up, stretching and strength exercises, which are much more extensive in scope than warming up in the water and which are designed to activate the cardiovascular system before the competition, should be performed instead of warming up in the water.

By interval compensation swimming is meant swimming certain distances between the individual training exercises which produce the actual training stimuli. In this type of active rest the process of rest and recovery takes place faster than in the case of passive rest. Products of metabolism are oxidized faster and the energy supply is replenished more speedily. Thus, through interval compensation swimming the swimmer is better able to prepare himself for the next training stimulus. Through interval compensation swimming the previous strains are compensated for and the body is prepared for the next work period. Generally interval compensation swimming is performed at a slow to intermediate speed, preference being given to strokes other than the competition stroke. The backstroke is particularly suitable for this purpose thanks to the ease of breathing in this stroke. On the other hand the effectiveness of interval compensation swimming can also be raised by using other strokes and breathing or similar additional exercises and by putting greater emphasis on certain swimming movements.

Compensation swimming is the final part of a training unit in the water. The purpose of compensation swimming is similar to that of interval compensation swimming. In this case too the aim is to speed up the process of degrading metabolic products and to give the body a chance to replenish its energy supply. Through compensation swimming the swimmer is able to recover better before starting with the next training unit.

Just as in the case of warming up in the water, the length of time devoted to compensation swimming should be between 10 and 25 minutes and the swimming speed should be between slow and medium. The total distance to be swum in compensation swimming should be between 400 and 2000 metres, depending on the swimmer's level of performance and on the type of workload preceding it.

Warming up, interval compensation swimming and compensation swimming are by no means conventional compulsory exercises which are to restrict the scope of the "actual" training. They are important and necessary components of training designed to develop an athlete's fitness and his or her related abilities using special techniques.

4.6.3.1.3. On development and improvement of co-ordination and related abilities

The following abilities associated with co-ordination are of particular importance for swimming as a sport:

- motor learning ability
- adaptability and ability to readjust
- ability to link up movements
- ability to regulate body movements

and

- ability to control body movements
- ability to move rhythmically
- ability to differentiate and
- ability to orientate oneself.

The four abilities mentioned first are basic abilities which together are approximately synonymous with the concept of agility.

The remaining four abilities can be seen as components of feeling for the water.

There is a very close connection between abilities associated with co-ordination, which constitute the general conditions, and the *skills* associated with co-ordination, by which we mean certain movement patterns, specific swimming techniques.

A high level of development of general and specific abilities associated with co-ordination promotes the development and improvement of skills, and vice versa, a mastery of a large number of moter skills and of skills associated with co-ordination promotes the improvement of abilities associated with co-ordination.

Abilities and skills involving co-ordination in their interrelation constitute essential performance conditions from the aspect of formation of optimum, effective swimming techniques, which means that the development and improvement of these motor abilities is important also in the basic training phase. There is a wide variety of methods for improving abilities associated with co-ordination.

The basic principle in developing abilities for co-ordination consists in confronting the athlete with new and growingly complex movement tasks, which make progressively higher demands and produce increasingly stronger stimuli for the development of abilities for co-ordination.

The totality of means and methods used in practical aquatic training for developing and improving abilities of co-ordination can be broken down into the following complexes:

1. All forms of *agility exercises on land,* such as gymnastics, exercises with partner assistance, floor exercises, obstacle exercises, agility races, etc.

2. *Water exercises* designed to develop agility. These include exercises used in synchronized swimming, twists and turns around the body axes, all turning techniques in both directions, etc. Water polo also helps to promote agility.

3. *Combinations* of arm and leg movements used in different strokes, e.g.:
● crawl arm movement with dolphin kick
● butterfly arm movement with crawl kick
● simultaneous backstroke with dolphin kick, etc.

In principle any combination of the arm and leg movements used in different swimming techniques can be employed as a means of developing and improving abilities to co-ordinate. But in concrete instances combinations that tend to reinforce a swimmer's proneness to faulty execution of a certain technique should be avoided.

4. *Methodical variants* within a stroke
The range of possible variations of co-ordinating different combined movements in a specific swimming stroke is restricted to the timing of breathing (breathing rhythm) and to rhythm of co-ordination of the arm and leg movements. In the individual instances this means

● consistently exercising breathing to both sides in the crawl stroke;
● alternate breathing in crawl and backstroke;
● two-beat breathing in crawl and butterfly swimming;
● bilateral breathing in the butterfly stroke;
● varying numbers of leg beats to one arm cycle (2, 4, 6 and 8 leg beats per arm movement cycle) and in dolphin swimming (1, 2 and 3 dolphin kicks per arm cycle).

5. Swimming with *foot and hand flippers*
These aids, which are used mainly in strength developing exercises, can also be effective to improve a swimmer's co-ordination abilities. Swimming with and without flippers, or swimming with and without hand flippers and "fist swimming" provide constantly varying resistance for the propelling extremities. In this manner high demands are made on the swimmer's adaptability and on his ability to control, regulate and differentiate body movements and in this way stimuli are produced for the development of co-ordination abilities.

6. *Varying the cycle rate and the swimming speed*
Such techniques as varying the movement cycle rate (rate of movement–number of movement cycles during the time unit, in general *per minute* [CR/min] while maintaining an even swimming speed or maintaining the same movement cycle rate while varying the speed depends largely on whether or not such equipment as pacemakers, etc., are available, which is seldom the case in basic training. For this reason this technique will normally be restricted in the basic training phase to varying the number of strokes (number of movement cycles [strokes] needed to cover a certain distance used to cover a given distance.

7. *Glide exercises*
Glides executed from racing starts and

push-offs and while swimming (the objective being to cover a maximum distance using a minimum number of propelling movements) develop the swimmer's feeling for the optimum swimming technique and for the most streamlined body posture and help improve abilities and skills associated with co-ordination.

8. *Comprehensive training*

Comprehensive development of technical skills should also be seen as part of the efforts to develop and improve an athlete's abilities of co-ordination. The development and improvement of all swimming techniques, special emphasis being put on medley swimming in training, also have a positive influence on the development of abilities of co-ordination.

The methods described above can be used in a wide variety of combinations. Collectively they act via sensomotor processes (sensomotor training) as development stimuli for improving abilities and skills associated with co-ordination.

4.6.3.1.4. On development and improvement of flexibility

In this context *flexibility* means an athlete's ability to do exercises requiring great suppleness (amplitude) of the muscular and skeletal systems.

It is determined by the active movement amplitude of the athlete's individual joints, which is essentially the elasticity of his ligaments, tendons and muscles.

High flexibility enables the athlete to achieve optimum effectiveness of his propulsive movements, to reduce the amount of drag created by his body in the water and to diminish the influence of movements tending to counteract the forward movement (arm recovery, leg recovery in breaststroke). High flexibility makes for optimum, rational (economical) swimming techni-

ques; the athlete's abilities connected with strength and endurance are put to full use through rational technique and translated into swimming performance. Certain conclusions can be drawn from these facts for basic training. The development of flexibility should be made an integral part of training from the very first training session. What are the most important things to bear in mind in developing flexibility in swimming?

Ankles:

The ability to extend one's feet toward the soles (planar flexion) is important in crawl, backstroke and dolphin strokes, but flexibility is equally important in foot circling. A connection has been established between the ability to extend the foot joints and the effectiveness of crawl and backstroke swimming.

The ability to flex the feet toward the shins is particularly important in the breaststroke. The greater the amplitude of flexion of the foot, the faster can the athlete get a grip on the water in the transition phase between the recovery phase (pulling up the legs) and the power phase (extending the legs).

Knee joints:

The flexibility of the knee joints in connection with the flexibility of the hip joints is particularly important in breaststroke. The ability to move one's lower legs as far out sideways as possible (abduction) is essential, because this determines the area of the thrust planes during the power phase of the leg movement.

Hip joints:

Maximum flexibility in executing leg spreading and straddle movements should be aimed at, but care should be taken to prevent strains.

High movement amplitudes in executing straddle movements (abduction) are important for the breaststroker despite the fact that the full movement amplitude is not used once the swimmer develops an optimum swimming technique.

The spinal column:

The significance of flexibility of the spinal column is often underestimated in developing an optimum swimming technique. And yet it is an important factor, for it is a necessary condition for adapting the trunk to the changing conditions during a movement cycle in such a manner as to minimize the body's drag in the water and thereby raising the efficiency of the swimming movements. The flexibility (suppleness) of the spinal column in all planes should be developed and improved; flexibility of the spinal column in the sagittal plane is particularly important for the breast and dolphin swimmer, while for the crawl swimmer and backstroker flexibility in the frontal plane is important. It is also essential for being able to twist the body (turning the shoulder line and the hip line in opposite directions around the central body axis). Special attention should be paid to improving the flexibility of the cervical section of the spinal column, because the greater the flexibility of this part of the spinal column, the less detrimental the influences of the movement of the head during breathing on the posture and movement of the trunk and the extremities.

Shoulder joints:

A high amplitude in the movement of the shoulder joints enables the swimmer easily to recover his arms in backstroke or to recover his arms with a high elbow in crawl and butterfly strokes. The ability to recover the arms keeping a high elbow helps the swimmer correctly, efficiently and quickly to get a hold on the water and to execute the power phase with a high elbow. High flexibility of the shoulder joints, elbows and wrists is an important condition for being able to develop an efficient swimming technique.

From what we have said above it follows that an optimum measure of flexibility has a direct bearing on the effectiveness of technique in all strokes. That is why flexibility should be developed systematically and regularly.

Exercises designed to improve flexibility should be an integral part of every athletic training unit and of every warm-up; they could also be used for compensation between workouts.

In terms of function the exercises to be used can be devised on the basis of the possibilities of movement *in different planes* of the extremities offered by the joints.

The stretching stimuli should be gradually increased in passive exercises (partner assistance, making use of the body weight or other weights or forces) and through active exercises (only through the contraction of muscles acting through the joint in question) in order to increase flexibility up to the optimum level strived after. The methodical approach is to raise the passive movement amplitude, to improve the active flexibility and to translate the improved flexibility into effective swimming technique.

Active flexibility exercises should always be at the beginning of any systematic programme of flexibility development and at the beginning of any workout unit. They are also very useful as warm-ups before training sessions and competitions. Basic principles in the development and improvement of flexibility are:

– one should exercise as often as possible;
– individual exercises should be repeated many times;
– active exercises should precede passive ones;
– one should not try to reach an objective "by force";
– one should exercise not only during formal training sessions but also perform exer-

cises adapted to suit individual requirements as "home work".

The exercises described below are designed,
individually or collectively, to be used as a
special training unit of its own whose purpose is to develop flexibility or in combination with strength-developing exercises.
They represent a selection which can be optionally modified and extended.

Ankle joints:

1. Sitting position with legs extended
straight in front; rotating the feet in the
ankle joint clockwise and counter-clockwise.
2. Sitting position with legs extended
straight in front; flexing the feet towards
the shins; forcefully flexing the toes and
slowly extending the feet.
3. Supine position; extending the feet and
then flexing them and rotating them outwards.
4. Standing in front of a wall with palms
pressing against the wall; slowly flexing the
elbows until the forehead touches the wall;
heels remain firmly in contact with the
ground.
5. Sitting in kneeling position, feet extended, buttocks resting on the calves; through
sudden extension of the knee and hip
joints and by swinging the arms over the
extended feet the athlete gets up to standing
position.

Knee joints:

1. Supine position; raising one knee until
the lower leg is at an angle of 90 degrees;
touching the posterior with the heel; alternating the legs.
2. Prone position; flexing the knees; gripping the ankles, pulling up feet until the
heels touch the buttocks. Alternating the
grip by holding the ankles from the inside
and then from the outside.
3. Sitting position with legs extended
straight in front; pressing feet against the
wall; heels touching the wall and the
ground; bending the trunk forward until

hands touch the wall when the arms are
stretched out; bending and stretching with
bouncing movements with knees remaining extended.
4. Kneeling position; legs straddled, toes
pointing outwards; bending and stretching
knee and hip joints with springy movement.
5. Changing from kneeling position with
feet extended to sitting position to the right
and left of the lower legs; arms help keep
body balance.

Hip joints:

1. Erect position, with legs slightly apart;
body remains in erect position; one knee
is flexed and the thigh is straddled (ab-
ducted); the exercise is rhythmically alternated.
2. Supine position with legs wide apart and
stretched out; one foot is placed with the
inner side against a resistance; the other leg
is straddled as far as possible; the exercise
is repeated with the other leg.
3. Supine position on a table or similar object; as close as possible to the edge; the
outer leg is allowed to hang down and is
then actively moved back in a plane parallel to the sagittal plane with the spine resting flat on the table. Repeated raising and
extending the leg. Other leg is then exercised in a similar manner.
4. Straddle-stand on flat ground, moving
legs further apart by sliding feet laterally
away from each other on the ground with
bouncing movement of the trunk (side
splits).
5. "Hurdle seat"; executed alternately with
springy movement.

Spinal column:

1. Upright stand, hands on hips; vigorous
hip gyration forward, sideways, backwards
and sideways, executed alternately in clockwise and counter-clockwise direction.
2. Lying on the back, hands beside the body,
palms down; flexing knee and hip joints;
lowering thighs to the ground to the right

122

and to the left, the legs are exercised alternately.

3. Lying on the back, feet drawn up, hands pushing against the floor above the shoulders; arching the body to form a "bridge" with spring-like movements, gradually diminishing the distance between the hands and feet.

4. Straddle-stand, hands clasped behind the neck; twisting the trunk (shoulder line) round the longitudinal axis alternately to the right and left with springy movements.

5. Sitting position with hands on the floor to support the torso; rotating the head in the clockwise and counter-clockwise direction.

6. Standing or sitting; alternating bending of the head to either side as if trying to touch the shoulder with the ear, the exercise is performed with springy movements.

Shoulder joints:

1. Vigorous windmill or paddlewheel arm rotation in standing position
– forward and backward
– forward to the right and backwards to the left and the other way round.

2. Lying on the back; arms spread out sideways at right-angles to longitudinal axis, palms turned up; alternate swinging of the arms across the chest in such a manner that the hands touch the ground on the other side of the body.

3. Lying on the back; arms along the body; palms turned up; sliding arms alternately away from the body, over the head and body to starting position keeping the arm close to the body, repeat with the other arm, repeat cycle several times.

4. Lying on the back; arms spread out at right-angles to the longitudinal axis of the body; flexing elbows at right-angles, rotation of upper arms in the shoulder joints in such a manner that the palms touch the floor near hip line and the backs of the hands touch the floor above the head (for greater flexibility the floor is touched with the hand edges).

5. Standing position; arms are raised to shoulder level with palms facing backwards; arms are swung back loosely with flexed elbows in such a way that the forearms swing back and up to the shoulder-blades with springy movement.

6. Standing position; arms raised alternately behind the head, forearm hanging down loosely, taking hold of the elbow and pulling it behind the head to the opposite side with the other hand using springy movements.

7. Standing position; torso bent forward slightly; hands are clasped at the back and loosely swung backwards and up while the torso is bent forward.

Elbow joints:

Lying on the back; arms slightly spread, palms turned up; cushions (rolled up towels) are put underneath the arms just above the elbows; forearms are swung up in a whip-like fashion until the fingers touch the shoulders and are then allowed to drop back again to initial position.

Wrist joints:

1. Standing or sitting position; arms spread sideways; rotating hands at the wrist joints.

2. Standing or sitting position; elbow resting on a support in such a way that the forearm and hand are in vertical position; the wrist joint is flexed forward and backwards with a springy movement.

It is essential that the physical training supervisor should constantly check and correct any faults.

4.6.3.2. Refining technique of swimming, starts and turns

The basic (elementary) forms of swimming, starting and turning techniques are acquired (with minor individual variations) in the course of basic instruction. The acquisition of these techniques is one of the main purposes of basic instruction (cf. ch. 4.2., p. 37). We have already mentioned in the sections dealing with abilities associated with co-ordination and flexibility that there exists a close relationship between the quality of athletic techniques and the level of development of the abilities of co-ordination or of flexibility. The level of development of an individual's abilities associated with condition, especially of his strength and endurance, determines to a great extent his technique. That is why the development and refinement of swimming technique should always be seen in connection with the development of abilities associated with condition, and that is why the process of perfecting the technique never ends. Continuous development and perfection of refined movements is a phase of the motor learning process that is just as important in basic training as it is in high-level competitive training. Modern conceptions concerning optimum swimming techniques from the point of view of biomechanics and physiology i. e., concerning the movements by means of which the swimmer can achieve the maximum result with minimum-physical effort, are the basis of the development and refinement of the different swimming techniques (cf. ch. 4.4., p. 63).

Refinement of the swimming technique should be the essence of *each* training unit, i. e., irrespective of the primary objective (development of speed, endurance, etc.) the coach should always keep an eye on the swimmer's technique, give him the necessary suggestions and correct his faults. In addition, it is also not only possible but also necessary to stress the development of the technique. Parts of training units or entire training units can be set aside for this purpose.

The technique used should be analysed to make sure that it is correct and efficient during parts of the training that are devoted to the refinement of technique. The coach or teacher should compare the techniques used by his swimmers with the movement pattern of the techniques which he has worked out for himself in the course of his career, differentiate between the primary and the secondary faults and lay down the necessary or expedient ways of correcting the primary faults.

The coach should explain to the swimmer the faults in his technique on the basis of the latter's theoretical knowledge of the technique, the correct technique and the swimmer's rendition of it are compared and he is advised on ways of improving it. Suggestions such as "change the head position", "keep legs closer together during recovery" etc. are then given to the swimmer during the actual training (either in an abbreviated form or through signs) to correct the faults gradually and to enable the swimmer to acquire the correct technique.

To develop the right conceptions of the movements involved in correct technique the following is necessary in addition to constant concentrated practice

● good and bad examples should be demonstrated,

● films and video recordings should be used as aids,

● drawings of movements should be used.

It is important to remember that technical proficiency should by no means be developed at "slow-motion" speeds, but that techniques of swimming, starting and turning should be developed, refined and reinforced under competitive conditions, i. e., at competitive speeds. The following are the aspects used for assessing the level and the degree of mastery of the swimming techniques and for achieving an optimum level of development of technique in its entirety:

● the position of the body,

- movement of the arms,
- movement of the legs,
- execution and timing of the breathing,
- co-ordination of the simple arm and leg movements and of breathing (complex movement),
- relations between stroke rate and stroke amplitude.

The following are some of the measures that have produced good results in correcting the most common primary faults in the different strokes in basic training:

Crawl stroke

a) Body posture

Faults:
- the planing angle of the trunk is too steep (exaggerated hollowing of the small of the back);
- the planing angle of the body is too small;
- exaggerated rolling of the trunk;
- the side opposite the "breath side" of the body is submerged too deep in the water.

Corrective measures:
- the head should be immersed deeper (up to the eye-brows);
- the head should be held higher (the mouth at the surface of the water);
- swimming in the gliding position (the arm completing a stroke is recovered and left stretched out in front until the other arm completes the stroke, etc.);
- "alternate breathing" (one breath to every three arm strokes);
- breathing on the weak side.

b) Arm movement

Faults:
- the power phase is not executed in a straight line;
- the power phase is too short, it is broken off too early;
- the stroke is executed too far from the longitudinal axis of the body;

- the hand trails behind the elbow (the "high elbow" position is not maintained);
- one or both arms are recovered too slowly;
- arm recovery is too wide and flat.

Corrective measures
- Swimming in "gliding" position with gradual transition to normal arm movement rhythm;
- swimming with clenched fists;
- swimming with clenched fists, opening them when they reach the hip line;
- swimming with eyes open under water without breathing or with goggles and a snorkel to watch he movements.

c) Leg movement

Faults:
- The kick amplitude is too high;
- the kick amplitude is not high enough;
- the knee joints are not flexed;
- thrust movements of the legs.

Corrective measures:
- The head should be held higher;
- stressing hip joint flexion when commencing the kick;
- swimming on the side and watching the movements;
- exercising in supine position (first the knee, then the foot should break the surface);
- suggestion: "kick the ball!";
- more vigorous downbeat in prone position.

d) Breathing

Faults:
- Exhaling too late as a result of which the inhalation is too short;
- the inhalation is too long as a result of which the stroke and timing are influenced detrimentally.

Corrective measures:
- Breathing exercises without arm movements;
- forced exhalation;
- swimming with one arm with the aid of a

float (bilaterally) using proper breathing co-ordination.

e) Co-ordination

(A wide variety of arm and leg movements can be used in the crawl stroke. In view of the various techniques used by world record swimmers, the use of the term "textbook variant" is hardly appropriate any more. Nevertheless, an even, rhythmic 6-beat stroke should be aimed at, taught and trained in basic training. In the course of further training the swimmer can then choose the 2-beat or 4-beat stroke if it is better suited to his or her disposition.)

Faults:
– No rhythmic co-ordination of the leg and arm movement cycles.

Corrective measures:
– Swimming with leg movements and keeping a mental cadence of the desired rhythm, then co-ordinating the leg movement with the arm stroke.

Backstroke

a) Body posture

Faults:
– Lying in a "cradle" (body not extended, buttocks too deep);
– hollowing the small of the back.

Corrective measures
– Leg movement, hands pressing against the buttocks, raised chin, executing the combined movements in this body position;
– pronounced drawing in of the chin with leg movements and combined movement.

b) Arm movement

Faults:
– Arms extended during stroke;
– delay in taking one or both arms out of the water;
– the lateral recovery of the arms is too low;
– entry is made across the saggital plane above the head;
– the entry of the arms is premature.

Corrective measures:

– Swimming with clenched fists with pronounced flexion of the elbows;
– swimming with clenched fists, opening the hands in the last third of the power phase;
– swimming only by arm movement with very swift arm withdrawal at the end of the push phase, later on in co-ordination with leg action;
– upper arms touch the ears during the recovery phase;
– pronounced extension of elbows during recovery.

c) Leg movement

The faults and the appropriate corrective measures correspond to those described for the crawl stroke.

d) Breathing

Faults:
– Unrhythmic breathing.

Corrective measures:
– Demonstrative inhalation during the recovery of the "breath arm", exhalation during the power phase of the arm;
– changing the breath arm.

e) Co-ordination

(Unlike crawl swimmers, the world's top male and female backstroke swimmers prefer the 6-beat stroke, apart from the few exceptions who prefer the 4-beat stroke. The 6-beat stroke should be taught and practised in basic training.)

Faults:
– No rhythmic 6-beat leg action.

Corrective measures:
– Swimming by leg action alone while keeping a mental count of the 6-beat rhythm, later on in co-ordination with arm movement.

Dolphin stroke

a) Body posture

Faults:
– The planing angle is too steep in relation to the surface.
– The trunk sinks too deep.

Corrective measures:
- Lateral breathing should be tried if necessary (to *both* sides if possible);
- stressed projection of the chin during the arm strokes;
- two-strokes breathing;
- swimming by arm action keeping the head in level position (eyebrows level with the surface), later on in co-ordination with the dolphin kick, maintaining same position.

b) Arm movement
Errors:
- The hands wobble during the power phase movement rather than executing it in a straight line;
- the power phase is too short;
- the arm recovery is too flat;
- premature arm entry.
Corrective measures:
- Swimming with clenched fists;
- swimming with clenched fists until the hands reach the hip line, from which point on the stroke is continued with open hands;
- trying to keep a high elbow during arm recovery;
- stressing the importance of entering the hands with the thumb side first far in front.

c) The dolphin kick
Faults:
- The kick amplitudes are too great;
- the undulation starts in the knees rather than at the hip joint and the lumbar vertebra.
Corrective measures:
- Swimming with clenched fists;
- practising the dolphin kick in supine position and on both sides and watching the movements;
- stressing the hip movement while reducing the knee action.

d) Breathing
Faults:
- The exhalation is made too late, as a result of which too little time is left for the inhalation;

- the inhalation is too long, this has an adverse effect on the arm stroke and co-ordination.
Corrective measures:
- Breathing exercises in conjunction with the dolphin kick, later on in co-ordination with the arm stroke;
- stressing the exhalation.

e) Co-ordination
(The co-ordination of the arm and dolphin movements used by the world's best male and female butterfly swimmers varies a great deal. The variants range from the two-beat stroke, in which two pronounced dolphin movements are made to each arm stroke, to the two-beat rhythm, in which only a slight dolphin movement using almost exclusively the knee joint is performed. A rhythmic two-beat stroke (one pronounced and one less pronounced dolphin movement per arm stroke) should be taught and developed during basic training.)
Faults:
There is no rhythmic two-beat stroke.
Corrective measures:
- Performing the dolphin kick and keeping count of the two-beat stroke, later on in co-ordination with the arm stroke.

The breaststroke
a) Body posture
Faults:
- The body's planing angle relative to the surface is too steep (exaggerated hollowing of the small of the back);
- buttocks raised too high.
Corrective measures:
Shortening the arm stroke and holding the head level (mouth level with the water surface);
- sequence of exercise: Leg movement with arms held crossed on the back; leg action with outstretched arms, the body position remaining unchanged; co-ordina-

tion of the arm movement, the body position remaining unchanged.

b) Arm movement

Faults:
- The arm stroke is too wide;
- the arm stroke is too narrow;
- the hands are held too flat (reduced thrust resistance);
- elbows kept too wide apart during arm recovery.

Corrective measures:
- Swimming with clenched fists;
- practising correct arm movement while holding a float between the thighs; repeat exercise without the float and then co-ordinate with the leg movement;
- turn palms up (supinate) during arm recovery.

c) Leg action

Faults:
- "Scissor" movement of the legs;
- legs are held too wide apart during recovery;
- legs spread too far apart;
- the lower legs are not spread slightly before beginning the drive phase of the leg action;
- the feet are not "kocked" before beginning the drive phase of the leg action;

Corrective measures:
- Practise leg kick in supine position and watch the movement;
- hands are held over the buttocks; breaststroke leg action drawing up the legs until the heels almost touch the hands;
- "slow-motion" swimming;
- increasing flexibility of the foot, knee and hip joints through special land exercises (cf. "Development and refinement of flexibility").

d) Breathing

Faults:
- The inhalation is too early.

Corrective measures:
- Forceful exhalation;

- practise correct and properly timed breathing with simple arm or leg movement; co-ordinate the combined movement and breathing.

e) Co-ordination

Faults:
- Legs are drawn up too early;
- legs are drawn up too late.

Corrective measures:
- "Slow-motion" swimming;
- practising with prolonged glide phase.

We have already pointed out the importance of simulating competitive conditions when developing and refining swimming techniques. The progression swimming method is ideally suited for stabilizing the technical details and fine points, which are first acquired at low speeds and perfected at competitive speeds.

It is important to bear in mind that while gradually building up his speed up to the competitive speed mark with a view to developing the details of the technique, the athlete should instantly discontinue the workout the moment he notices that he can no longer keep up the pace using the correct technique.

Another aspect of the competitive swimming technique is the relationship between the stroke length and stroke frequency. In this connection we should like to note that the methodical trend of development is first to lengthen the stroke length (optimizing the technique of the individual cycle) and then to increase the stroke rate. The emphasis is shifted to the lengthening of the stroke length and slightly reducing the movement frequency only once the swimmer reaches his optimum stroke frequency. This once again proves the close connection between refining the abilities associated with condition and improving the abilities of co-ordination, skills and the swimming technique in general.

The following are among the corrective measures that have proved successful in correcting the most common faults made in turns and starts:

Turns
(irrespective of the turning technique in question)
Faults:
– The turn is started too late;
– the twisting movement started too late;
– the twisting movement is too slow;
– the push-off is inadequate;
– the push-off is too deep or too shallow;
– incorrect body posture during the push-off and glide phases;
– swimming movement started too early;
– swimming movement started too late.
Corrective measures:
– Consistent maintenance of the competitive speed during the exercise;
– executing the twisting movements out of the swimming movement without touching the wall;
– push-off and glide exercises with fixed objectives;
– finding the optimum glide distance before starting the swimming movements;
– developing springiness or stretching on land.

Starting dive and backstroke start
(irrespective of the technique used)
Faults:
– the reaction to the start signal is too slow;
– the take-off is too weak;
– the arm swing is inadequate or absent altogether during take-off;
– the take-off angle is too flat (the swimmer falls onto the water surface instead of diving);
– the take-off angle is too steep;
– the dive is too deep;
– the swimming movement is started too early or too late.

Corrective measures:
– Check starting position (shifting the balance in the starting position);
– reflex training on land;
– developing springiness on land;
– jumping over a rope using the starting dive;
– correcting the position of the head during the flight phase, during the entry and during the glide phase;
– finding the optimum distance of the glide phase before starting with the swimming movement (exercising at competitive speeds).

4.6.3.3. On the land training of swimmers

We have pointed out several times how the development and refinement of physical abilities can be supported and promoted through land training. In principle, all abilities needed for achieving high swimming performances can be developed to a considerable extent through land training. This applies especially to general athletic instruction, to the general development of the individual physical abilities, to suppleness, agility and to the development of the more specific strength qualities (maximum strength, stamina, springiness). This even applies to a certain extent to the athletic technique, whose development can be prepared and supported through simulation and pulley weight work in which the "high elbow" and other movement patterns are stressed. General endurance can also be developed to a considerable extent on land, although there is a qualitative difference between developing general endurance on the one hand and such qualities as maximum strength and stamina on the other. Abilities of strength can be developed faster and more effectively on land than in the water, but the higher a swimmer's performance class, the less effectively his general endurance acquired on land can be made use of in swimming. But endurance work on land with a view to developing general endurance is an integral part of the basic training programme. To underline this point we must repeat that land training with its multitude of ways of developing the abilities needed by swimmers is neither an "appendage" of swimming training, nor merely a way of adding variety to training, it is rather an independent structural element of training work as a whole. The ratio of time spent in training in the water and on land is an important factor in working out the workload structure. Thus it follows that land training, which can be planned in the same way as training in the water, should be analysed just as systematically and planned just as thoroughly as training in the water. This holds true not only for the scope of the workload of athletic training on land but also for choosing the individual means and methods. Some points must be differentiated and stressed in planning and organizing athletic instruction on land.

It has proved expedient already in the basic training phase, for instance, to devote more time to general athletic instruction in the case of boys than in the case of girls.

If we take a period of several years of training or one year or period of training, we will notice a continuous shift from land training in the first part of the training period to more water training towards the end.

Similarly, more time is devoted to general exercises and methods in the first phase of athletic instruction on land, while the share of time spent doing specific exercises and using specific methods increases gradually towards the end. This shift is particularly evident in strength training. This gradual shift from general to specific exercises and

methods in land training applies both to shorter periods and to cycles of several years.

4.6.4. Planning basic training

The entire pedagogically guided process of training from the beginning of basic training up to the point when an athlete reaches the top performance level brings forth the best results only if the work is done systematically, methodically and purposively. A thoroughly worked out training plan is a very important means of achieving this end.

There are certain principles that must be observed in planning the training programme. We shall first give a brief outline of the principles and then deal with the planning of swimming training and with the main areas of basic training.

All forms of training planning, from long-term planning embracing several years up to the thorough preparation of a training unit, are absolutely essential for achieving the best possible, successful and efficient development of the athletes' potential and of their motivation. Long-term planning is particulary important in this connection. It is the starting point and the guideline for all sport-term planning and thus a decisive factor in determining the basis for the purposive development and training of the athletes' abilities and skills.

The following elucidations are in the main based on principles of individual training planning; due allowances should be made when applying them to group training.

The training plan should contain the following essential elements:

(1) *Analysis of the preconditions*
They include the training age, the training condition, physical and psychic preconditions of the athlete or training group.

(2) *Setting objectives*

This includes setting the intermediate and final performance objectives, objectives of the individual training components (endurance, strength, speed, agility, flexibility, technical skills) and educational goals.

(3) *Setting the tasks*

The individual tasks are worked out on the basis of the final objective to be achieved on the one hand and the given preconditions on the other. They can be broken down into the refinement of technical skills, development of physical abilities, theoretical instruction and educational tasks.

(4) *Choosing the means and methods of dealing with the tasks*

The choice of the means and methods will depend in any case on the tasks set.

(5) *Co-ordinating and scheduling the training components*

The main aspects of the training plan should be broken down into periods, phases, cycles, days or training units. This also applies to the ratio of water training to workouts on land, to the share of time to be devoted to strength training, endurance training, technique refinement, etc., and to organizing the scope and intensity of training.

(6) *Training organization*

The general conditions of the training facilities (indoor swimming pool, open-air swimming pool, lane length, indoor or outdoor land training facilities, etc.) and the organizational forms (group training, individual tuition, special tasks to be dealt with by the athlete on his own, etc.) should be taken into account in this part of the training plan.

Obviously the factor determining the thoroughness which the above mentioned aspects or sections of a training plan are dealt with will depend first and foremost on the length of the period covered by the plan. The shorter the period covered the more detailed the plan tends to be. On the other hand, a training plan (sub-plan) covering a two-week cycle will not have to analyse in detail the existing conditions. On the whole the training plans are worked out to cover specific periods, the content and form of such plans will have to be tailored to the requirements in question:

a) Training plans covering periods of several years, or long-term plans.

b) Annual training plans.

c) Detail training plans (Covering periods, phases, sections, cycles, days, training units).

4.6.4.1. Training plans covering several years, or long-term plans

Plans covering several years, or long-term plans, are of equal importance in training swimmers of all ages, be it basic training or top performance training. The main forms of long-term planning in the top-performance class are organized in phases with such international highlight events as the Olympic Games, World and European Championships and European Cup Competitions. Long-term plans geared solely to the Olympic Games cover a four-year cycle; whereas training plans co-ordinated with the European Cup Competitions can be based on two or three year cycles, irrespective of the objectives set.

To ensure a smooth transition from the lower to the successively higher stages of systematic training good results have been achieved in gearing the basic training plans to the high-performance training cycles, adjustments being made to take into account the annual competition seasons or local conditions.

Long-term plans should contain the components mentioned earlier. It is particularly important to co-ordinate the training plan with the pupils' curricula. – It is also very important to assess the swimmers' level of performance within the framework of the analysis of the preconditions. The individual physical abilities and the level of mastery of the swimming technique should be assessed or objectified in any case. In most cases long-term objectives, i. e., the concrete performance targets to be achieved within the period covered by the plan, will consist in setting the task of achieving a certain performance class within the period specified, qualifying for certain important competitions or qualifying for being put on the best performers list. Irrespective of how the long-term objective is fixed or formulated, it is always based on a concrete performance target expressed in terms of the distance and time in which a swimmer is expected to swim it at the end of the period covered by the plan. The intermediate performance objectives set for the individual years are designed gradually to improve the swimmers' performance until they reach the final target performance at the end of the long-term plan.

In basic training such concrete performance objectives are usually set for all four strokes. It is advisable to assign special tasks only once a young swimmer clearly begins showing promise in one of the strokes. The plan for a child starting basic training at the age of 9 to 10 can be based on Chart 10, there being only minor differences in performances between boys and girls in the younger age groups.

Long-term and intermediate objectives should also be set for the development of the essential physical skills within the framework of planning performance development for one or several specific competitive event.

Objectives such as complete mastery of the techniques of the four strokes, emphasis being laid on certain types of exercise (e. g. breathing on alternate sides in crawl, head position in backstroke, learning the deep turns and their use in training and competition, etc.), will also be set in conjunction with the development of skills.

Objectives of the development of individual physical abilities are set on the basis of tests and measurements.

In principle, long-term and intermediate objectives should spur the athlete on to

Chart 10   Long-term planning of performance for the first two years of basic training (example)

Performance planning schedule	Distance	Type of Stroke			
		Freestyle (min)	Backstroke (min)	Butterfly (min)	Breaststroke (min)
Initial performance	25 m	0:18.0	0:21.0	0:31.0	0:25.0
	50 m	0:46.0	0:50.5	–	0:55.5
Target performance for age class 9	25 m	–	–	–	–
	50 m	0:40.5	0:45.0	0:48.0	0:50.0
	100 m	1:32.0	1:41.0	1:55.0	1:50.0
	200 m	3:36.0	3:40.0	–	–
Target performance for age class 10	25 m	–	–	–	–
	50 m	0:38.5	0:42.0	0:44.0	0:46.0
	100 m	1:24.0	1:33.5	1:35.0	1:43.5
	200 m	2:59.5	3:18.0	–	3:46.0

higher achievement and they should provide a means of continually checking the effectivness of training. That is why setting *realistic* performance objectives is very important in the practical planning of training.

In *planning the main tasks* based on the objectives the following essential aspects should be included:

Development of physical abilities;

refining the technique;

theoretical and tactical instruction in relevant fields of sport;

the educational aspect should be borne in mind throughout the training process.

In planning the main tasks within the framework of *developing* physical abilities it is important to outline the *essential components* of training, because in principle the individual physical abilities are developed *simultaneously*. But it is still necessary to decide when and to what extent the individual abilities of endurance should be trained and when the athlete should concentrate on strength training. The extent and phases in which general agility, flexibility and ability to relax are to be developed should also be planned systematically. A considerable amount of time is devoted to the training designed to improve *technical skills* especially in the basic training phase. The way in which optimum and competition-seasoned techniques of all four strokes, of starts and turns are to be acquired and the sequence in which this is to be done should be outlined in the long-term plan.

Once this has been achieved the main tasks of technical training within the framework of the long-term training plan will be confined to technical adjustments and to the correction of minor recurring faults and defects. The main purpose of *theoretical instruction* is to develop the athlete's ability to think on their own and to take an active part in shaping their own training.

All further tasks of theoretical training are based on this ability.

Tactical abilities are developed mainly through competitive experience. Provisions for continuing the development of these abilities should also be made in the long-term plan and especially in basic training. This is accomplished through theoretical instruction, by discussing tactical problems in the training group and by developing and improving tactical qualities in training and in test meets and tapering competitions.

It is particularly important to lay down the essential *educational tasks* within the framework of the long-term plan. They should also include component tasks and individual steps aimed at achieving the educational objective in question, which should be specified in the annual training plans and detailed training schedules.

The sequence and combination of the individual primary and secondary tasks should be arranged and co-ordinated in the long-term and annual training plans in *laying down the methodical principles of training*.

The establishment of the *workload pattern* for the entire training period is essential (cf. Chart 11).

The training workload as the sum of all training stimuli designed to improve the athlete's shape is determined by the scope of training and by the training intensity. In this connection establishing the proper *balance between the scope and intensity* in the training programme is particularly important. The balance can be shifted by gradually increasing one of the factors and reducing the other.

(REMARK: The quantitative scope of training is determined by the sum of kilometres swum in training or by the total training time in hours or minutes, while the term "training intensity" refers to the qua-

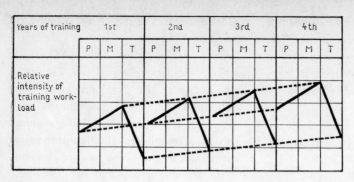

Years of training	1st			2nd			3rd			4th		
	P	M	T	P	M	T	P	M	T	P	M	T
Relative intensity of training work-load												

Chart 11   Planning the training workload over four years (after *V. P. Filin*)

litative aspect of training, i. e., the amount of stress experienced by the training athlete. In swimming sports, training intensity can be adequately measured and expressed by the distance-to-time ratio, i.e., by the average swimming speed.)

Other important aspects of the methodical organization of the training process are:
– structuring the training patterns of the individual years of the long-term training plan (periodic pattern),
– adjusting the balance between water training and athletic training on land,
– competition scheduling.

It is particularly important *to co-ordinate the training plan with curricular commitments* owing to the fact that the great majority of those taking part in basic training are young athletes of school age. It is not enough merely to co-ordinate the organization and scheduling of the curricular and athletic activities. The training plan should be co-ordinated in such a way that the pupils meet their curricular obligations (they should be able to reach the required standard of the class, their marks in the main subjects should not drop below a certain minimum standard, etc.). The athlete should realize that his performance in school and in sports constitutes a unity, and if his performance in school drops below a certain standard the coach or training supervisor should have the option of reducing or even temporarily suspending that

athlete's training to give him a chance to improve his scholastic performance.

4.6.4.2.   The annual training plan

The annual training plan, which covers the entire year, is set up on the basis of the long-term plan and forms an integral part of the long-term training programme.

An *individual annual training plan* should contain the following data:
1. The athlete's personal data;
2. results of performance analysis (assessment of the standard of performance);
3. results of personality analysis;
4. list of educational tasks;
5. performance objectives:
(a) Performance target to be achieved by the end of the year in specific competitive events. (Owing to the fact that the emphasis during basic training is on all-round swimming instruction, at first performance targets should be set for all four strokes, and later on, when the swimmer begins to show promise in one of the strokes, a performance plan should be worked out with special emphasis on that stroke, which is tentatively chosen as the athlete's main stroke);
(b) performance objectives set for the individual performance-determining factors or physical abilities, such as maximum arm pull strength, maximum number of movement repetitions on the pulley weigth or

134

rubber rope device at fixed resistance, maximum swimming speed over 25 metres, broken down if need be by arm movement, leg movement, combined movement, movement amplitude of the shoulder or foot joints;

(c) dates set for achieving the final and intermediate objectives;

6. breaking up the training year into periods and co-ordinating the training components;

7. fixing the total workload in terms of training hours or training kilometres;

(a) workload structure (workload to rest ratio);

(b) water to land training ratio;

(c) breaking down the total training kilometres to be swum in the water and the total number of hours of athletic training to be done on land into the individual training sections and training components;

8. planning the annual organization of the part of training devoted to developing individual physical abilities and improving the technique and tactics, and in conjunction with this:

Laying down methods, means, workload structure within the individual training components, progress check exercises and schedules;

9. planning theoretical instruction (content and organization);

10. planning competitions (tapering competitions, main competitions, competitive highlights);

11. measures for monitoring and assessing training work;

(a) listing all monitoring methods;

(b) scheduling the progress checks;

(c) arranging sports medical examinations and check-ups.

(1) *Periodization of the annual training programme*

Periodization of training means the scheduling, rational organization, the structure of the entire training process over prolonged periods. Principles underlying the development of athletic form and of the training condition are the basis of efficient periodization. Athletic form develops in phases. The soviet scientist MATVEYEV differentiates between three phases:

1. The phase in which athletic form is developed, i. e., the phase in which the athlete shows optimum readiness to strive for higher athletic achievement.

2. The phase of relative stabilization of athletic form.

3. The phase of temporary loss of athletic form. If the training process is to yield optimum results, then the process and the structure of annual training should be in compliance with principles governing the development of athletic shape, which means that training carried out over an extended period should be broken down into the following periods:

Chart 12 Development and perfection of technical skills in the course of basic training

Stroke	1st phase			2nd phase	
	1st year of training	2nd year of training	3rd year of training	4th year of training	5th year of training
Backstroke	50 m	50 m	100 m	200 m	200 m
Crawl	50 m	100 m	200 m	200 m	400 m
Butterfly	25 m	25 m	50 m	100 m	200 m
Breaststroke	50 m	50 m	100 m	200 m	200 m
Medley	–	–	100 m	200 m	400 m

Training sections	Periods	1st phase 50 starts per year			2nd phase 60 starts per year		
		Individ. compet.	Relay compet.	Compet. distance	Individ. compet.	Relay compet.	Compet. distance
I	Preparatory period	6	1	25 m	6	2	50 m
	Main period	8	2	25/50 m	8	2	50/100 m
II	Preparatory period	4	1	25/50 m	6	1	50/100 m
	Main period	8	2	50/100 m	8	3	50/100/200 m
III	Preparatory period	6	2	50/100 m	8	2	100/200 m
	Main period	8	2	100/200 m	10	4	100/200/400 m

1. The period in which athletic form is acquired.

2. The period in which transition to the next cycle of development of an athlete's form is made possible.

The points of reference of the periodization of a training year is the point or points in time at which the best competitive results are to be achieved. Generally they are the dates on which the main competitive events take place. The training year is periodized on the basis of this schedule of competitive events. In the basic training phase periodization is geared mainly to the school year pattern.

The essence of periodization consists in scheduling the training workload and in planning the scope and intensity of training (cf. Chart 14) and the use of the different training methods and means (cf. Chart 15). Various *forms of periodization* of annual training have evolved in the field. Two useful variants are:

(a) Simple periodization broken down into the preparatory period, competitive period, transition period (cf. Chart 16);

(b) dual periodization broken down into:

1. preparatory period, 1st competition period, 2nd competition period;

2. competition period, transition period (cf. Chart 17).

There are also other forms of periodization that can be used in certain circumstances. They include triple and multiple periodization.

Owing to the fact that basic training concerns almost exclusively children of school age, the following form of periodization is recommended. If August is left out as a vacation month, triple periodization can be used. A year's cycle would then look as follows:

1st training section
preparatory period: 9 weeks
main period: 6 weeks
transition period: 2 weeks

2nd training section
preparatory period: 9 weeks
main period: 6 weeks
transition period: 2 weeks

3rd training section
preparatory period: 9 weeks
main period: 3 weeks
transition period: 3 weeks

Multiple periodization in basic swimming training offers favourable conditions for adding variety to the year's training programme. It can be adjusted to the curricular programme and to various highlight events during the indoor and open-air swimming season and the young swimmers can be accustomed to frequent competition.

(2) *Tasks and contents of the individual periods*

In principle all main training tasks should be properly co-ordinated in all training periods. Differences in training in the different training periods consist solely in the way the individual training components are organized.

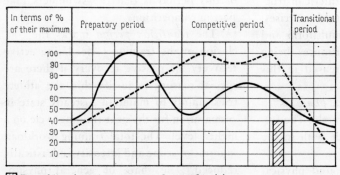

Chart 14 Periodization of the training year with regard to scope and intensity (as proposed by *Matveyev*)

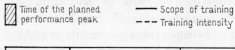

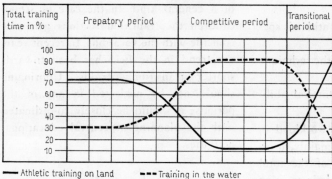

Chart 15 Periodization of the training year with regard to the ratio of water training to athletic training on land

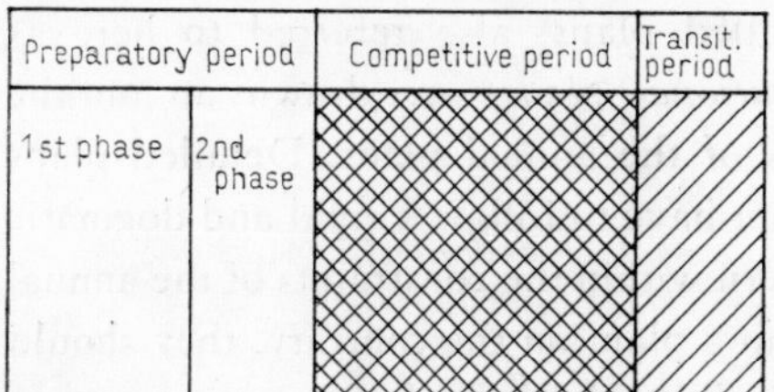

Chart 16 Simple periodization (after D. *Harre*)

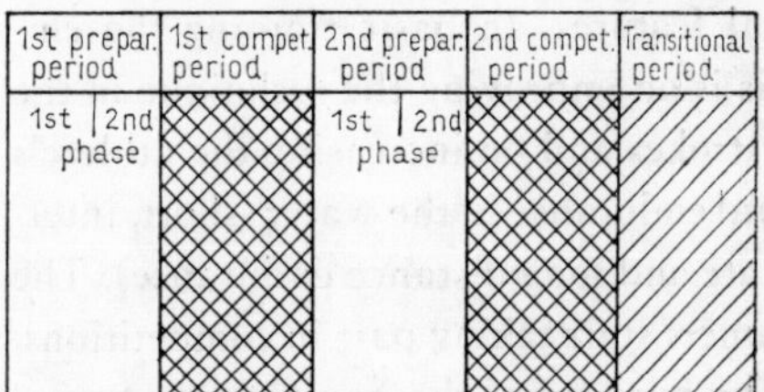

Chart 17 Double periodization (after D. *Harre*)

(1) The *preparatory period* consists of two phases:
(a) the phase of general basic preparation
b) the phase of special preparation.

The *first phase* is designed to create the conditions necessary for developing athletic form. The following tasks should be accomplished in the course of the first phase:
a) improving the process of physical preparation;
b) developing various co-ordination abilities in the water and on land.

The workload of all-round athletic instruction on land, with its manifold exercises, and in the water, with its multiform and varied exercises, (longer distances being preferred), is gradually increased in this phase of training.

The purpose of the *second phase* is to develop the athletic form directly. The following tasks should be dealt with in the course of this phase:
a) raising the level of all-round physical preparation;
b) shifting the emphasis to special physical preparation;
c) continuously improving the athlete's specific training state;
d) developing and improving the technique of the four strokes;
e) acquiring and improving tactical abilities.

The gradual increase in the workload in this phase of training is due mainly to increased intensity. The part of the total training time devoted to athletic training on land diminishes and begins acquiring special features. In basic training the emphasis is on improving the technique in the four strokes and on increasing the athlete's general endurance in the water (short, intermediate and long distance endurance). The swimmers start taking part in competitions.

(2) The purpose of the *competition period* is to maintain the athlete's shape and to translate it into swimming performance in competitions. The main goal of this period is continually to improve competitive performance. The scope of training is gradually reduced and becomes relatively stabilized, while training intensity reaches its peak and remains relatively steady. The share of total training devoted to athletic exercises on land reaches its lowest level during this phase, while water training becomes specialized and is adapted to competitive conditions. The characteristic feature of this period is that the swimmers take part in competitions.

(3) The *transition period* marks the conclusion of the training cycle. Using active recovery, or passive recovery if there are special reasons to justify this, the athlete tries mainly to maintain a steady state in preparation for the next training cycle on a higher level. The total training workload in terms of scope and intensity is drastically reduced. The share of general physical training on land is substantially increased. The swimmer takes part mostly in athletics of a general kind. In the case of school children the transition sections generally coincide with the vacations. In recent years the trend in the field has been towards shorter transition periods. Upbringing should not be neglected in any of the periods; it should be closely co-ordinated with the planning of general educational activities.

4.6.4.3.   Detailed planning of training

Detailed plans, also referred to here as *operational plans,* are drawn up on the basis of the annual plans. Detailed plans do not have to follow a rigid and dogmatic pattern within the constraints of the annual training plan, on the contrary, they should be flexibly adjusted whenever necessary to meet the given conditions or requirements.

This is where the instructor's or coach's experience and knowledge and his ability to work creatively will come in handy.

The principal forms of detailed planning are:

● section planning (covering periods of three to six weeks);

● cycle planning (one- and two-week cycles have brought particularly good results in swimming training);

● daily planning;

● planning a training unit (training preparation).

Detailed planning in all its forms is based on an analysis of training and of the performance progress made in the training section and on the objectives or tasks of the superordinate plan.

The detailed plan should always be based on the objective of the training and on the tasks set. These tasks determine which methods are to be used and the scope of training and its intensity. The detailed plan should contain data about the type and sequence of the individual exercises, about their duration (distance), about their intensity (swimming speed), about the number of repeats and about the length and organization of rest periods. The focal points of technical and tactical instruction should also be mentioned. The daily plan or the training unit should always be worked out in detail so as to enable the athlete or the group to perform the exercises on their own without supervision if need be (this does not apply to the lower age groups).

4.6.4.4. Planning tapering programmes for major competitions

This is an important part of planning the training of competitive swimmers. Proper planning adapted to the performance capacity and the psychological qualities of the individual swimmer is essential for translating the properties, abilities and skills acquired by the swimmer through training into good competitive performance.

The planning of tapering programmes for competition is not so important in basic training owing to the fact that special training is not one of the main tasks in the first phase of long-term systematic training. The closer the level of basic training approaches that of competitive training the more important becomes peaking for competitions and its planning. The purpose of tapering swimmers for competitions is to enable them to achieve the best performance they are capable of during the main competition season.

In principle a tapering programme is a condensed recapitulation of the year's training programme using simple periodization.

The training workload for a three- to six-week period is arranged as follows: A brief period of active rest (passive rest is used in exceptional cases) is followed by a phase of general and special tapering exercises of high intensity and broad scope. This is followed by a period of gradually increasing specialization in the physical tapering programme. The scope and intensity of the workload increase in the first phase, while in the second phase scope is drastically reduced and the intensity is increased still further. About one week before the contest the training workload is reduced to light, steady-state training of active rest intensity. The workout pattern of the last two to three days should in each case be adjusted to the idiosyncrasies of the individual swimmers. Partly passive rest is best for some athletes in this tapering phase.

Another aspect of tapering the athlete for the season's decisive competition consists in preparing him for the specific conditions of the competition. This includes:

● acquainting him with his potential opponents,

● working out the tactical approach,
● preparing the swimmer for the specific conditions of the competitions (time of day and site of the competition, climatic conditions, water temperature, etc.),
● practising relay swimming with the relay partners.

4.6.4.5. Documentation and analysis of training

We have already mentioned in connection with the elaboration of training plans that setting the performance targets and scrupulously analysing the preceding training period (be it a year or a shorter period of training) are both very important in planning training work. This means that the training work done, the results achieved and the experience gathered should be noted down in detail, i. e., documented.

There are the following forms of documentation:

1. the coach's training diary,
2. workload record,
3. the athlete's diary,
4. results of competitions, performance checks and tests, including physiological tests,
5. results of special medical examinations.

The *coach's training diary* contains a running account of the content and course of the training units completed. It also contains notes on any deviations from the original plan or tapering programme. Moreover, the diary contains notes about time checks and tests and about the physical condition, the athlete's determination and miscellaneous observations.

The *workload record,* which is usually prepared each week, is in itself a sort of analysis of the facts contained in the diary. In it the content of the training is processed and analysed from aspects such as the total scope of training, amount of training done

at different speeds, average section length, distances swum using the different strokes, amount of arm or leg movement exercise, amount of time spent doing athletic land training and type of exercises done, etc. A running graphic record of the values reached in the form of diagrams makes it easier to review the record and to obtain on-the-spot information.

The *athlete's training diary* is less important during basic training owing to the fact that in the great majority of cases one cannot expect a child to give a critical assessment of the training work, of the results achieved and of his condition. The value of having children keep a training diary lies mainly in its educational aspects and in helping the child to consciously take an active part in training.

Compiling the results of competitions, checks and tests are also a form of processing the information contained in the coach's diary. The effectiveness of the training work done can be quantified and improvements or drops in performance or minor fluctuations in an athlete's form can be clearly seen on the basis of such compilations. Regular *physical examinations by a sports physician* offer another possibility of monitoring the effectiveness of training and the athletes' reaction to training stimuli based on their organic condition.

The training work done can be compared with the training work that had been planned with the aid of these notes. The notes are particularly important for comparing such aspects as the total workload, the scope of training, the intensity and the proportions of the different types of training. The performance actually achieved can be related to the content and organization of training by analysing the notes.

If the results achieved correspond to the objectives, then this can generally be seen as an expression of correct planning and implementation of the training plan. On the other hand, if there are discrepancies between the aims set and the results achieved, then the reasons for this should be sought. If they are due to faulty planning the remaining training schedule should be immediately corrected and adapted to the athlete's actual performance potential. Only in this manner can truly optimum and successful training planning, training work and performance development be achieved.

4.6.4.6. Planning eductional aspects

Every training process is a paedagogic process in which education and upbringing form a unity. This means that in addition to developing an athlete's *fitness* (physical abilities, technical and tactical abilities and skills) it is also necessary consciously, persistently and systematically to develop and improve the athlete's *willingness to strive for better performance* (the level of his consciousness, his traits and willpower and other personality characteristics). The process of upbringing, which in a narrower sense is political and moral education, should be organized systematically because spontaneous influence by the coach is not enough to promote the development of an athlete's willingness to strive for better performance, as a result of which balanced development of an athlete's fitness on the one hand and of his willingness to strive for better performance on the other is neglected. The coach's tasks include helping the pupil develop a scientific world outlook, perseverance, determination, an ability to think and act on his own, to promote team spirit, etc.

The planning of work connected with upbringing should always be based on an *analysis* of the situation existing in the training group and on an analysis of the personality of the individual athletes. The focal points of educational work, the tasks to be dealt with in this connection, the measures to be taken and the intermediate objectives are then worked out in the form of a *character training plan.* The specific tasks that can be included in this plan are measures to help the athletes to be punctual (punctual commencement of training), to be honest (they should swim the full training distance), to develop hygienic habits (they should take a shower before swimming), to act independently (swimming before the competition to warm up), etc. A character training plan does not have to be as detailed as the plan covering the development of physical abilities and of technical and tactical abilities and skills. But it should always contain focal points, tasks and measures for the different periods of training. Such a plan helps the coach to carry out and to check his systematic, purposive and conscious upbringing work. A successful development and improvement of the athlete's willingness to strive for better achievements, which is essential for improving athletic performance, can be ensured only through continuous upbringing work and through regular checking of the results achieved.

Good results have been achieved in practical training by merging the instruction and character training plan into a *single* training plan.

5.   Basic Diving Instruction

Historical records showing that diving, just as swimming, is an old art date back to antiquity. Apart from sagas there exists reliable evidence that the military training of Greek, Roman and Germanic warriors, for instance included jumping into the water under extremely difficult conditions and swimming.

The *inhabitants of Halle,* who have made an important contribution to the revival of swimming in the modern era, were enthusiastic divers. In his Philonexia *Fulda* writes: ". . . and it is not easy to find a boy of six or seven around Halle who is not fond of jumping off the bridge and swimming." (24) In his „Gymnastik für die Jugend" GutsMuths writes with the greatest respect about the impressive swimming and diving skill of the people of Halle. Tychy and Lutz, who were also from that part of the country, founded a diving club known as "Tychische Frösche" in 1840. It is seen as one of the first swimming clubs in Germany. In 1843, two members of "Tychische Frösche", Hermann Otto Kluge and Karl Euler published a description of 89 different dives, which included tuck and pike dives, fall-in dives, headers, twist dives and somersault dives. This seems to confirm the assumption that the art of diving originated in Halle.

The first competitive diving events were held somewhere between 1880 and 1890. Numerous swimming clubs were founded in that period and the first national and international diving competitions were held. The rules of competition were still very sketchy then and they underwent changes almost every year. But the experience gathered in the process enabled the German divers to win a total of eight medals in the three Olympic Games from 1904 to 1912. Later on the diving events were dominated by American athletes, a fact that is attributed mainly to the two world wars. The two bronze medals won by German divers in the 1936 Olympics had little bearing on this development. It was not until the 1960 Olympics in Rome that a German diver managed to break the American monopoly again. Her name was Ingrid Gulbin-Krämer and she belonged to the GDR Olympic team. She won two gold medals, one in springboard and one in firmboard diving. During the Olympic Games held in Tokyo in 1964 she again won two medals: a gold medal in springboard diving and a silver medal in the firmboard event.

The three categories of diving are:
informal diving,
springboard diving,
firmboard diving.

Informal diving does not figure in competitive sports. For this reason it is not restricted by any rules concerning posture, competition facilities, etc. As a rule such diving is done from heights of about one metre above the surface of the water at places which are not dangerous.

Springboard and firmboard diving is subject to rules covering body posture and specific aspects of the diving facilities, because these forms of diving are part of competitive sports. They have been a permanent part of the Olympic programme since 1904. In competitive events, springboard diving is done from one-and three-metre springboards, while firmboard dives are performed from 5-metre, 7.5-metre and 10-metre firmboards.

Rules of competition distinguish between six diving groups, dives of groups I to V being performed from springboards and firmboards, while dives belonging to group VI are done only from firmboards. The classification is based on the starting position and on the direction of spins.

I. Forward dives (athlete facing the water, the dive being executed from standing position or using an approach run, forward spin);

II. Back dives (diver facing the board and executing the dive from standing position, backward spin);

III. Reverse dives (diver facing the water and executing the dive from standing position or using an approach run, backward spin);

IV. Inward dives (diver facing the board, forward spin);

V. Twist dives (facing the water or the board, executed from standing position or using an approach run, the body twists are done about the longitudinal axis, also in combination with forward and back dives from the other groups);

VI. Armstand dives (performed from armstand position forward or backward).

5.1. Informal diving

Informal dives, just as springboard and firmboard dives, are broken down into groups. But the aspects according to which the breakdown is made are much simpler. The main feature of each dive is the criterion determining the classification, and it plays a decisive role in determining the name of the group into which the dive falls. The names of the dive groups are collective names and should be used in plural form in order to prevent confusion with competitive dives and dive groups.

The following breakdown should be seen as an attempt to systematize informal dives. Organizational aspects, which will be mentioned subsequently, have not been taken into account.

1. Feet-first dives
2. Fall-in dives
3. Headers
4. Handstand dives
5. Rolls and somersaults
6. Double dives

(1) *Feet-first dives*

Feet-first dives should be seen as a comprehensive term for all dives in which the diver enters the water feet first without spinning about the transverse axis. They can be executed as forward dives from standing position facing the water or as backward dives facing the board. The take-off can be from one foot or both feet.

Examples:

Equal-pace takeoff, straight take-off, tuck dive, straddle dive (Fig. 35), straddle pike dive, pike dive, twist dive.

(2) *Fall-in dives*

As the name implies, a fall-in dive is not a dive in the true sense of the word. The diver does not leave the take-off point by

Fig. 35

Fig. 36

Fig. 37

Fig. 38

using his jumping muscles, but merely by shifting the body's centre of gravity and allowing his body to fall in through the force of gravity. Fall-in dives are included in the informal dives as a group thanks to their importance for purposes of education and instruction.

Examples:
Forward fall-in dives:
from crouch position (Fig. 36);
from trunk bend forward position;
from horizontal balance position.
Backward fall-in dives:
from squat stand;
from trunk bend forward position;
from standing position.

(3) *Headers*

In popular usage here, headers are considered only those dives that are done forwards with a running or standing take-off. The takeoff can be with one or both legs. The upper arms should be pressed firmly against the ears, the hands are kept together and enter the water first.

Examples:
frog jumps (Fig. 37);
starting dives or lunge dives;
lunges;
headers with different leg positions (e. g. spread, straddle, tuck).

(4) *Handstand dives*

The characteristic feature of handstand dives is that the ultimate impetus influencing the trajectory of the body's centre of gravity comes from the diver's hands and arms. It makes no difference if one or both arms are used. The diver can enter the water head first or feet first. The takeoff level for handstand dives can be raised by using benches, handrails or other apparatus or by leap-frogging over partners standing with bent backs.

Fig. 39

Fig. 40

Examples:
Leap-frog dives over partners (Fig. 38);
leap-frog head-first dives over handrails
(Fig. 39);
handstand dives, handsprings, straddle-
vault dives (Fig. 40);
squat dives; cart-wheel dives.

(5) *Rolls and somersaults*
In the case of somersaults the entire spin is
performed in the air, while in the case of
rolls parts of the body may touch the board
in the process. That is why rolls should be
practised first before starting with the
somersaults. But both rolls and somersaults
should be first practised with the tuck position.

Examples:
Forward roll with tuck;
forward roll piked;
backward roll with tuck (Fig. 41);
backward roll piked;
forward somersault with tuck (Fig. 42);
backward somersault with tuck.

Fig. 41

Fig. 42

Fig. 43

Fig. 44

Fig. 45

(6) *Jumping in pairs*

Jumping in pairs is perhaps the most popular of the group jumps both as far as the divers and the spectators are concerned. When looking for matching partners one should take into account the height, weight and the dexterity of the divers.

Examples:

Twin jumps:

(a) The partners stand beside each other holding hands, arms or hips and dive feet- or head-first.

(b) The partners stand facing each other sideways to the pool and jump feet- or head-first. The spin is round the dorsoventral axis. Running dives can also be performed in this manner.

Pickapack feet- and head-first dives (Fig. 43);

stand-handstand jump (Fig. 44);

jockey jump (feet- and head-first), in which one partner sits on the other's shoulders;

kangaroo jump (Fig. 45).

(7) *Organization of informal diving*

The fun of informal diving can be increased by having several pupils execute the dives simultaneously. Training intensity can also be increased with this type of diving; this has a particularly beneficial influence on learning the dives that are compulsory in the school swimming programme and in beginner's training. These dives can be executed side-by-side or in succession, the learners can hold on to each other or jump separately, they can perform the dives from a running start or from a standing or sitting position. It is important that the learners should always grip the edge of the pool deck with their toes or that their heels project beyond the edge of the pool deck when diving if the pool deck is slippery. Running dives should be performed only if there is no danger of slipping anywhere along the approach run. But before starting with the diving exercises, the depth and the condition of the bottom of the pool or lake must be known.

The following are some of the most popular forms of organization:

Group and chain jumps

In addition to a high intensity the advantage of group and chain jumps is that the timid ones, put in the middle, soon get used to jumping in a group and overcome their fear. But it is important to remember that in the case of group jumping the takeoff should be simultaneous and that in the case of chain diving the takeoff intervals should not be too long, because otherwise collision accidents can happen. An additional advantage of chain jumps is that the coach can watch each pupil individually (Fig. 46). All jumps mentioned up till now can be executed as group or chain jumps without the pupils' holding on to each other. In the case of group jumps we recommend that the learners should hold hands, link arms or hold on to each other's hips or shoulders.

Forward or backward fall-in squat stand or trunk bend dives can be used for chain jumps in which the pupils hold on to each other. Jumping into the water in a chain formed by pupils sitting close behind each other along the edge of the pool is another popular form of the chain jump (Fig. 47). If the appropriate facilities are available these group and chain jumps can also be executed as running dives.

Jumping over obstacles is the last organizational form we shall mention here. Forward feet- and head-first dives, pike roll and forward somersault can be executed over a bench, a pole, through a hoop or over a person standing with his back bent. It is particularly important to make sure that the take-off area is not slippery and that the pool is sufficiently deep for such dives.

Fig. 46

Fig. 47

5.2.   Basic springboard diving instruction

The term "elementary school" of springboard instruction can be frequently found in diving instruction manuals here. But unfortunately different authors use different definitions of the term. For this reason we shall use the term "basic springboard diving instruction", which we shall first define and explain.

The starting point is that the content of basic springboard diving instruction should be such as to provide an adequate foundation for subsequent tapering training and competitive training.

We classify basic diving instruction into *basic exercises* on the one hand and *jumps and key dives* on the other. But one should not overlook the organic connection existing between the two. This classification was chosen for methodical reasons, because the basic exercises must be seen as a preparatory stage leading up to the jumps and key dives. The basic exercises help the beginner to get used to his new environment, which includes the springboard, the fligth phase and the immersion. The novice also learns the starting position and the forward and backward dive from standing position, which are the basis for all further take-offs. In the course of the basic exercises the beginner also learns the basic approach, which is part of the jumps and key dives. The approach technique is perfected in the process of learning the jumps and key dives. A purposeful system of gymnastic exercises will help the beginner improve the execution of all jumps and key dives; the learning process can be speeded up through posture and movement exercises.

The purpose of teaching the key dives is to acquaint the diver with further basic elements of diving and to prepare him for the more advanced stages of tapering and high-level competitive training.

The objectives of jumps and key dives are:
– The purpose of learning the jumps is to learn the forward and back standing take-off and the three modifications thereof (tuck, pike and straight) and to learn the feet-first entry.
– The purpose of learning the key dives is to acquire a feeling for applying the right amount of vertical spin with each of the takeoffs of groups I to IV and to learn the head-first entry.
– The purpose of the twist jumps and dives is to acquire a feeling for the lateral spin (in the case of feet-first twist jumps the twist is executed only round the body's longitudinal axis, but in the case of head-first twist dives this is done in conjunction with a half somersault).

– The aim of learning to somersault is to acquire a fine feeling for controlling the body's angular momentum and for changes in the mass moment of inertia and its influence on the angular velocity and in this way to improve the performance of the kinaesthetic motor analyser, of the optical analyser and of the vestibulary analyser.

5.2.1. Basic springboard exercises

(1) *Springboard familiarization exercises*
The transition from jumping off the edge of the pool to diving from the springboard is a systematic process of adapting to the springboard through familiarization exercises. The line of flight of the body's centre of gravity does not matter in the case of popular jumps and dives, but in springboard diving it is very important to achieve maximum height and steepness of the body's centre of gravity in all springboard jumps and dives. Developing a keen sense of balance is the main objective of springboard familiarization exercises. Physiologically, springboard familiarization exercises involve complex training of the sense of touch of the touch-corpuscles of the soles, of the muscle sense, which is made up of sensations coming from the tendons, muscles, ligaments and joints and of the vestibulary system. Due to the complex physiological processes involved the process of springboard familiarization is a lengthy one and familiarization exercises should be continued throughout the training process.

Sample exercises
All forward and backward informal jumps and dives should be repeated from the one-metre springboard from a standing position.
– Walking along the springboard
The learner should walk along the spring-

board taking short steps before jumping off. Later on the learner should practise all feet-first forward jumps mentioned earlier. The jumps should first be practised with single footed and later on with double footed takeoff.

– Running along the board

Same exercises as those done walking except that they should be done at a higher speed.

– Bouncing along the board with both feet held together

The learner bounces along the board keeping his feet together. He should try to concentrate on jumping higher rather than making long jumps. Later on the learner can start practising jumps and dives after the last bounce off the board. The learner can also do a half twist after the penultimate bounce on the springboard and then jump off backwards.

– Board rocking

The pupil stands with his feet slightly apart with his body erect, his head raised and his eyes focused straight ahead.

By flexing and stretching his hip, knee and foot joints the pupil sets the firmboard in motion and experiences its resilience. Later on he should raise his heels with each rocking movement. In the process the foot "rolls" on the springboard from the heel to the ball and back without leaving the board yet.

The pupil should keep his arms relaxed at his sides. The rocking exercise should always be completed by jumping off into the water, any jump or dive the pupil already masters can be used.

– Standing board bouncing

Bouncing is more difficult than rocking, for here the pupil's feet leave the board and his arms are used to assist him. The starting position and the stance are the same as with the rocking exercise. The board is depressed more vigorously with the bouncing

exercise. The pupil should use his jumping muscles to assist the upward drive. He also swings his arms loosely in front of him to get added takeoff drive. The pupil should try to bounce four to six times at the end of the board. After that he should either stop bouncing or execute a controlled takeoff. The next series of bounces should be started from an approach run.

(2) *Starting position and standing takeoff*

In starting position the learner stands at the front end of the springboard with his legs extended and his feet together. When doing forward dives and jumps the ends of the pupil's toes should be flush with the front edge of the diving board. In the starting position for backward dives the diver's heels should project beyond the end of the springboard. The diver holds his body erect, his stomach drawn in and his shoulders slightly back. His body rests on the balls of his feet, his leg muscles tensed, his arms are extended along the sides of his body. He looks straight ahead.

After pausing briefly in this position the diver starts preparing for the takeoff. He raises his arms loosely to the upward lateral position raising his heels from the board in the process. The load on the springboard is relieved through these movements, as a result of which it recoils upwards. Then the diver lowers the full weight of his body on the board, flexing his foot, knee and hip joints, swinging his arms downward and thereby exerting extra pressure on the board and depressing it again. But before the springboard reaches its lowest point of depression the diver begins to extend his legs in order to depress the board still more. At the same time he swings his arms upwards, elbows flexed, in preparation for an optimum takeoff. The force of the board's recoil throws the diver upwards. Just before leaving the springboard the diver

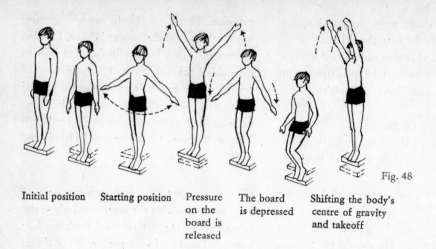

Initial position   Starting position   Pressure on the board is released   The board is depressed   Shifting the body's centre of gravity and takeoff

Fig. 48

should shift his body's centre of gravity from the imaginary line vertical to the plane of the board to the direction of flight, for if the diver failed to do this he would land on the springboard again as in the case of the board bouncing exercise (Fig. 48). These instructions apply to both forward and backward takeoffs.

(3) *The approach*

According to the rules of competition the approach should be done without hesitation, in a straight line and the diver should take at least four steps (including the takeoff bounce).

The approach consists of the starting position, approach, takeoff bounce and takeoff. The diver should assume the normal position before the approach. In this position the diver's body is erect, his eyes focused on the tip of the board and his arms hang loosely on his sides. He then takes at least three steps of normal length and accelerates his walk slightly, swinging his arms slightly or holding them loosely at his sides. During the last step the diver moves both arms back simultaneously in preparation for the takeoff bounce.

The diver should push off for the takeoff bounce about 60 cm before reaching the tip

of the springboard. When the body's centre of gravity is above the jumping leg the diver vigorously pushes off with this leg, bringing up the swinging leg from the rear to the front to a position in which the swinging leg's knee and hip joints are at rightangles.

At the highest point in the line of flight during the takeoff bounce the swinging leg is brought up along the jumping leg, which is extended at this point, and the hips are pushed slightly forward. During the takeoff bounce the outstretched body is flexed somewhat in the hip, knee and foot joints in order to tense the muscles for the takeoff. Landing on the springboard for the takeoff the diver touches the springboard first with the balls of his feet and then with his heels swinging his arms down vigorously. The sequence of movements that is initiated then is the same as that described for the standing dive (Fig. 49).

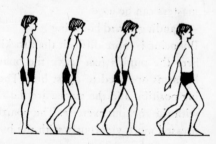

(4) *The entry*

The jump or dive is completed once the diver's body is fully submerged in the water. The entry is also very important in the judgement of the dive. According to the rules of competition the entry must be made vertically or almost vertically with the body fully stretched out. But this rule can be complied with only if the diver's body enters the water vertically and if the diver keeps his muscles tensed until he reaches the bottom of the pool. Only in this way can the diver's body enter the water like a pointed pole drawing in its wake the water it displaces and thus causing minimum splash.

It is relatively easy to make an entry as described in the foregoing if the jump is made without spinning around the body's transverse axis. The degree of difficulty is directly proportional to the angular velocity which the body reaches around its transverse axis during the flight phase. A diver should always try to reduce his angular velocity to a minimum before making the entry. This is done by stretching out one's body from the tuck or pike, thereby increasing one's mass moment of inertia. A diver cannot completely check his body's spin around the transverse axis; i.e., his body continues spinning also during the entry phase. If his body started the entry in a vertical position it would "go over" beyond

the 90-degree angle. This means that the diver's body should start the entry at an angle of less than 90 degrees so that by the time the diver has completed the entry his body should have reached the vertical. It is obvious, therefore, that those parts of the body that are still outside the water retain their angular velocity, while the submerged part is checked somewhat by the water. That is why the diver should counteract this spinning force by tensing his muscles from the costal arch to the tips of his toes.

Summing up we can say that in the case of any dive involving vertical spin the spin should be counteracted during entry by tensing the hip, stomach and leg muscles.

The following entry exercises are recommended:

Feet-first entries

1. Forward jump from the sitting position (from edge of pool deck and from 1-metre board);
2. from stretched hang from 1-metre board;
3. from stretched hang from 3-metre board;
– arms held up
– arms by the sides;
4. all feet-first jumps.

Head-first entries

Beginners should first start with fall-in dives before progressing to other head-first entries. Fall-in forward dives from the bent trunk position from the pool deck edge and

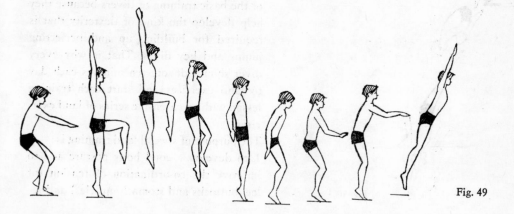

Fig. 49

from higher positions are the most commonly used form of fall-in dive.

In the starting position for the fall-in dive the beginner stands with his feet together, knees straight and the tips of his toes flush with the edge of the pool deck. His arms are either in a lateral slightly raised position or held up and his body is bent forward and down. His eyes are focused on the intended point of entry, which is determined by his height and by the height from which he jumps. Leg muscles are tensed by raising the heels. By shifting his weight forward the diver lets his body fall forward. With his feet pressing in the direction opposite the direction of his body spin, the learner points his hands in the direction of the point of entry. Just before making the entry the learner clasps his hands and presses his upper arms tightly against his ears.

Other entry exercises from the 3-metre board:
– from the sitting position (tucked) (Fig. 50);
– from the piked sitting position;
– from the forward roll;
– from the standing position with outstretched arms and feet (Fig. 51).

Fig. 51

The following exercises are recommended for practising backward head-first dives:
– backward straight fall-in dives from the 3-metre board;
– backward fall-in dives from forward trunk bend from 1- and 3-metre boards (Fig. 52).

5.2.2. Special land exercises for divers

Special land exercises are an important part of the basic training of divers because they help develop the kind of dexterity that is required for building up and perfecting jumps and key dives. That is why every diver should devote ten minutes each day to land exercises and start each training lesson with an extensive series of land exercises.

The purpose of special land training is:
1. to develop a good body posture and to improve the co-ordination of tension (of leg, buttocks and stomach muscles) and re-

Fig. 50

Fig. 52

laxation (of the thoracic and arm muscles);
2. to develop the technique of basic movement patterns;
3. to develop the suppleness of the joints that play an important role in diving (foot, hip and shoulder joints) and to develop general agility and joint flexibility;
4. to develop general physical fitness.
The following special exercises are recommended for this purpose:
a) Posture exercises
In all exercises belonging to this group the diver should tense the muscles of the lower extremities, of the pelvis and of the stomach while relaxing his arm and shoulder muscles.
– Standing on his toes the athlete raises and lowers his shoulders.
– Lying in supine position the athlete raises his legs and holds them in this position.
– Lying in supine position the athlete is raised by a partner to stretched out standing position.

– Lying in prone head-first dive position the athlete raises his legs and thorax.
– In long sitting position he raises his legs and spreads and closes them several times.
– Sitting in long sitting position the athlete "curls in" his toes and stretches his feet.
– The athlete tenses his leg, stomach and buttock muscles in ordinary hang position.
– Headstand same as ordinary hang.
– Handstand same as ordinary hang.
b) Movement exercises
Normal position: straight jumps accompanied by takeoff arm movement, approach run exercises (the takeoff bounce should be made from a higher level).
Normal position: Each knee is drawn up to the body and extended alternately.
Long sitting positions: Both knees are drawn up to the body and extended without touching the floor.
Supine position: Both knees are drawn up to the body and extended, arms imitate back tuck dive movement.
Ordinary hang: The knees are drawn up and extended.
Supine position: Angle or "V" sits (pike exercises).
Ordinary hang: Raising and lowering of extended legs.
Forward and backward rolls from standing position.
c) Supplying exercises
Floor beating with hands.
Sit ups with chest touching the legs.
Overhead leg swing in supine position with toes touching the floor.
Forward and backward arm circling in standing position.
Alternate forward and backward swinging of the arms in the standing position.
Raising the knees from the kneeling position and bending backwards at the same time.
Slowly stretching the knees and rising on the toes in bench position.

153

Sitting in the squatting position with a partner sitting on his feet the athlete slowly extends his knees to long sitting position.

d) Strengthening exercises

These exercises are of a general character and are described in any gymnastics textbook. But special attention should be paid to strengthening one's stomach, leg and back muscles.

Special exercises have already been described in the section dealing with basic exercises because they play an important role in progressing to jumps and key dives. But this does not mean that no further exercises are required for further progression. Appropriate exercises should be an integral part of the training programme of any athlete, be he a beginner or an intermediate- or championship-level diver.

5.2.3.   Jumps and key dives

5.2.3.1.   The feet-first jumping technique

Feet-first jumps are important not only because they are the first jumps a beginner learns, but also because they are used by advanced-level divers for perfecting their stance and sense of balance. Even championship-level divers use them for training purposes.

It is not advisable to proceed to more complicated dives before the beginners have mastered the fine points of the feet-first jumps. The simplicity of feet-first jumps lies in the fact that they are translation jumps, which means that they do not involve vertical spins and that the drive produced during takeoff should coincide with the centre of gravity of the body in order to prevent any spin around the transverse axis of the body.

The sequence of the jumps described in the following should be regarded as a methodical routine. It was worked out on the basis of a pedagogical experiment carried out by the Institute of Swimming Sports of the German College of Physical Culture (DHfK). [15]

– The plain jump forward

As the body leaves the board the arms should continue their swing forwards and upwards until they are straight above the head. The feet and legs are kept close together at a slight angle forward. Buttocks and stomach muscles are tensed and the shoulders slightly drawn back. At the highest point the legs are bent slightly backwards. The extended arms are lowered laterally as the body descends. The legs are again angled slightly forward and the head is tilted into normal position. The hands are on the front of the thighs as the body makes the entry.

– The tuck jump backward

The takeoff is made facing the board. As the learner jumps off his arms, bent at the elbows, swing up in front until they are level with the head. At the same time the hip and knee joints are flexed as compactly as possible. The hands grip the shins and draw up the lower legs. The back is slightly arched and the trunk is bent slightly over the knees. While the trunk retains its position the legs are quickly stretched out downwards. Then the body is straightened, the arms slide along the legs. All muscles are tensed during the entry and the eyes are on the springboard.

– The plain backward jump (Fig. 53)

The learner faces the springboard in the starting position and jumps backwards and up when taking off; all other aspects of the technique are the same as described for the plain forward jump.

– The tuck jump forward (Fig. 54)

The learner jumps forward and up; all other elements of the technique are the same as those described for the tuck jump back-

Fig. 53

Fig. 54

top of the flight the learner stretches out the body by lowering the legs and sliding the hands up the legs until they reach the thighs, against which they are held firmly during the entry.

– The forward jump piked (Fig. 55)
The same applies here as in the case of the backward jump piked.

5.2.3.2. The half-twist jump technique

Feet-first twist or screw jumps are used primarily to teach the beginner how to twist the body around the longitudinal axis of the body. Thus, they should be seen not so much as jumps in their own right but as preliminaries to more difficult dives listed in the table of official dives. The half-twist jump can be executed either forwards or backwards from the standing position. The take-off is the same as that used for the other feet-first dives, except that the body must be given a twist. This is done by throwing up the hands after the takeoff and the diver's body starts out in an outstretched position. The arm movement sequence is de-

ward, except that the forward bend of the trunk is not as pronounced.

– The backward jump piked
Having taken off backwards and up the learner raises his outstretched legs forward and quickly flexes his hip joint until the legs reach the horizontal position and the trunk is bent forward, enabling him to touch the toes with his fingers. After reaching the

Fig. 55

signed to intensify the twist. If the twist is to be made to the right the left arm is swung downwards and across the chest with the elbow bent just before the top of the flight. The head is turned to the right while the right arm is stretched out vertically parallel to the pivot axis. The half-twist must be completed just after the top of the flight. To check the twist the arms are spread out sideways and then brought to the sides for the entry. The entry is made in the same way as in the case of plain forward jumps (Fig. 56).

5.2.3.3. The head-first diving technique

All jumps that involve half a spin around the transverse axis of the body are designated as dives in international official tables of dives. The difficulty of any jump involving rotation around the transverse body

Fig. 56

156

axis consists in having to put the body in a *spin around the transverse axis.* From the mechanical point of view a spin can no longer be imparted to the body after the take-off, because there are no opposable resistances in the air that can be used to give the body such a spin. But it is possible to influence the body's angular momentum (angular velocity) by changing the mass moment of inertia. The closer the mass particles are to the centre of a body's rotation, the higher that body's angular velocity, and vice versa. But the original angular momentum can only be imparted to a body through the takeoff. This means that the diver must give his body the necessary amount of spin at takeoff, regardless of whether he is doing a forward or backward dive, and that the centre of gravity of the body must not coincide with the line of the board's lift force. Fig. 57 shows a feet-first jump in which the board's lift force is in alignment with the body's centre of gravity. In this case there can be no rotation around the transverse axis. Fig. 58 shows how the body is given a forward spin by the line of the board's lift force being behind the body's centre of gravity.

The angular momentum is determined by the lift force and the takeoff angle, i.e., the distance between the centre of gravity of the body and the line of force of the board's lift. This means that by increasing the distance between the body's centre of gravity and the line of force the same angular momentum can be imparted to the body as by correspondingly increasing the lift force (this applies to both forward and backward takeoffs). Figures 59 to 62 show the mechanics of the takeoffs of the first four groups of dives, which can be regarded as "pure" dive groups by virtue of the fact that they are distinguished by the starting position and the direction of rotation. (The basic features of these groups can be recog-

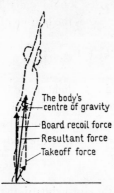

The body's
centre of gravity
Board recoil force
Resultant force
Takeoff force

Fig. 57   Feet-first jumps

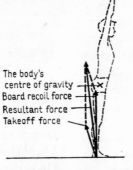

The body's
centre of gravity
Board recoil force
Resultant force
Takeoff force

Fig. 58   Jumps with forward spin

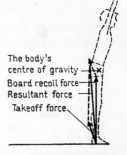

The body's
centre of gravity
Board recoil force
Resultant force
Takeoff force

Fig. 59   Forward jumps

The body's
centre of gravity
Board recoil force
Resultant force
Takeoff force

Fig. 60   Backward jumps

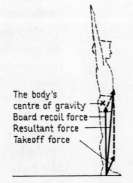

The body's
centre of gravity
Board recoil force
Resultant force
Takeoff force

Fig. 61   Reverse dives (Gainers)

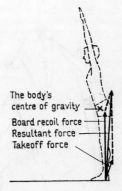

The body's
centre of gravity
Board recoil force
Resultant force
Takeoff force

Fig. 62   Inward dives

nized in Group V, which comprises twist dives.)

Despite some basic differences between the four groups of dives, they also have some common features with respect to the body movements during the flight phase, notably between forward and spring-and-submerge dives and between back and gainers. This fact should be taken into account in instruction and it has a certain bearing on training (the pairs of dives are mutually complementary).

Forward dives facing the water
(Forward jumps, cf. Fig. 59)

Forward dives facing the water can be executed from the standing position or with an approach run.

– The forward dive with tuck
(Fig. 63)

The takeoff should be executed at a slight angle. The stretching of the legs and the upward movement of the arms should be simultaneous. The head should be raised, the eyes should be turned to the highest point in the flight curve.

Flight phase:

After the feet have left the springboard the buttocks are "raised", the knees are brought up to the chest by flexing the knee and hip joints. At the same time the diver grasps his shins and presses his arms firmly against the body. The top of the flight is reached in this compact tuck or hunch position. The eyes are now turned to the point of entry. In the second part of the flight

Fig. 63

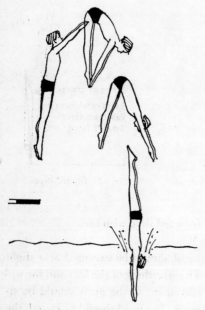

Fig. 64

phase the diver should open out by straightening the legs in line with the body (the exact moment when this should be done depends on the angular velocity) and then straightening the arms sideways and overhead.

Entry:

When the hands touch the water the upper arms should be held tightly against the ears. The body should enter at an almost verti-

cal angle and the muscles should remain tensed until the diver reaches the bottom of the pool.

– The forward dive piked (Fig. 64)

Takeoff:

The takeoff is executed at a slight angle in the same manner as the forward dive with tuck. But the angular momentum should be somewhat greater in order to give the body enough angular velocity.

Flight phase:

Once the feet leave the springboard the buttocks are vigorously "raised", the outstretched legs are forced forward in the direction opposite to the direction of rotation. The legs are in a nearly vertical position. At the same time the trunk is bent forward and then downwards in a pike position. The hands touching the insteps, or, in the case of a free pike position, they are held sideways. These movements should be completed by the time the culmination point is reached.

The body is swiftly stretched out from the pike position, the legs still exerting a slight pressure against the direction of rotation and the arms are moved sideways and up. The eyes are focused on the point of entry.

Entry:

The entry is made in the same manner as in the case of the forward dive with tuck. The body should be kept completely straight at the hip joint and the legs braced against the direction of rotation in order to prevent "going over".

– The "swallow dive" or forward dive straight (Fig. 65)

Takeoff:

The takeoff is the same as in the case of other head-first dives. In addition, the feet should be vigorously pressed backwards and up during the last phase of the flight in order to give the body enough spin.

Flight phase:

As the feet leave the board, the leg and pel-

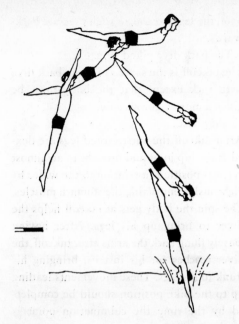

Fig. 65

vic muscles should be tensed firmly and the feet should continue pressing backwards and up. The eyes should be kept focused on the intended culmination point, the arms are held up. During the ascending part of the flight the arms are lowered from the upward to the sideways position. The head is dropped slightly backwards in the neck, which results in a slight tensing of the body. After passing the culmination point the arms are again brought up together, the eyes are focused on the point of entry.

Entry:

The entry is made in the same manner as with all other forward dives.

Back dives with head-first entry
(Head-first back dives, cf. Fig. 60)
All head-first back dives are executed from standing position. The takeoff thrust and the body's backward lean should be co-ordinated in order to ensure the right amount of spin for the dive in question. The buttocks should not be moved backwards nor the hip joint bent during the backward

lean. The shoulders, the head and the arms should be moved backwards. But this does not mean that the trunk should be jerked backwards right away, but rather that the body's centre of gravity should be slightly shifted in this manner.

– The back dive with tuck (Fig. 66)

Takeoff:

The sequence of takeoff movements starts when the springboard reaches its lowest point of depression. The arms are flexed at the elbows and swung forward and over-head and the jumping joints are extended; the body balance is shifted slightly to the rear. Throughout the sequence of takeoff movements the eyes are on the rear end of the board.

Flight phase:

The arms are swung up when the feet have left the board. The eyes are focused on the hands. The knees are quickly drawn up

Fig. 66

159

until they touch the chest and the hands grasp the shins. These movements are completed by the time the top of the flight is reached, and the body has completed $1/4$ of a turn around its transverse axis.

During the second flight phase the legs are stretched out in line with the body backwards and up and the eyes are fixed on the toes (the exact moment of the opening out depends on the body's angular velocity). Then the arms are swung out sideways to the entry position, at the same time the head is forced back and the eyes focused on the point of entry.

Entry:

When the hands, which are held close together, touch the water the body should be completely stretched out and all muscles tensed. The head is tilted forward in such a way that the upper arms touch the ears. The diver continues the dive in this rigid state until he reaches the bottom of the

pool, the legs exerting a sligh pressure backwards.

– The back dive piked (Fig. 67)

The takeoff is the same as for the back dive with tuck except that the body must be given a more vigorous spin.

Flight phase:

After takeoff the outstretched legs are flexed at the hip joint and brought to an almost vertical position in relation to the water by vigorously contracting the stomach muscles. The spin the body gets at takeoff helps the diver to bring up his legs. After having loosely flung back the arms after takeoff, the diver reaches for his insteps, bringing his trunk to his legs. These movements leading up to the pike position should be completed by the time the culmination point is reached.

During the second part of the flight phase the body is stretched out smoothly until the legs and the trunk are in a straight line, the angle of the legs in relation to the flight trajectory remaining unchanged because they counteract the direction of rotation, while the trunk moves backwards and down in the direction of rotation. The hands slide the legs up to the thighs and are then brought up sideways and into the entry position. At the same time the head is tilted slightly backwards and the eyes focused on the entry point.

Entry:

See back dive with tuck.

– Back dive straight (Fig. 68)

Takeoff:

The takeoff is the same as that of the back dive with tuck except that the backward lean is more pronounced.

Flight phase:

When the feet leave the board the outstretched body is pushed up and backwards, the stomach, buttocks and leg muscles being tensed. The arms are swung up, the shoulders pressed back and the head kept

Fig. 67

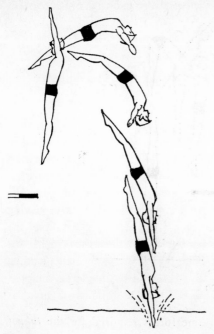

Fig. 68

in its normal position. At the apex the head and shoulders are swiftly moved backwards and the arms sideways, a slight hollow being formed in the small of the back as a result.

During the descent part of the flight phase the arms are brought up from the sideways to the entry position. Just before entry the back should be slowly straightened by moving forward the head and shoulders.

Entry:

The entry is made in the same way as in the case of the other head-first dives.

Reverse dives straight

(Half-gainers, cf. Fig. 61)

Half-gainers can be done from standing position or with an approach. Their movement sequence during the flight phase and during entry is the same as that of back dives. This is due to the fact that the backward body spin is used in both cases. That is why we shall dispense with a description of the flight and entry techniques, because in prin-

ciple that same technique as that used for back dives is used.

The main difference between these two groups of dives consists in their different starting positions. Owing to the fact that a different position of the body's centre of gravity and a different takeoff force are the only aspects that are different in the case of half-gainers (the technique features the same basic characteristics as that of the back dives), we shall only give a general description of the takeoff.

Three different forces are involved in half-gainers:

a) a horizontal force by means of which the diver "gains" distance from the board,

b) a vertical force propelling the body upwards,

c) a force that gives the body its spin around the transverse body axis.

These forces are produced in the following manner:

a) the horizontal force is produced mainly by the jumping joints in a forward and updrive at takeoff and by the body's forward movement if an approach run is used;

b) the vertical force is produced by the board's recoil and by a sudden stretching of the legs and arm swing;

c) the spinning force is produced by shifting the centre of gravity behind the resultant of the takeoff vector and the board recoil vector.

The half-gainer takeoff:

While the board is being depressed the arms are brought down and the knees and hip joint slightly flexed, the leg muscles are vigorously tensed. The body's centre of gravity still remains above the support surface. The takeoff movement is initiated before the springboard reaches its deepest point. The takeoff movement sequence consists in raising the head and slowly moving the trunk backwards. The body's backward movement is speeded up during the board recoil phase (the speed of this movement depending on the type of dive) and the arms are quickly moved forwards and up. The body's centre of gravity should be moved behind the line of the resultant force and the leg takeoff completed by the time the springboard reaches its normal position. The centre of gravity is shifted by bringing back the arms, the head, the shoulders and the chest without hollowing the small of the back. The legs and the pelvis are driven forwards and up by a vigorous push-off with the feet (Fig. 69).

Inward dives
(also known as back-front pike, cf. Fig. 62) The resemblance between the reverse dives and the back dives is the same as that between the inward dives and the forward dives. In both types of dives the direction of rotation is forward, but the starting position varies. Thus, the technique used during the flight phase and when making the entry is the same for the inward dive as that used for the forward dives.

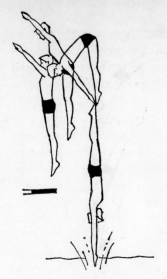

Fig. 70

The same forces required for the *takeoff used for the inward dives* are the same as those used for the reverse dives.
a) The horizontal force is produced by the legs pushing off backwards and up;
b) the vertical force is produced by the springboard recoil and push-off;
c) the force of rotation is produced by shifting the body's centre of gravity on front of the resultant force vector.
Inward dive takeoff technique (Fig. 70):
The body's centre of gravity remains above the support surface while the board is being depressed by the weight of the body and by the winding up movement. Once the board has reached its lowest point of depression the diver begins to swing his arms upwards just before he commences the take-off movement sequence. The body leans slightly forward as the board moves up, the hip joint being slightly flexed while the legs complete their extension. The arms have already reached the highest point of their upward movement. The head is held in its normal position and the line of sight is shifted to the end of the board. The arms are pushed in the direction of rotation during

Fig. 69

162

the last phase of the upward movement which ends with a vigorous push-off backwards and up. In this series of movements the upward swing of the arms preceding the takeoff sequence mentioned earlier has a favourable effect on the subsequent spinning movement owing to the fact that now both forces act in the direction of rotation. This is especially important for dives involving multiple spins around the transverse axis, and less important for the inward dive straight.

Fig. 71

The somersault with tuck technique
We call all dives in which the diver's body makes at least one complete rotation around its transverse axis somersaults, irrespective of whether the entry is made head first or feet first.

Only somersaults with tuck of Groups I to IV are included in basic diving instruction.

Apart from the takeoff force and the amount by which the body's centre of gravity is shifted, all somersaults with tuck resemble dives (head-first entry). That is why we shall not go into the takeoff technique again.

– Forward somersault with tuck (Fig. 71)
Takeoff:
The takeoff is done in the same manner as that of the forward dive with tuck except that the forward lean should be more pronounced.

Flight phase:
Once the feet have left the board, the heels are brought up to the buttocks and the head and shoulders towards the knees while the arms are swung down to the shins, which increases the spin and improves the compact tuck position. The chin is brought down to the chest and the back is bent. The body should have completed half a spin by the time it reaches the culmination point. The rest of the somersault is completed during the descent part of the flight. The legs are stretched out before the body reaches the vertical position (the exact moment depending on the angular velocity), the hands sliding along the legs and up to the thighs, the head and trunk are straightened out and the legs are slowly "pushed" down for entry.

The entry:
The eyes should be focused on a distant point during the entry. The body is fully stretched out, the leg, stomach and buttocks muscles are kept rigidly tense, the shoulders are drawn back and relaxed, the arms are held along the body, the hands resting on the front part of the thighs. The body is kept in this position until the diver reaches the bottom of the pool.

– Back somersault with tuck (Fig. 72)
Takeoff:
The takeoff is the same as that of the back dive with tuck except that the angular momentum and the backward lean are more pronounced.

Flight phase:
The legs are drawn up to a tuck once the feet leave the board and the head tilted

163

Fig. 72

back slightly. At the culmination point the body should be in a compact tuck and half of the somersault should have been completed by that time. The head precedes the spin, and the eyes focused on the water after the culmination point. Just before the somersault is completed the legs are stretched out in line with the trunk (the exact moment at which this is done depending on the body's angular velocity), and the hands are slid along the legs from the shins to the thighs.

Entry:

The trunk is straightened out and the head tilted back for the entry. Keeping his body rigid and his arms relaxed along the sides the diver retains this attitude until he reaches the bottom of the pool.

– Reverse dive with tuck (Fig. 73)

Takeoff:

The takeoff is the same as that used for the half-gainer except that the angular momentum is greater.

Flight phase:

After the arms have been swung up and the feet have left the board the diver quickly draws up his legs to a compact tuck. The direction of movement of the knees is towards the culmination point. At the same time the head is tilted back and precedes the direction of rotation.

During the descent the feet are stretched out towards the tip of the springboard after $3/4$ of the somersault have been completed, the trunk and head straightened out and the hands put on the thighs in front.

Entry:

His eyes focused on the opposite side of the pool, the diver makes the entry in the same manner as in the case of the back somersault with tuck.

– The inward somersault with tuck (Fig. 74)

Takeoff:

The same takeoff is used as that with the inward dive except that the angular momentum is more forceful. This is achieved through a more vigorous push-off, greater

Fig. 73

Fig. 74

lean, faster tuck and drawing in of the head. Divers often hold up their hands in the starting position in order to achieve a more powerful spin by forcefully swinging the arms down in the direction of the spin. But this results in a more shallow flight trajectory.

Flight phase:
After the takeoff the buttocks are raised backwards and up and the heels are quickly and forcefully brought up to the buttocks. At the same time the trunk and the arms move forwards and down in the direction of rotation. The hands grip the shins and draw the body into a close tuck. Having almost completed the somersault, the diver stretches out his legs in the direction of the tip of the springboard, straightens out his trunk and head and places his hands on his thighs in the front.

Entry:
The legs are stretched out to the front and down towards the point of entry, the hip joint being fully extended. The eyes are focused on the tip of the board. The diver

maintains this position until he reaches the pool bottom.

The technique of the half-twist jumps
In the chapter entitled "The half-twist jump technique" (5.2.3.2.) we described the spin around the body's longitudinal axis and pointed out that the angular momentum for the twist is produced during takeoff.

But in the case of the forward dive half-twist the diver's body must be spun not only around the longitudinal but also around the transverse axis. Analyses of films made of movement sequences and practical experience show that an angular momentum is imparted only around the body's transverse axis at takeoff, while the rotation around the longitudinal axis is begun when the body is already in the air.

Theoretically this can be explained by the fact that the body's spin around the transverse axis can be transformed into a twist around the longitudinal axis. Mass moments of inertia play an important role in the body's rotation around its axes. The body's longitudinal axis is the axis of the lowest mass moment of inertia, the transverse axis is the axis of the mean mass moment of inertia while the dorsoventral axis is the axis of the greatest mass moment of inertia. A body rotating around the axis of the mean mass moment of inertia (transverse axis) has a tendency to change into a rotation around the axis of the lowest mass moment of inertia. This law of mechanics is made use of in the forward dive half-twist in order to transform the body's spin around the transverse axis into a twist around the longitudinal axis by appropriate movements of the head, arms and shoulders.

– Forward dive half-twist straight (Fig. 75)
Takeoff:
The takeoff is the same as that used for the forward dive straight.

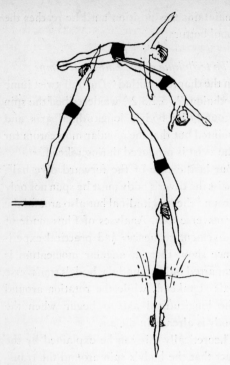

Fig. 75

Flight phase:

The first part of the flight phase is similar to that of the forward dive straight. The diver begins the twist around the longitudinal axis at the culmination point. In the case of the forward dive half-twist this is done by moving the left arm to the right, pushing the left shoulder forward and down and slightly flexing the right arm and raising it up and backwards. The diver's eyes are fixed on the water over his outstretched left arm. Once the body has completed one quarter of the twist around the longitudinal axis the head is tilted back and the right arm slowly stretched out to the side, in which process the body completes the half twist. The arms are then brought up for the entry.

Entry:

The entry is the same as that for back dive straight. It is particularly important that the diver tenses the legs and pelvic muscles so as not to overtwist the jump or not to "go over" sideways as a result of relaxed hip muscles.

– Forward dive $1/2$ twist piked

Takeoff:

The same takeoff is used as that of the forward dive piked.

Flight phase:

The first part of the flight phase is executed like a forward dive piked without a twist being noticeable around the longitudinal axis. After reaching the culmination point the diver opens out and starts the twist movement by moving his right arm (if he wants to twist to the left) in front of his legs and moving his right shoulder down. The opposite shoulder is lifted and the slightly flexed, loosely held arm is moved back. This twist movement, which is introduced by the arms, is transmitted to the trunk and amplified by extending the hip joint. After completing the $1/2$ twist the diver tilts back his head and focuses his eyes on the point of entry. He joins his arms for entry.

Entry:

The entry is made in the same manner as in the case of back dives.

Fig. 76

– Back dive ¹/₂ twist straight (Fig. 76)
Takeoff:
The takeoff is the same as that of the back dive straight.
Flight phase:
The same movements are executed after takeoff as in the case of the back dive straight. The twist is initiated before reaching the culmination point. This is done first by twisting one's head in the intended direction of twist and then swinging the left arm (if the twist is to be to the left) back and down from the sideways position. The loosely held right arm, which is slightly flexed, and the right shoulder are lifted to support the twist movement. When the eyes are focused on the point of entry and the left arm is in the same position as in the forward dive straight, the right arm, which was kept in a flexed position up till that time, is extended sideways and the head is slightly tilted back. This completes the twist around the longitudinal axis and the body begins its descent. The arms are moved together for entry.

Entry:
The entry is made in the same manner as in the forward dive straight.
– Reverse dive ¹/₂ twist straight (Fig. 77)
Takeoff:
The takeoff of the half-gainer is done in an outstretched position.
Flight phase:
Just before the body reaches the horizontal position with the arms held sideways, the right arm (if the twist is to be to the right) is swung back and down, while the left arm and left shoulder are pressed forward and up, the left arm being moved close to the body's longitudinal axis in the process. The head is moved in the direction of rotation, preceding the twisting movement of the rest of the body. The eyes are focused on the point of entry over the right arm. Having executed just over a quarter of the twist, the diver stretches his arms forward to sideways position just as if he were doing a forward dive straight, and tilts back his head. The half twist around the longitudinal axis is completed in the process.

Fig. 77

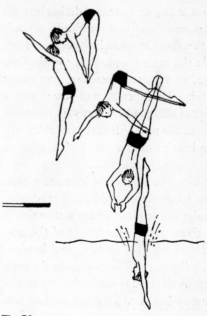

Fig. 78

167

Entry:

The same entry is used as with the forward dive straight or with the back dive $1/2$ twist.

– Inward dive $1/2$ twist piked (Fig. 78)

Takeoff:

The takeoff is the same as that of the inward dive piked.

Flight phase:

The movements during the flight phase correspond to those of the forward dive $1/2$ piked.

Entry:

The entry is the same as that of the forward dive $1/2$ twist piked.

5.3. The methods of basic diving instruction

In this section of the book we shall try to set forth the methods used in basic diving instruction. But before we start we should point out that no attempt should be made to conform to any set system of diving instruction because there is a multitude of variables that must be taken into account. They include the athlete's physical constitution, his age, movement experience, movement sensitivity, intelligence, will-power and a number of other factors that vary from one athlete to the next. All these variables will have a bearing on the course of instruction decided upon.

In addition, the methods of instruction must also be adapted to the objective conditions that exist at the place where instruction is to be given, such as the height of the pool deck above the pool surface, pool ladders, stairs, railings, etc. The essence of the present section devoted to methods of basic diving instruction is to give the student, the training supervisor, teacher and coach a

basis for their own creative work. For this reason the methods described here should by no means be regarded as perfect and universal. Every teacher should enhance them with his or her own experience and knowledge to suit his or her particular requirements.

5.3.1. General methods of instruction

There are certain characteristic features common to all jumps and key dives.

The following sequence is normally adhered to in diving instruction, in which the general paedagogical principles should also be observed:

(a) demonstration and explanation;

(b) preparatory exercises on land;

(c) preparatory exercises in the water;

(d) preliminary exercises from ladder or steps;

(e) preliminary exercises from edge of pool deck;

(f) preliminary exercises from 1-metre board.

Either the composite or the analytical method is used, depending on the objective. In principle, all jumps and dives are first executed from standing position and later on with an approach run.

The general order in which basic springboard diving instruction should be given is shown in Chart 18. The exercises in the chart arranged side by side should be taught at the same time, while those arranged vertically should be taught consecutively. It goes without saying that here too minor adjustments can be made to adapt instruction to the individual student and to the objective conditions.

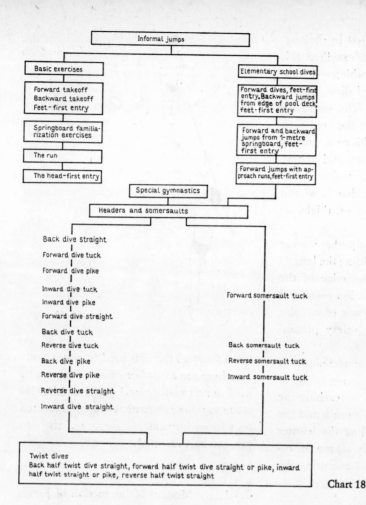

Informal jumps

Basic exercises

Forward takeoff
Backward takeoff
Feet-first entry

Springboard familia-
rization exercises

The run

The head-first entry

Elementary school dives

Forward dives, feet-first
entry. Backward jumps
from edge of pool deck,
feet-first entry

Forward and backward
jumps from 1-metre
springboard, feet-
first entry

Forward jumps with ap-
proach runs, feet-first entry

Special gymnastics

Headers and somersaults

Back dive straight
Forward dive tuck
Forward dive pike
Inward dive tuck
Inward dive pike
Forward dive straight
Back dive tuck
Reverse dive tuck
Back dive pike
Reverse dive pike
Reverse dive straight
Inward dive straight

Forward somersault tuck

Back somersault tuck
Reverse somersault tuck
Inward somersault tuck

Twist dives
Back half twist dive straight, forward half twist dive straight or pike, inward
half twist straight or pike, reverse half twist straight

Chart 18

5.3.2. The use of aids and partner assistance

The reaching pole is the most familiar aid used in diving instruction. A high-jump bar or a bamboo pole with the aid of which one can reach the 1-metre board from the edge of the pool deck is ideally suited for this purpose.

The pole is used either to help the diver position his arms, feet, head or trunk properly or to mark the height or horizontal distances which he is expected to jump; the pole being held in front of or behind the respective part of the body.

The essential objectives are to prevent fall-ins before the takeoff (the pole being held in front of or behind the diver's body) or to mark the desired culmination point, the desired point of entry or other points of orientation. The diver should touch the bar with his hands and feet when doing forward dives piked.

The pole can be used in a wide variety of ways, for this reason we cannot describe all its applications in detail here.

A water jet, whose range of application is just as extensive as that of the pole, is another important aid. But the water jet has the advantage that the learner is not afraid to collide with it.

A bathing robe belt about as thick as a fin-

ger and two metres long used in conjunction with the pole is another excellent aid.
It is particularly useful in teaching such complicated dives as the inward dive, inward
somersault and full gainer. The instructor
can use this aid standing on the pool deck
edge to help the diver achieve a greater
amount of angular momentum and to help
him achieve the right flight trajectory by
pulling with it on the belt that is wound
around the learner's knees or thighs as
shown in Figs. 79 and 80.

The instructor can also help the learner
practise various dives by guiding the latter's
body after takeoff from the edge of the
pool deck up to the culmination point and
giving it the necessary amount of angular
momentum (the necessary safety precautions should be taken).

Jumping in twos is another technique of
helping the learner. An experienced diver
can be particularly helpful in teaching the
learner do the full gainer with tuck and the
inward somersault by holding the learner
at the hips. He does this by taking off together with the learner and executing the
spins in unison.

Fig. 80

In addition to the aids used in water practice there are a number of aids that can be
used in preparatory land exercises (they include various gymnastic elements executed
on various instruments, the use of the sus-
pension harness, etc.).

5.3.3. Method of instruction of jumps and key dives

Now that we have dealt with the principles
of instruction let us turn to the methodical
routines involved in teaching the individual
jumps and key dives. These dives and key
jumps and the associated methodical routines have been compiled in systematically
arranged tables. The dives and key jumps
are arranged in groups rather than according to the methodical sequence (cf. Charts
19–23).

Fig. 79

Chart 19   Methodical routines of feet-first jumps.
The athlete must be able to do forward and back jumps before he can do the corresponding jumps with half-twist. He should practise the appropriate arm movement for the twist on land before practising these jumps in the pool from the edge and from the 1-m board

	Forward straight	Forward piked	Forward with tuck	Back jump straight	Back jump piked	Back jump with tuck
Preparatory exercises on land	Straight jump on ground and from box	Piked sitting position Straddle jump from box	Tuck position Tuck jump from box	Straight jump	Pike position Straddle jump from box	Tuck position Tuck jump from box
Preliminary exercises from pool deck edge	Tumble dive Lunge jump Straight jump	Straddle jump Straddle jump piked Feet-first jump piked	Cowering plunge Tuck jump Feet-first jump with tuck	Lunge jump Straight jump with out-stretched arm Straight jump	Straddle jump Straddle jump piked Straight jump piked	Squat plunge Tuck jump Feet-first jump with tuck
Preliminary exercises from 1-metre board	Feet-first jump without arm control					

Chart 20   Methodical routines of forward and inward dives

	Forward dive straight	Forward dive piked	Forward dive with tuck	Inward dive straight	Inward dive piked	Inward dive with tuck
Preparatory exercises on land	Prone position Starting position[1]	Preparatory exercises on handrail[2]	Preparatory exercises on handrail[2]	Starting position with assistance[1]		
Preparatory exercises in shallow water	Dropping in dive position	Jump to hand-stand with flexed hips	Jump to hand-stand with tuck			
Preparatory exercises from stairs or ladder	As in shallow water	Fall-in dive Takeoff and entry in piked position	Cowering plunge with 1/2 spin	Inward feet-first jump[3]	Inward „monkey"[4] Inward dive[5] with partner assistance	Inward dive[5] with tuck without stretching with partner assistance
Preliminary exercises on pool deck edge	Frog leap Long jump Starting jump Straight dive			Inward feet-first jump[3]	Inward dive[5] with partner assistance	Inward dive[5] with partner assistance
Preliminary exercises from 1-metre board					Same as from pool deck edge	Same as from pool deck edge

FOOTNOTES:
1 The instructor kneels in front of the athlete and props up his hips.
2 When doing preliminary exercises the student grabs hold of the handrail and practises raising his buttocks after a vigorous takeoff. The partner should stand by to help if necessary.
3 In an inward feet-first dive stretched the diver pushes his feet back vigorously and enters at an acute angle.
4 The student does a close pike after takeoff and enters the water with hands and feet simultaneously.
5 See Fig. 79.

Chart 21 Methodical routines of back dives and half-gainers

	Back dive straight	Back dive piked	Back dive with tuck		Reverse dive straight	Reverse dive piked	Reverse dive with tuck
Preparatory exercises on land	Takeoff[1] with partner assistance	Raising legs and torso in supine position	Takeoff[2] Tuck, stretch and moving arms backwards		Takeoff[1] with partner assistance	Same as in back dive piked	Takeoff[1] with partner assistance
Preparatory exercises in shallow water	Diving in breast-deep water				Feet-first reverse jump[2]	Forward squat jump	
Preparatory exercises from stairs or ladder	Fall-ins into hip-deep water Dives from progressively higher steps	Back crouch jump			Feet-first reverse jump[2]		Reverse dive with partner assistance With partner assistance as shown in Fig. 80
Preliminary exercises from pool deck edge	Back fall-ins straight Dives straight	Fall-ins with pike Crouch jump	Fall-ins with tuck Squat plunge and back dive				
Preliminary exercises from 1-metre board	Back fall-ins straight Dives from medium knee bend	Fall-in with pike	Fall-in with tuck Fall-in with tuck and straight				

FOOTNOTES

1 The takeoffs are executed with the instructor supporting the learner's hips and helping him during the first phase of the flight. The learner should achieve the right amount of spin. – Another preliminary exercise that can be performed in connection with the half-gainer is to practise the takeoff after bouncing on the board.

2 The term „feet-first reverse jump" is used here to mean a jump in which the learner enters the water feet first at an acute angle.

Chart 22 Methodical routines of dives half twist

	Forward dive half twist	Back dive half twist		Reverse dive twist	Inward dive half twist
Preparatory exercise on land	Practise arm swing and head position standing and in prone position	Practise arm swing and head position standing and in supine position		Takeoff with half twist Feet-first reverse jump half twist (cf. Chart 21) Reverse dive half twist	Inward jump half twist Inward dive half twist
Preparatory exercises in shallow water	Falling over in straight position with half twist	Same as forward dive half twist			
Preliminary exercises from edge of pool deck	Fall-in dive straight half twist Takeoff with half twist	Fall-in dive straight half twist Dive half twist			
Preliminary exercise from 1-metre board	Fall-in dive half twist Dive half twist	Same as from pool deck edge			

172

Chart 23   Methodical routines of somersaults

	Forward somersault with tuck	Back somersault with tuck	Reverse dive with tuck	Inward dive with tuck
Preparatory exercises on land	Shoulder circle backward on ground and over box	Shoulder circle backward		
Preparatory exercises in shallow water	Half somersault in breast-deep water			
Preparatory exercises from stairs or ladder	Flying roll Closed somersault[1]	Closed somersault[1]		
Preliminary jumps from edge of pool deck	Flying roll Closed forward somersault[1] Somersault from medium knee bend	Somersault from knee bend with vigorous arm swing		
Preliminary exercises from 1-metre board	Shoulder circle forward from board Somersault from knee bend	Shoulder circle backward from board Somersault from medium knee bend	Somersault with partner assistance as in Fig. 80	Somersault with partner assistance as in Fig. 79

FOOTNOTE:
1 The term „closed somersault" is used here to mean a jump in which the learner does not straighten out his body when making the entry.

5.4.   Basic training in diving

The purpose of basic training
The purpose of basic training is to develop a basis for the subsequent stages of the overall training process. Basic training comprises general physical basic training and basic diving instruction.

The tasks of basic training
The basic training stage represents first and foremost a process of general development whose aim is to prepare the beginner for the subsequent stages to such an extent that he can meet progressively higher demands without suffering physical harm. The most important task is to strengthen the learner's general state of health and to develop all his organs and systems.

Strength, speed, endurance, flexibility and agility are developed to a sufficiently high level in the course of *comprehensive athletic training* to meet the demands of diving instruction. During this period of training the student should also acquire a rich stock of experience in executing various types of movement in order to make it easier for him to learn how to dive. In the process of *learning the techniques* basic diving instruction should be arranged in such a manner that the learner proceeds from elementary to more advanced stages. A score of five points should be used as a guide value in marking each jump. The training workload during the technical training phase should be proportioned and adapted to the age in an optimum manner to derive maximum benefit. The intensity of each training unit should be proportioned in such a way as to keep the amount of exertion the learner is exposed to during the training programme within tolerable limits. Thirty to fifty jumps and dives can be executed by a group of four to five learners in the course of a training unit of 60 minutes, the exact number of dives depending on the aim set for the training unit.

The desire to engage in sports regularly should be awakened in young people through *socialist upbringing*. In addition beginners should be encouraged to strive for high levels of performance. Diving is a particularly good sport to help develop willpower.

The substance of basic training

The substance of basic training depends on the aim and tasks set. The emphasis is on exercises designed to promote general development.

Training elements from gymnastics (especially obstacle training), ballet, various games and trampoline jumping are used in basic training and in technical training. Special body posture exercises associated with diving should take up a considerable share of the time allotted to training on account of the fact that these exercises have a major bearing on the judgement of a dive. About 40 to 60 per cent of the total training time should be devoted to general athletic training. The substance of technical training comprises basic exercises, jumps and key dives. The exercises should be repeated many times over in order to stabilize the movement patterns, to refine the diver's sense of movement and orientation in order to enable him quicker to learn the more difficult dives in build-up and competitive training.

According to experience gathered to date *basic training should start* at the age of eight or nine. The total period of basic training lasts two to three years. But to extend the overall training process as much as possible basic training should be started as early as possible. The earlier in life a learner starts his basic training, the longer will be the total period of training, because a six-year-old, for instance, has not reached the physical and psychological level of development that would enable him or her to complete basic training in diving in two to three year's time.

6.   Basic Water Polo Instruction

The first water polo game was played in Glasgow in 1869 when it was decided that a "soccer match in the water" would have greater advertising value in promoting a swimming match. First attempts to draw up rules were made by the London Swimming Association in 1870. Despite repeated attempts to work out rules that would find general acceptance, the game remained wild and uncontrolled for a long time. The number of players varied between seven and eleven and the goal width between three and six metres. The goals were marked by flags. The goal keeper used a rowing boat part of the time.

In Germany, the first water polo game was played in Berlin in 1894. But at that time it was not yet possible to hold matches on a broader scale because every club had a different set of rules. Water polo was included in the programme of Olympic events in 1900, but the basis for international competitions was established only after a set of rules drawn up in Great Britain had found general acceptance.

Water polo began to flourish in Germany when the first German Water Polo Championships were held in 1912. The First World War checked the development of the game, but Germany won the Gold Medal in water polo at the 1928 Olympics.

Today, the European teams have taken a clear lead in water polo. The Soviet Union, Hungary, Yugoslavia and Italy are among the world's best teams.

Steady development of water polo resulted in frequent changes in the rules.

Replacement by substitutes, which was introduced in 1961 and which can be done mainly during one of the 4×5 min intervals between periods of play and after the scoring of goals, has enhanced the modern active game.

Water polo makes particularly high demands on strength and intelligence of movement. It is one of the most energy-consuming games. That is why it is understandable that more time is required for training athletes for competition in this discipline than in other games.

Despite the high demands and the initial difficulties connected with this game, water polo would deserve more promotion. It is a particularly valuable game with regard to its character training and health-promoting properties. Another reason for its popularity among the swimming disciplines is that the game is exciting and fun to play. Systematic training is the key to success also in the case of water polo.

6.1.   Special swimming technique

A player must have a good command of the swimming techniques involved in the game. A great deal of skill and experience is needed to execute appropriate swift movements with and without a ball, to react instantly to constant changes in the situation in the fast moving game by starting, turning, attacking individual players, shooting out from the water to parry or catch the ball. A knowledge of the most effective movement patterns of some basic forms is required. We shall dispense with the fine points and details in describing these techniques for two reasons: Firstly, the movements during a game are not restricted by any rules, and secondly, the different situations involved in a game and the need for the player to keep making decisions on the best way to respond to a given situation do not admit of a standard set of movement patterns, on the contrary, they call for broad variability.

6.1.1. Swimming techniques used for locomotion in water polo

General skills in the crawl stroke, backstroke and breaststroke are the basic requirements. In principle the techniques described for basic swimming instruction also apply to learning the different strokes used in water polo. Special features and variations should be seen as supplementary skills to be acquired at a more advanced stage of training.

The use of crawl in water polo

The water polo player should be able to crawl in such a manner as to keep his chin about at the surface of the water. The steep planing angle of the torso is maintained through vigorous leg thrusts. The swimmer is able to keep his head above the water—without consciously pushing his head up and making the necessary arm and hand movements—only after he achieves a certain swimming speed. That is why the slowly swimming beginner should be forced to keep his head up high from the very start.

The shorter the distance to be swum, the faster should be the crawl stroke rate. The water polo player swims at maximum speeds only distances of 5 to 25 metres. For this reason the player should have a command of the technique that is suited for the highest possible stroke rate.

Obtaining a purchase on the water at the beginning of the arm stroke is dispensed with, the hand is frequently slapped into the water after recovery.

Maximum use is made of the middle part of the power phase, the last push of the arm before withdrawing it from the water being very brief.

Arm recovery above the surface is a whip-like movement, the arms being kept close to the surface in the process. This type of recovery using a fast stroke rate also makes the opponent's defensive measures more difficult. There are still other departures from the normal technique which the water polo player is often permitted but which are seen as faults here. They include rolling from one side to the other with each arm stroke and lateral bending at the hips, which are seen as a sign of laxity and as bad habits, and which have a detrimental effect on speed.

Dribbling

Dribbling is used here to mean handling the ball while crawling. The crawl technique remains essentially unchanged. The ball is pushed forward with the head, or to be more precise, with the nose or by the bow wave (Fig. 81). This form of ball handling can be compared with balancing, except that the ball does not have to be supported from below but pushed from behind in such a manner that the tip of the nose pushing

Fig. 81

the ball and the ball's centre of gravity are in a straight line. Minor deviations can be corrected through appropriate head movements.

In this manner a skilled dribbler can push the ball without using any other part of his body than his head. Although we should add that this can be done only when swimming in a straight line and if there is no interference from opposing players.

Considerable deviations are inevitable in games and when beginners start learning the technique.

A player can use his arms if he is unable to achieve the right measure of ball control with his head. Arms can be used very effectively for controlling the ball, because they constantly move on either side of the ball in the course of their swimming movement anyway. To prevent the ball's escaping, the player makes shorter but quicker arm strokes. The hands enter not so far in front of the ball as in the normal crawl stroke without a ball. The slightly flexed arms start their pull when they are next to the ball.

If it is necessary to use an arm to bring the ball into line again, this should be done in such a way as not to push the ball too far to the other side, otherwise the ball describes a zig-zag course which must be constantly corrected by using the arms, which slows down the swimmer's speed. If the ball is controlled properly a swimmer's speed while dribbling is hardly any slower than when swimming without a ball.

6.1.2.   Stopping, starting and turning in the water

In water polo, just as in the case of other goal games, it is important to free oneself from the opposing player covering one in order to build up a play, to receive the ball or to pass it or to take a shot at the goal. This can be achieved more through agility, fast evasive movements and turns and quick starts and stops.

Stopping

To stop suddenly or to execute a short backward movement the player must push against the water in the direction opposite to that in which he is swimming. This is done best of all by pulling up the legs to a tuck and in this manner checking one's movement by exerting a braking action on the water with one's thighs. At the same time the arm that was submerged in the power phase is pushed back against the swimming direction, the palm of the hand being used for the retroactive push. The opposing player covering one is shaken off briefly by such a sudden stop.

This brief instant should be used for receiving or passing the ball. The stopping movement affords a good position for this purpose. It also causes the swimmer's body to turn about its transverse axis. His drawn up legs can immediately execute a vigorous kick enabling the player to shoot up from the water or to dart backwards. The arm that is used by the swimmer to check his forward movement is also used for receiving the ball.

The start

The purpose of the starting or ready position, which should always be prone or slightly inclined to the side, is to enable the player to execute quick and vigorous forward lunges without having to make extra preparations for this purpose. The most effective movement to propel the body forward is a vigorous scissors kick. To execute this kick the player must keep his legs bent and slightly spread out. The arms, which should not be fully stretched out, are held close to the surface below the head. To re-

Fig. 82

main above the surface the player moves his hands slightly to and fro. When starting, the swimmer executes a vigorous scissors kick along with an arm stroke and pushes the other arm forward (Fig. 82). In this way the swimmer's stopping movement enables him to start with the crawl stroke after the start. The breaststroke or sidestroke is immediately transformed into the crawl leg stroke.

The turn

The purpose of the turn in the water is to change one's direction of swimming by more than 90 degrees as fast as possible in the act of swimming. Oblique turns of less than 90 degrees are relatively simple. The arms press outwards and the body is bent sideways at the hips in such a way that the trunk points in the new direction.

But in the case of turns of more than 90 degrees another technique, which is subdivided into phases for the sake of clarity, is used (Fig. 83).

(a) crawl stroke;

(b) the arms and legs are drawn up for stopping and in preparation for raising the trunk;

(c) the trunk is raised in erect position with the aid of a slight scissors kick. At the same time the hands push down obliquely to support the raising of the trunk and to initiate the turn;

(d) the turn is initiated from the hips. It is not necessary to make a turn of 180 degrees, 90 degrees is enough. Then the body is allowed to drop in the new direction, the arm pointing in this direction being slightly extended;

(e) the player starts swimming in the new direction by executing the start described in the foregoing.

The movement sequence involved in making a left turn and shown in Fig. 83, can be performed in the same manner in the other direction. The player must be able to perform the turn to either side, because if there is a member of the opposing team swimming alongside it is always better to turn away from him.

Swimmers who are particularly agile prefer oblique turns followed by swimming in a tight curve until they reach the desired direction. With this technique the body remains in a relatively level position; right after the oblique turn the swimmer performs a leg thrust before resuming the crawl kick. Combination turns in which the two techniques are blended can also be used.

Fig. 83

6.1.3. Maintaining a high position above and shooting up from the water

The ability to keep one's body as high as possible above the water and to lunge is very useful in many situations in water polo. We have already pointed out the advantage of keeping the head high above the water in order to survey the situation more effectively. The higher the player receiving the ball is above the surface of the water, the less the likelihood of the ball's being intercepted. Staying up and shooting up with little or no forward movement are particularly useful in encounters at close quarters, in disrupting the opponent's play-making, in ball reception and passing and especially in goal-keeping work.

Maintaining a high position above the water

Being able to keep one's body as high as possible above the water when in front of the goal or receiving the ball is very important. The higher the attacking player can keep his body above the water, the more intense his activity and the lesser the chances of the defending team's undertaking undetected disruptive measures. The goal-keeper and defending players trying to intercept balls thrown by the opponent should also be able to keep their upper part of the body above the water. The leg action should be similar to that used in the breaststroke. In maintaining a position of readiness the player should use the alternate leg kick technique, while at close quarters the simultaneous kick action should be used. The hips are flexed to such an extent that the upper part of the body is almost in a horizontal position. The arms are bent in such a way that the hands are at chin level or just in front of the chin. Keeping the palms down the player performs vigorous paddling movements with his hands.

With the aid of these leg and arm movements the player can raise his back and a considerable part of the upper part of his body.

Shooting up from the water

When a player tries to parry or catch a high-flying ball or to throw it without fear of interception he should be able to shoot up as high as possible from the water. This is done in a manner similar to that described for maintaining a high position above the water except that the player performs the movement only once but with great speed and vigour in order to leap up as high as possible from the water.

To shoot up, the player pushes down with both hands simultaneously, extends his hips and executes a powerful scissors kick. As the body shoots up the player throws up one hand. If the body is to shoot up at an oblique angle, then the hands should push down and more or less to the sides (Fig. 84).

A player who has mastered this technique can shoot up high enough for the upper edge of his bathing trunks to be seen above the water. Good water polo players can reach up to 1.50 metres above the water. An effective scissors kick should be seen as the essential part of the overall movement. There are some additional points in this connection that apply to the goal-keeper, who must be able to shoot up from the wa-

Fig. 84

ter in order to protect the goal. He must keep his body in a somewhat more erect position when in a position of readiness and move around within the goal without giving up the position of readiness. It is particularly important for the goal-keeper not to sink back into the water right after the leap, but to stay above the water with his arms raised for several seconds. This calls for very vigorous and fast leg thrust movements.

6.2. Ball handling techniques

Initial experience in elementary ball handling is obtained by the beginner in ball games involving the use of one hand on land. At that stage the details of ball management are not important. It should only be made certain that the fingers are kept spread out when receiving, holding, moving and throwing the ball. The broad area of contact achieved in this manner enables the player to control the ball reliably and to acquire a feeling for the ball.

To acquaint the beginner with the special requirements more effectively he is allowed to touch the ball only with the hand and to keep the ball above the shoulders whenever possible.

6.2.1. Ball reception

Recovering the ball from the water in order to carry or pass it or to try to score a goal is a special field of practice.

If the appropriate technique is not applied consciously and if the skill is not systematically acquired, the player will forfeit many good opportunities on account of not being fast enough and lacking the sure touch when receiving the ball. There are two ways of recovering the ball from the water in modern water polo: The ball is either raised from below or pushed down and allowed to bob up. Raising the ball from the water by holding it between the hand and the forearm is an obsolete method and is hardly ever used today.

The scoop hold

The ball's position in relation to the body and its distance should be such as to permit the player to recover it. The player either jogs the ball into a convenient position from which he can make the recovery, depending on the situation in the game.

If the player is going to throw the ball with his right hand the ball should be at his right side or in front of him at a distance at which it can be conveniently reached by him with a slightly flexed arm. Recovery right next to the body or with an outstretched arm is difficult and unreliable. To scoop up the ball the player lifts the ball from beneath with his fingers spread out and lifts it for the throw (Fig. 85).

To execute the scoop quickly the player should move the ball back to the throwing position as he picks it up. That is why the hand is placed below and ahead of the ball so as to enable the player to haul it back for the throw. At first beginners tend to balance the ball gingerly, but as they acquire experience they begin controlling the ball more by making appropriate speed adjustments. The scoop is particularly useful for

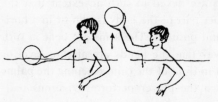

Fig. 85

the beginner because it is easy to learn and because it is not pushed down into the water (which is contrary to the rules of the game).

The twist hold

The ball can be recovered faster if the player reaches out for it from above using the twist hold. In actual games players usually reach out for the ball directly or set it up for a more convenient recovery position. In either case the twist hold can then be performed in one continuous movement, which is not possible in the case of the scoop hold, which involves making an extra preparatory movement. The twist hold is performed by gently dipping the ball into the water from above. Care should be taken not to push the ball down too deep or too long, because this may result in a rule violation and a free throw being awarded to the opposing team.

After dipping down the ball the player allows it to bob up by raising his hand only a few centimetres and then executing a half twist in the clockwise direction (Fig. 86) with his hand, which stays in contact with the ball and lifts it at the end of this movement. A quick transition should be made from the hand twist to the throwing position in a manner analogous to that described for the scoop hold.

6.2.2.   Carrying the ball

Dribbling is the most commonly used and fastest way of carrying the ball. But situations often arise in a game which make it

Fig. 86

necessary for the player to move forward with the ball lying on his hand. Holding the ball in this manner the player can proceed towards the opposing team's goal ready to throw the ball until he is challenged or his advance checked by the opposing team. Owing to the fact that only a minor change in a player's position is often enough to give him a good opportunity to score, major advantages can be achieved by carrying the ball only a short distance. In such situations the ball is thrown at the last moment, i.e., just before the player carrying the ball is intercepted. The player in possession of the ball can either have a shot at the goal himself or pass it to one of his team mates who are in a better scoring position. This type of approach which looks very menacing is often used only to draw away one of the opposing team's players from a team mate who is situated in a better position for a shot at the goal and to pass the ball to him.

When carrying the ball in one hand a player cannot use the crawl stroke, which is preferred in water polo, because the player holds the ball above the water with one hand which is slightly flexed and held to the side and above the head. The body's transverse axis is at an angle to the water surface in such a way that the shoulder of the arm holding the ball is above the surface. The body's longitudinal axis, which is normally almost horizontal when the player is in motion, is also at an angle, the legs being held deeper in the water. The free arm is kept submerged and is used for locomotion and to keep part of the trunk above the water. For this reason the hand can be swayed from side to side instead of executing a straight stroke. The legs perform scissors kicks. The position of the ball-carrying arm should be as nearly as possible the position from which the ball is thrown.

6.2.3.   Types of throw

There is a wide variety of throwing forms used in water polo. This is due partly to the many positions from which the ball can be thrown. The body can be in a vertical, prone, lateral, supine or oblique position when making the throw. This is also due to the fact that the player must have a wide variety of throwing techniques at his command in order to be able to throw the ball in the direction he wants to throw it without its being intercepted, which is more likely to happen in water polo because it is easier to cover an opponent in this game than in others. Another reason for the great variety of throwing techniques used in water polo is that the throwing technique chosen will depend on what the goal-keeper is doing or is likely to do and on the way the ball is passed, received and recovered from the water.

There are six basic types of throw, all of which can be used for passing and for taking shots at the goal.

The straight shot

The characteristic feature of this throw is that the striking movement of the lower arm is stressed after the elbow joint had been tightly flexed. The basic form of this throw is the simplest, most common, most accurate and sharpest of all the throws used in water polo (Fig. 87).

Fig. 87

The body is in a vertical position when making the throw. While one arm is raised for the throw the other hand pushes down vigorously against the water in order to push the body as high up above the water as possible with the help of a forceful scissors kick with the leg of the throwing side being pushed back. The more free and relaxed the body shoots up the harder the player can throw the ball. The shooting up of the body should be seen as part of the body movement sequence of throwing the ball.

The most powerful and longest throws can be made with this technique, because this is the only throw in which the body can be used to such advantage. The force of the shot is diminished also with this technique if the player's body is inclined forwards or sideways or if the throw is made from the supine position.

A particularly frequent variant of the straight shot is made by rolling over from the prone to the supine position and then making the shot. It is used to pass the ball from the crawl stroke position if the player in possession of the ball is covered by an opposing player following him. It is also used for goal shots while in motion and from stationary position. This variant is useful when the ball has to be thrown in the direction of the feet while the player is in a supine position.

The sequence of movements involved in this throw starting from the prone position is as follows: The player gets hold of the ball lying in front of him from above with his almost outstretched arm and rolls over on his left side. The outstretched arm is twisted round the ball in such a way that it moves underneath the ball (Fig. 88). This is followed by a straight shot from the supine position. If the throw is to be hard and accurate the player should use the full arm swing and push the ball down as it

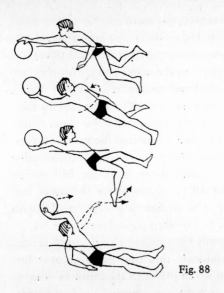

Fig. 88

leaves his hand otherwise the ball will fly too high. The throw should be practised until the player can execute it at rest and while dribbling. The throwing sequence should be initiated even before the roll is completed.

The stretched arm throw

The stretched arm throw is performed with an outstretched arm. Its advantage lies in the fact that with this throw it is more difficult for the goal-keeper to predict the ball's trajectory than in the case of the straight shot. In addition this throw, which is executed relatively far from the side, enables the player to take shots at the goal that would be easily intercepted if they were made using the straight shot. In executing this throw the player should also try to rise as high from the water as he can.

Much in the same manner as making a standing discus throw, the player first twists the throwing side of the body back and then whips it forward, the arm describing an almost horizontal arc (Fig. 89). When the forward movement begins, the player's hand is almost behind the ball, the fingers gripping part of the far side of the ball so as not to lose the ball through centrifugal force prematurely. The angle of the ball's trajectory is determined by the point in the arc described by the hand at which the player releases the ball. At this point the ball flies off at a tangent in the desired direction.

The stretched arm throw can also be performed as a feint shot by hauling one's hand back but not actually throwing the ball.

The back flip

The palm of the hand is turned back and the arm is flipped backwards. The back flip can be executed with a flexed or with an extended elbow. This throw is necessarily inaccurate, because the player does not see where he is throwing the ball. But its advantage is that the throw is executed before the cover man or the goal-keeper realizes what happened. The back flip can be made while swimming or while treading water. The sequence of movements involved is as follows: The ball floats in front of the player. To get it out of the water the player depresses it slightly. As the ball bobs up the player's hand twists around it in such a way that his thumb points down-

Fig. 89

wards. The wrist is sharply flexed. The player's fingers should grip part of the far side of the ball so as not to let the centrifugal force carry the ball away prematurely (Fig. 90). As soon as he has lifted the ball out of the water, the player should flip it back with a flexed or extended elbow.

Pushing the ball and knuckling

The basic movements involved in the throws described up till now involved a striking and a whipping action. The third basic movement involved in throwing the ball using pushing and knuckling is a shoving movement. By their very nature these throws are not very powerful. But they are very useful by virtue of the fact that the player can pass the ball or take a shot at the goal while crawling without having to slow down, to change his position or to haul back.

These two throwing techniques often produce good results when shooting at the goal from short distances thanks to the fact that they can be carried out quickly and that the goal-keeper has little time to anticipate the shots. In modern water polo each player must be able to throw the ball while swimming at a fast pace. This can be done best with these two throwing techniques.

When using the *pushing* technique, the ball is in front of the crawling swimmer. When crawling, the swimmer's position does not allow him to haul back. That is why the ball is pushed to the front. But before he can do this he must get the ball out of the water, which is rather difficult at first. The player puts his hand on the ball in front of him. His elbow is bent at right angles, the elbow pointing to the side. He dips the ball slightly into the water and allows it to bob up, the hand remaining in contact with it and twisting around it. He raises his forearm slightly and extends his wrist to the back in such a way that the hand is behind the ball relative to the intended direction of the ball's flight. Since the ball is only about 10 to 20 cm above the water and since it is without any support, the push must be executed immediately (Fig. 91).

Not only the arm, but also the trunk is used by suddenly thrusting that side of it forward which performs the throw in order to put as much force behind the ball as possible. The arm should not be twisted to the left when making the throw, in other words, the thumb must point to the left when the hand releases the ball. The arm should not touch the water during the throw.

Knuckling is an even more effective technique for taking shots at the goal from short distances because the goal-keeper has hardly any time at all to respond to the ball's sudden and unexpected bound.

In executing this throw, for instance while dribbling, the left hand is slid under the ball, and it is advisable to turn it in such

Fig. 91

Fig. 90

a manner that the palm faces the ball so as not to push the ball up and forward, but somewhat to the right and slightly above the water. When the ball is in front of the right shoulder, the arm whipping forward should hit the ball with the fingers and thrust it forward in much the same way as with the pushing technique (Fig. 92). Beginners tend to lift the ball up to forehead level, but when watching an experienced player the ball's rise is so slight that one gets the impression that the ball bounds forward from floating position.

Fig. 93

(5) *Forward and backward volleying*

The characteristic thing about volleying is that the ball is thrown from its floating position without being raised above the surface of the water. Volleying is also a useful technique. Normally the arm and the hand are under the water at the beginning of a throw. The water's drag on the arm diminishes the effectiveness of the arm's striking, pushing or pulling movement. That is why special importance should be attached to that part of the throwing movement sequence in which the wrist is above the water.

The drawback of volleying, which is that there is little force behind the ball when it is thrown in this manner, is compensated by the fact that the throw is almost always fully unexpected, which gives its user the advantage of the element of surprise over opposing players trying to intercept the ball

and over the goal-keeper. The following are three of the techniques used in volleying:

a) The ball is in front of the player. The hand of the slightly bent arm that is kept submerged is moved under the ball with the palm turned upwards. Executing a sudden pulling movement the player throws the ball backwards or obliquely backwards over his head.

b) The ball is at the player's side. The player holds his hand submerged in a manner similar to that used when throwing the ball with a stretched arm. The palm, which is in contact with the ball, faces the front and up. The ball is thrown forward by part of the lower arm being whipped out above the water and the wrist being flexed.

c) While dribbling and crawling, the player's hand enters the water and without twisting slides underneath the ball (Fig. 93). The fingers, which are kept slightly parted, are extended as far back as possible. The arm, which is slightly flexed, is extended suddenly, whereby the ball is thrown forward and up with the back of the hand. The ball cannot be thrown very far using this technique; it is used almost exclusively if the player is in trouble.

(6) *The relay*

The relay can be used to pass the ball to another player not far away or to surprise the goal-keeper. With this technique the player does not catch the ball when receiving it, but relays it in the desired direction by letting it bounce off his hand or arm.

Fig. 92

The relay has the advantage that it can be done without interference from opposing players, for according to the rules of the game the player in possession of the ball may be attacked only when he handles the ball. This technique is normally used in front of the opposing team's goal and not so often in field play. The player passing the ball to his team-mate who is to relay it should throw the ball hard, aiming it at the relayer's neck or head. The latter puts out the back of his hand or his forearm holding it flat above the water so that the ball can bounce off in the desired direction (Fig. 94). If the point of impact does not coincide with the trajectory of the ball's centre of gravity, then the ball will bounce off at an angle of less than 180 degress. Although the relayer will not be able to determine the angle very accurately, the relay, once mastered, is very useful when it comes to catching the goal-keeper off his guard. Even if he anticipates the manoeuvre he still needs a lot of luck to catch this kind of ball.

A weak throw is relayed only if its trajectory is not too flat. Weakly thrown balls flying in a high arc are relayed in a slightly different manner: The relayer uses the back

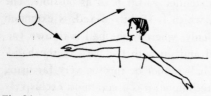

Fig. 94

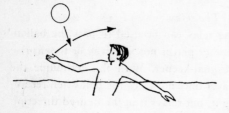

Fig. 95

of his hand or his palm, with which he pulls, pushes or hits the ball in the desired direction (Fig. 95). The relay technique is used for passing only in cases where the player is hard pressed or if the play requires split-second timing. In other situations preference should be given to throwing, which is more accurate.

(7) The lob

The lob is a term used to describe the ball's trajectory rather than any particular technique of throwing the ball. The lob's special advantage, which can sometimes be put to good use, is that owing to the goalkeeper's limited ability to jump up, the ball can be given such a steep trajectory that it drops into the goal behind the goal-keeper without his being able to catch it.

Any of the techniques of throwing the ball described in the foregoing can be used for lobs, although the difficulties involved here are so great that the straight shot is about the only technique that can be used with any chance of success. The most important thing to bear in mind is to give the ball a steep trajectory so that it enters the goal at an almost vertical angle. A high degree of co-ordination is needed between the force with which the ball is thrown, the angle at which it is thrown and the lateral aim.

6.2.4. Catching and parrying

Great concentration is needed on the part of the goal-keeper and even more so on the part of the field players when catching the ball. The degree of skill that is required here is just as high as in the case of any other ball control technique, except that here it is even more important. We can only mention some fundamentals, for even the most detailed description of the various movements involved would not suffice to describe a skilled player's control of the ball.

A sequence of preparatory movements precedes the actual catching of the ball. Its purpose is to put the player in the most convenient position for receiving the ball, which can be done at rest or while swimming. While the ball is in flight the player who is to catch it can manoeuvre himself into the proper position according to his estimation of the ball's trajectory, speed and direction so as to be able to put out his hand in such a way as to be able to catch it. If it is the goal-keeper that is catching the ball, he should use both hands if possible.

(1) *Catching technique used by field players*
According to the rules of the game a field player may touch the ball only with one hand at a time. For this reason the arm that is not used for catching the ball is kept submerged and used for maintaining the best possible body position before, while and after catching the ball. The player should try to rise high enough to reach the ball with this arm slightly flexed. He can shift his body somewhat to the side if he wants to catch the ball more to the side rather than above his head.

The player stretches out his hand towards the approaching ball with the fingers parted and slightly tensed. At the moment of contact his hand points straight up or it is inclined slightly to the front (Fig. 96).

The player should not try to check the ball's flight instantly. He should allow his arm and his trunk to yield somewhat, in this manner braking the force of its flight gradually by allowing the arm to move back and the trunk to arch backwards. The tension that is produced in the body in the process can be used in preparing for the throw that is to follow. The real master executes these movements smoothly and without any splashing.

(2) *Catching technique used by the goal-keeper*
The goal-keeper is the only man of the team that is allowed to touch the ball with both hands at the same time. The goal-keeper should take full advantage of this rule and try to use both hands whenever he can in order to get better control of the ball.

To be able to catch the ball, which is normally thrown as hard as possible, and not to allow it to slip through, the hands should be held in such a way that the index fingers and thumbs almost touch each other instead of trying to catch the ball with both hands on the sides of the ball. The player's hands form a flat concavity in which the ball is received. The catching action itself is performed quickly and the ball is drawn down onto the water. The goal-keeper should try to draw even those balls down which come at him far from the side and which he can reach only with one hand, for only in this manner will he be able to get full control of the ball. The goal-keeper should strike the ball back into the field or parry it to the side only if he cannot bring it under his control. If the goal-keeper has no choice but to slam the ball back into the field, he should try to hold his arms or hands in such a way as to hit the ball to the side and above its centre.

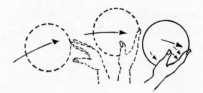

Fig. 96

6.3. Methods used in teaching the special techniques involved in water polo

The development of skills in crawl, back-stroke and breaststroke is described in section 3.3. entitled "Basic swimming instruction". There are no fundamental differences in learning how to swim for water polo. The better the player masters the different movements involved and the better he develops his physical abilities that are required for speed and endurance in the three strokes in the course of his basic training, the easier he can learn the different skills involved in water polo.

In those relatively few cases in which the beginner to be taught how to play water polo is a non-swimmer, special emphasis should be laid on the use of PVC balls as swimming aids during the first phase of basic training.

6.3.1. Development of special swimming techniques

Much time is devoted during basic instruction to exercises designed to develop and perfect swimming skills. The water polo player should always have the most effective swimming technique and ball handling technique at his command in any of the constantly varying situations with which he is confronted in the course of a game. The range of forms of movement which can help the player take advantage of or avoid water resistance is so vast that we shall deal only with exercises that can be performed only for the most important basic techniques.

In addition to the three basic strokes mentioned, it is also useful for the water polo player to be able to use the sidestroke and the crawl arm stroke (alternate arm stroke) in combination with the breaststroke leg action.

(1) Alternate arm stroke and sidestroke

It is easy to learn the scissors kick if the swimmer, lying in the prone position, inclines his body sideways at a steep angle using the leg action he learned in connection with the breaststroke. When the swimmer is on his side or when his hips are inclined sideways at a steep angle he will tend to perform the scissors kick automatically. The arm on the side of the body that is raised higher executes a crawl arm stroke, the pull phase of the arm stroke coinciding with the scissors kick. The other arm that is kept stretched out in the initial phases of training, is subsequently used for support by pulling while the legs are being drawn up. On completing the pull the arm is stretched out again under water. The swimmer must be able to do the sidestroke on either side. As soon as the beginner has acquired a basic co-ordination on the one side he should start practising on the other side.

The alternate arm stroke is learned on the basis of the crawl arm movement because it plays a vital role in propelling the swimmer. During the initial phase, the beginner supports the crawl arm stroke with any kind of leg action or scissors kicks. Later on he starts co-ordinating the leg and arm movements by doing one leg movement with every second arm movement and ultimately with every third arm movement.

Swimmers who already know how to do the crawl stroke, backstroke and breast-stroke are not taught the arm and leg movements associated with the sidestroke and the alternate arm stroke separately.

(2) *Transition from developing skill to developing performance*

Short distances of 15 to 25 metres are normally used for practising until the swimmer has developed the necessary measure of elementary co-ordination. The length of breaks is determined by the time it takes to correct mistakes, recover concentration and rest. At this stage the training sessions should be focused on one of the strokes.

In the process of transition from elementary to advanced co-ordination these distances are extended to up to 100 metres. Frequent changes of the stroke should be avoided during a given training session. It is important that the learner should get enough rest during the breaks.

When the swimmer has mastered or has nearly mastered advanced co-ordination, more and more time should be devoted to performance and progressively less time to technical improvement, although corrections of movement errors should countinue to be made during training. The competitive spirit, fulfilment of speed, targets (which are set individually) and the use of special difficult exercises determine the character of the swimming exercises.

All distances from 15 to 400 metres are swum using the crawl stroke, but distances not exceeding 50 metres should be swum using the other swimming styles. The stroke may be changed frequently and the recovery breaks can be shortened until the rest periods are as long as the swimming times. The following exercises of increased difficulty should be performed when practising the different strokes:

(a) Crawling with head raised above the water. A folded water polo cap lies on the swimmer's head; it may not fall off during swimming.

(b) Handling the ball with the head while crawling (dribbling) without correcting the ball's movement with the arms too much.

(c) Carrying the ball using the sidestroke. Only the arm that is deeper in the water is used for swimming, the other arm being used to hold the ball up above the water.

(d) Throwing the ball from one hand to the other while doing the backstroke.

(e) Holding the ball up with both hands. The leg action is the same as that used with the breaststroke, the body being kept in a more vertical position.

(f) Alternations between crawl and backstroke in rapid succession.

In water polo, the player uses the crawl stroke about 90 per cent of the time for swimming more or less straight stretches at a fast pace. The other strokes are used only in special situations during play and only for short distances. Their special importance lies in the fact that they can be used to teach the player almost all the basic movement skills which he must master in order to learn the more advanced technical skills.

This means that developing a high degree of efficiency in executing the various movements involved in the different strokes is the first and most important methodical stage in the process of developing the other special skills.

A sidestroke cycle is the most expedient movement to use for sudden forward movements from a position of rest in the water. Leg kicks that are used with the alternate arm stroke are used in situations requiring sharp turns and sudden accelerations.

Most throwing movements are supported by scissors kicks. Vertical simultaneous leg kick is the most effective leg action for shooting up as high out of the water as possible. We hope the few examples given above will suffice to illustrate the importance of mastering the skills of breaststroke, sidestroke and alternate arm swimming in order to develop performance.

(3) Braking and using the hips

Special exercises must be performed for developing braking and hip flexibility, which are required for executing the complex movements that are often necessary in the course of a game.

The simplest way of practising the use of hips for making turns is to crawl along a slalom course, i. e., a course with lane markers on either side which the swimmer must touch alternately with his right and left hips, swimming in a zig-zag pattern in the process.

As regards braking, this is practised by swimming fast using the crawl stroke and then just stopping. It is important to make certain that the braking movement should be performed suddenly, using the thighs and arms. Once the swimmer has learned to check his forward movement completely, another element should be added to the exercise, i. e., having come to a complete halt the swimmer should raise his body out of the water slightly and throw himself in the opposite direction. To raise his body and propel it in the opposite direction the swimmer executes a leg kick which starts from the position the swimmer's body is in when he stops. Immediately on having lunged in the opposite direction the swimmer starts crawling.

(4) Starting, turning, rising and shooting up

The various technical skills associated with starting, turning, rising and shooting up, which the swimmer must acquire in addition to the common strokes should be practised with not more than ten repeats each at the beginning. The degree of strain involved in these exercises, which must be performed quickly and which require a great deal of strength and involve not only the trunk muscles but also the muscles of all extremities, is often underestimated. Owing to the fact that in the early phases the accent is on concentration and correction by the instructor and by the swimmer himself, many repeats are not necessary.

Having learned how to perform the movement sequences effectively, the swimmer can do up to twenty repeats of the same or similar kind (with or without short breaks). These repeats then are done more in the way of stamina training using special exercises.

Competitive forms and swimming against the clock should also be used. Some of them can also be performed with the ball to make the training more effective.

a) Starting in the water from the goal line, which the player must touch with his neck, and swimming to the 4-metre line and measuring the time it takes the swimmer to do this.

b) Making sharp turns, slalom swimming between lane markers in competition with and without timing over certain fixed distances with the number of times the swimmer must touch the lane markers being specified.

c) Making turns between lane markers spaced 5 metres apart in competition with and without timing. The start, the turning point and the finish are to be marked by ropes; their number must be specified.

d) The swimmer should try to touch the crossbar for as long as he can, the instructor timing him. The swimmer should touch the crossbar with the fingers of one hand or of both hands, depending on his age, height and level of development. Objects are hung from the crossbar for younger swimmers to touch.

e) Shooting up from the water. The swimmer practises touching a measuring staff attached to the goal-post, a record being kept of his best three jumps and of the average height reached by him in ten jumps performed in the course of one minute (this is the best time to use for this exercise).

f) Starting from the 4-metre line (the head must be touching the line) to the goal, stopping, shooting up to touch the crossbar, turning and swimming back to the 4-metre line. The time is stopped when the swimmer's head crosses the line.

The last example comprises several things that the swimmer must do. A large number of exercise and performance monitoring and competition setups can be built up using field markers or ropes, crossbars, the 1-metre springboard in conjunction with other objects.

6.3.2. Developing ball handling proficiency

Thanks to the fact that the ball is one of the favourite toys used from the earliest childhood, most swimmers are familiar with the elementary throwing techniques by hitting, throwing or pushing it. That is why attention is focused on one-handed ball handling in the early phases of training. The swimmer must master the one-handed ball handling techniques before he can learn the ball control techniques used in water polo.

(1) Preliminary land exercises

In the first phase of training the learner's feeling for the ball should be developed through one-handed land exercises. It is not possible for the learner to master the various difficulties posed by the ball handling techniques used in polo, which are new to him, by starting to learn these techniques in the water, where the difficulties are compounded by the water's drag, which impedes the learner's movements, by making it more difficult to balance the ball and to co-ordinate the movements involved in throwing the ball, etc. The amount of physical stress which the learner is exposed to

on land should not be too great on account of the fact that the swimming exercises which he is called upon to perform are in themselves very strenuous.

The initial exercises are carried out without the help of a partner:

a) The ball is held in the outstretched arm, thrown upwards and caught with the same nearly outstretched hand.

b) The ball rests in the palm held level with the top of the head. The ball is thrown upwards and caught.

c) The ball is held at shoulder level in a slightly bent arm. The ball is pushed slightly up, the hand is twisted around it and the ball is bounced against the floor. As the ball bounces up it is touched with the hand from above and brought back to the starting position.

d) The ball is held at shoulder level and hauled back and thrown against the wall, caught to the side of the head and returned to initial position. The distance from the wall is only 1 metre at the beginning (Fig. 97).

e) The force with which the ball is thrown against the wall and the speed of the cycle is gradually increased and the exercise is repeated without interruption. The distance is increased up to 6 metres.

These exercises are followed by similar throwing and catching exercises in groups of two, three or four. Such exercises can

Fig. 97

also be carried out in bigger groups, but two or more balls should then be used at the same time, because otherwise there will be a sharp drop in the intensity of the exercises. One row, two rows and circle are the most common player arrangements used in these exercises.

When the learners have acquired a certain amount of skill in handling the ball with one hand, games and contests should be organized in order to make the exercises more exciting for the learners. The time or the number of balls not caught should be used as the criterion for scoring. Only games in which the ball can be handled with one hand should be chosen for practising.

(2) *Receiving and transporting the ball in the water*

All ball handling exercises should, if possible, be performed several times in shoulder-deep water before they are done in water of normal depth. In this way that part of the more difficult movement combinations is reinforced that is connected with the handling of the ball on the surface. The easiest ball reception technique and the first one taught is the one in which the ball is held with the palm. It is first practised at rest until the player is able to perform the sequence of movements involved in palming the ball, hauling back and assuming the throwing position fluently and quickly. The most intensive way of performing this exercise is by throwing the ball to a partner who returns the ball in the same manner. In this way the learner starts practising aiming from the very beginning. Palming is then practised in the same manner in water of normal depth. Approaching the ball and dribbling are then linked up with palming and throwing the ball. The twist grip is learned and improved upon in the same manner.

Ball transport is a very important aspect of water polo owing to the fact that the arm carrying the ball cannot be held completely still, which makes it necessary to keep balancing it.

As a preliminary exercise for transporting the ball the swimmer should hold the ball just above the water to the side of his hip in the manner described in connection with the sidestroke. What makes this exercise more difficult is holding the ball up higher. But the most difficult thing to do in connection with this exercise is to swim fast using the sidestroke and to move the arm into throwing position for throwing the ball forward.

(3) *Catching and throwing the ball in the water*

The special significance of catching and throwing the ball while in the water is reflected by the fact that these two skills are taught not only during basic training, but that 10 to 30 minutes of each training unit—which is a relatively long period—are spent practising these skills even by players with a higher level of qualification. Perseverance and concentration are required in order to master these skills. Practising with partners and in small groups at rest and while moving slowly and with passing distances of 3 to 15 metres is often included in the programme.

The preferred method of throwing is the straight shot, which can be used in all variants. The act of catching is performed in a wide variety of ways due to the inaccuracy involved in throwing the ball, which makes it necessary for the catcher to react accordingly. This means that to catch high balls the player must shoot up from the water, while to catch balls that veer off to either side he has to lunge to the side and perform the proper catching movements at the same time.

The first thing that must be done when catching a ball is to bring the ball to rest on the hand without touching the water before throwing it again.

Later the catching movement is coupled with the throwing movement immediately following it. The reception of the ball, which checks its flight, should be carried out in such a manner that in the act of catching the ball the player assumes the best possible position for throwing the ball again in any direction. In the course of the training the swimmer learns how to rotate about the longitudinal axis of his body in order to improve ball control in this phase of handling the ball (Fig. 98).

All other techniques of throwing the ball in addition to the straight throw are included in the basic training until the beginner has mastered the elementary movements. Later on they are practised as long passes and shots at the goal.

Goal shots should be practised from distances of 4 to 8 metres. Throws from resting position should be followed by throws while dribbling or after receiving a pass while swimming and finally while being slightly or fully covered by an opponent.

Fast passing between three to five players in front of a goal and then taking a shot at the goal is a favourite form of exercise, whose variants range from elementary catching and throwing up to aggressively approaching the goal.

Fig. 98

The conditions prevailing during such exercises are adjusted to the level of development or objective, e.g.:

a) A shot may be taken at the goal only after the ball has been passed at least three times without touching the water.

b) Only one type of shot may be used when shooting at the goal.

c) The players move in front of the goal in a circle or in some other formation or haphazardly. Shots may be taken at the goal only while swimming.

d) The same or a smaller number of players are assigned to interfere.

e) Two groups of equal strength play in front of a goal.

6.4. Tactical principles

The term „tactics" covers a broad range of measures that can be taken by one or the other side in a scrimmage in order to gain a maximum advantage over the other side. They include taking into account such things as the weather and lighting conditions, appraising the special features of the pool in choosing sides, sizing up the opposing team, making appropriate adjustments, using a certain system, etc.

But before players can perform tactical exercises in the water they must have reached a certain level of swimming and ball-control skills. This is why only essential tactics are taught in basic water polo training. Elementary tactics are explained to players on the basis of the principles, described below, while further tactical instruction in the initial phase is given in conjunction with practice games. Whenever a tactical error or inaccuracy is made during such a practice game the practice game should be interrupted and the players positioned again in such a manner that the tactical error can be corrected. This is done by explaining to them the error made and how to correct it and then blowing the whistle as a signal resuming the play. It is advisable to instruct one of the two teams before the game to put up only a token defence. In this way the other team is given a chance to build up and make their play deliberately. The tactical measures should be discussed thoroughly enough in advance so as to reduce to a minimum the need for the instructor to intervene.

6.4.1. Offensive tactics

As soon as a team is in possession of the ball it goes on the offensive. We shall not try to explain chess-like moves or combinations based on certain formations. For the beginner it is enough to comply with the general tactical principles to bring an offensive play to a successful conclusion:

(1) When a game is started or re-started after changing sides, the charging player should be followed closely. If the player reaches the ball before his opponent closes in he should throw the ball to the back. If the player is being covered too closely he throws the ball over the player following him to the back. The back should wait, if possible, until his team is in a good position for the ball to be passed.

(2) Attacking players should try to get away from the players covering them and to take up good positions for continuing the attack.

(3) The play should not be allowed to deteriorate into a static game as was commonly done in the past. It is particularly important that the players up in front and in the centre should keep moving all the time, because this makes it more difficult for the opposing players to cover them.

(4) The ball is passed to a team-mate according to the following basic principles:
– The ball may be thrown to a player only when he is not covered.
– The player receiving a forward pass should be able to receive the ball without interrupting his speed or changing his direction of swimming.
– When passing the ball to the centre forward when he is covered, the ball should be thrown in such a way that it lands in the area controlled by him.

(5) If the situation is such that the player in possession is not forced to make a long pass, it is safer to relay the ball over several short passes or to dribble it closer to the desired destination.

(6) In order to diminish the risk of losing the ball, the player should try to pass the ball before a player from the opposing team approaches the ball close enough to reach it. If this cannot be done, the player should secure the ball by staying between the ball and the opposing player (Fig. 99), thereby keeping the ball out of the opponent's reach.

(7) If the player in possession of the ball is in trouble the team-mate next to him should manoeuvre himself into such a position that the player being set to can easily pass the ball to him.

(8) The backs or other players in the backfield should try to manoeuvre themselves into a position from which they can break through with or without a ball without

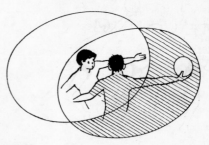

Fig. 99

being closely followed. A breakthrough gives the attacking team a superiority in numbers in front of the opposing team's goal as a result of which the attacking team can usually score a goal. The player making the breakthrough should swim towards the centre of the goal. The forwards move somewhat to the sides in order to let him pass. If the dribbling player reaches the goal without being covered he should try to score himself. But if there is another player in an equally favourable situation, the player making the breakthrough should pass the ball to him, because his arms have been weakened by the effort of making the breakthrough.

(9) Only balls thrown from within a certain area in front of the goal stand a chance of scoring (Fig. 100). The forwards should try to be in this area whenever possible. It is not advisable to take shots at the goal that have little chance of hitting it. It is better to keep passing the ball until a better scoring position is achieved. From the very start players should be trained not to keep the ball too long, because according to the rules of the game a team may not stay in possession of a ball for more than 45 seconds without taking a shot at the goal.

(10) Forwards and other attacking players should not bunch up in front of the opposing team's goal. It is easier for the defending team to regain possession of the ball in the hustle and bustle that results in crowded situations, and it is difficult for the team in possession to secure the ball. (Fig. 100)

(11) If the referee penalizes one of the players by taking him out of the game, the team in question "plays it safe", i.e., the team keeps passing the ball to players not being covered until a shot can be taken at the goal with a good chance of scoring.

(12) If the team plays a good and clear tactical game with each player knowing exactly where to be and when to be there, it is not necessary for the players to "talk" to each other. Besides, such "talk" is usually counterproductive in a game, because it alerts the defending team to weak points in its position.

(13) A forward who is not covered feints several shots at the goal before making the actual shot. The shot should always be aimed at points which are difficult if at all possible for the goal-keeper to reach.

6.4.2.   Defensive tactics

If the opposing team is in possession of the ball or if it is certain that it is about to gain possession of it, the other team should go over to the defensive. The defence can be effective only if all opposing players are properly covered. The purpose of the defence is to disrupt the opponent's play, to prevent shots at the goal and to recover the ball from him. To do this the defending team should comply with the following principles:

(1) If the team fails to get possession of the ball at the start, it should try to cover the opposing team's players as quickly as possible. The players in the back should quickly try to estimate in what formation the attacking team is approaching and spread out accordingly to cover the attackers. The forwards should not diminish their speed even if it is obvious that they cannot reach the ball. In this way the charging player is forced to throw the ball back to its defence. The sooner the attack is checked, the more difficult it becomes for the attackers to organize their play.

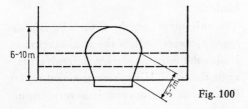

Fig. 100

(2) It is often difficult to keep an eye on the game as a whole and on the ball and the player to be covered at the same time. This often makes it necessary to keep turning one's head by 180 degrees. In such situations it is best to concentrate most of one's attention on the player to be covered.

(3) The rule of thumb for the covering player to bear in mind during the first few games is to try to stay as close as possible to the player he is covering on the side between him and the covering player's goal. However, in the following case it is advisable to make an exception:

– If there is a forward from the opposing team very close to the defending team's goal, then it is better to cover him from the side from which he might be expected to receive the ball. In this way the covering player has a better chance of intercepting balls meant for the forward. The space between the forward and the goal is too small for the ball to be thrown there without being intercepted either by the goal-keeper or one of the backs.

– If it becomes obvious that an opposing player is very one-sided in his ability to handle the ball, then the defending player can concentrate more on the more active hand of his opponent and stay closer to that side.

(4) If a player, normally this will be a back, manages to break loose from the player covering him to make a breakthrough, he must be followed immediately even if the situation seems hopeless. If another player is in a better position to pursue the one making the breakthrough he should do so, while his team-mate takes over the cover of the player the other one was covering up till then. If the player making the breakthrough cannot be caught up with, then the players in the back should try to reduce the attacking team's numerical superiority in front of their goal to a minimum. They

should try to block his way to the centre of the goal. This too can be done by switching positions in the manner described above, i.e., the defending players switch the men they are covering in such a way that the man in the most unfavourable position is released, or they go over to zone defence tactics as soon as the charging player penetrates into the dangerous zone. The more players there are in front of the goal, the easier it is to frustrate the opponent's attempt to score.

(5) If a player has been taken out of the game, the team penalized should immediately take up a defensive position. In such a case all players from both teams are usually in the half of the field occupied by the team with the diminished number. As soon as the attacking team takes a shot at the goal, the defending team as a whole and the fastest swimmers in particular should start for the opponent's goal. In this manner even the numerically smaller team gets an advantage over the opposing team if its goal-keeper manages to catch the ball and often converts this advantage into a goal.

(6) The goal-keeper should always stay a little in front of the goal line. If the opposing team's player making the goal-shot is straight in front of the goal, the goal-keeper's best chance of catching the ball is if he is equidistant from the two goal-posts. But he can also intentionally leave a little more space on one side in order to tempt the man making the shot to aim at the bigger hole, which enables the goal-keeper to anticipate the shot. The more off to the side a shot is expected to come from, the more the goal-keeper should move over to that side of the goal.

The only player on the team who is a *defensive player only* is the goal-keeper; he is also the most important defensive player on the team. His sphere of action is very limited but his function is a very responsible one. An error made by a field player can be put right in most cases, but one made by the goal-keeper results in a quantifiable advantage for the other team.

The goal-keeper's skill depends a great deal on his tactical understanding of the game, which is expressed by his ability to be at the right place at the right time. A good goal-keeper often makes the impression that his skill is never put to the test, because all the balls he catches are aimed straight at him. But in reality this is proof of his great skill; it shows that he assesses the situations correctly and knows where the ball will go even before it leaves the hand of the player making a shot and responds accordingly. Each time the goalkeeper gets the ball the play is reversed, which means that the team that was on the offensive takes up a defensive position, and the other team proceeds to attack. The position of the team that was on the defensive is then often very favourable for launching an attack, because the team that has been attacking has been trying to keep its distance from covering players, which means that when the goal-keeper gets the ball some of the attackers are not covered. Owing to this the goal-keeper should not keep the ball longer than is absolutely necessary, he should try to take advantage of the situation to pass the ball to one of his team as quickly as possible. To be able to respond instantly, the goal-keeper should always pay attention to the situation. He should not lose track of the situation even when he is concentrating on the player taking a shot at the goal. An alert goal-keeper not only protects the goal, but he also plays a vital role in improving his own team's chances of scoring a goal.

6.5. Suggestions for basic water polo instruction

There are no fundamental differences between the basic training for water polo players and that for swimmers. But there are some features specific to water polo that should be borne in mind.

Initial training for water polo players should be organized in such a manner that it is fun to take part in. The future player's enthusiasm is aroused and his willingness to take part in training regularly grows when he fulfils the first performance requirements and when he is told about his future prospects.

But there are relatively many conditions that have to be satisfied before the players can play this very exciting ball game in accordance with the rules of the game. That is why simple ball games such as water rugby should be played in shallow and deep water before proceeding to the more advanced forms of the game. The impression the instructor gets from the training group's performance level is decisive for proportioning the exercises and training when drawing up the training programme. Generally, the best land-to-water training ratio at the beginning of the first year of training is 40 : 60 per cent, at the end 30 : 70 per cent. Specific water polo training can be started only when the learners feel completely confident in the water, when they have mastered the different strokes and when they have learned the fundamental ball handling techniques.

6.5.1. The objective, tasks and scope of basic training

The objective of basic training, which is normally carried out with children and youngsters, is to enable the players to take

197

part in matches at the lowest level. Normally, when a new team is being formed the swimmers have already acquired the necessary range of physical abilities and an average level of proficiency in the crawl stroke, backstroke and breaststroke.

Based on these physical abilities and proficiency the following tasks should be carried out in the various phases of training the water polo players:

1. In the field of swimming instruction:
refining the crawl stroke with and without a ball;
learning and refining overhand swimming and the sidestroke;
developing general endurance;
developing speed using the crawl stroke;
learning and improving special swimming techniques.

2. In the field of ball control instruction:
developing a feeling for the ball in handling it with one hand;
developing confidence in catching and lifting the ball;
learning and refining the throwing techniques.

3. In tactical training:
learning the rules of the game;
learning the tactical principles and being able to apply them in theory and practice.

The objective of the training programme can be reached in one to three year's time with three training sessions a week, depending on the age of the trainees and on their initial level of aptitude and physical condition. Each training unit is 60 to 90 minutes long.

6.5.2.   Planning of basic training

The more exacting the demands of an athletic discipline, the more important it is to co-ordinate and proportion the training workload. The various skills and physical qualities required of the players by water polo should be systematically developed at certain times of the year, the focus being shifted according to the objectives set. Owing to the fact that various faculties associated with condition and co-ordination are developed in basic training first, without having to prepare for any highlight events marked by major seasonal matches, it is not as important to divide the training year into transitional, preparatory and main training periods in basic training as it is in competitive training. In competitive training, dividing the training year into such periods is also designed for periodic alternation between periods of stress and relative relaxation. But this consideration, too, is not so important in basic training, because the athletes have plenty of time to relax between the three weekly training sessions.

But a certain measure of adjustment to this periodic division is advisable also in basic training for the following reasons: Attention must be focused on certain areas of training in the course of the year in order to ensure that the training programme has a logical sequence of development; performance checks should be carried out by organizing training games as highlight events in order to stimulate the player's interest in training.

Each training year should culminate in two peaks (this is also common in other games). Consequently, there is double periodization, the individual periods and their sequence, the mains tasks and means being patterned after the example shown in the foregoing.

The *transition period* in the first year of training is practically a preparatory period during which the learners should acquire the basic skills required for swimming and ball control training.

Chart 24 An example of basic water polo training programme

Main tasks	Main exercises
TP 5 W	
Basic endurance and agility	Sundry games on land and group games in the water
Feeling for the ball	Throwing and catching the ball with one hand on land singly or with partner
Refining the crawl stroke	50-metre stretches, 3- to 5- minute breaks, correction and self-analysis
TP I 20 W	
Learning new strokes	Overhand and side-stroke. Exercises of up to 100 metres
Feeling for the ball	Catching and throwing 1 and 2 balls with partner or in groups on land, lifting ball and passing in the water, catching and throwing ball with a partner in the water
Learning the throwing techniques	Straight throw, volleying and pushing for passing and shooting at goal
Speed in crawl	15- to 25-metre stretches at high speed, up to 10 repeats, 3-min breaks
Applying skills	First training games using smaller field and shorter playing time, simplified rules
Learning the rules	Theoretical instruction
MP II 5 W	
Developing confidence and speed in catching and throwing	Passing over greater distances, fast passes in groups with several balls
Speed and special endurance in crawling	See PP II and realistic practice exercises in front of the goal
Checking development in games	Games with analysis of technique, swimming and tactics

Main tasks	Main exercises
MP I 5 W	
Refining the throws	Straight throw, volley, pushing used for passing and shooting at goal
Learning to dribble	10- to 25-metre stretches with correction and self-analysis
Performance checks	Crawling against clock 50 metres, dribbling 25 metres, 50 metres sidestroke, measuring straight and push throws
Practice games	Practice games with tactical analysis
PP II 15 W	
Refinement of strokes, basic endurance	Lengthening the lengths up to 200 metres using crawl and sidestroke, up to 100 metres using overhand stroke and backstroke at intermediate intensity
Learning special swimming techniques	Making sharp turn, starts in water, shooting up in individual and group exercises
Refinement of catching and throwing techniques	Group exercises and score games with one and with several balls on land, in the water Goal shot exercises while swimming and while at rest
Learning new throwing techniques	Volley, backhand and shots with straight arm at the goal and passes
Speed and endurance in crawling	25-metre distances at high intensity with and without a ball, up to 12 repeats, 1.5 to 3 minute breaks
Applying the skills	Practice games, field and playing time depending on the level of development
Learning the rules	Theoretical instruction

Abbreviations: TP = transition period; PP = preparation period; MP = main period; W = weeks

In the years after that the transition period is designed mainly for active recreation. As a rule, passive recreation is not necessary. It is prescribed only in special cases by the sports physician. The training year is based on a 50-week year to allow for breaks in the training needed for special occasions. The preparation periods, which are considerably longer than the other periods, are designed for further development. The workload peaks during a year occur during the preparation periods; at the beginning of each preparation these increased workloads are characterized by a greater scope of training and at the end by higher intensity of training.

The *main periods* are designed to check what level of performance has been achieved, this level of performance being maintained for a certain length of time.

The more detailed planning aspects covering periods of 1 to 2 weeks are worked out in an operational plan in compliance with the main tasks and means of fulfilling them. The following sequence has proved practical and expedient in setting up individual training units, which are usually designed to carry out several tasks. Exceptions from this sequence should be made only in special cases justifying such exceptions: warmups on land or in the water for 5 to 10 minutes;

exercises requiring a great deal of concentration;

exercises designed for developing springiness;

exercises designed for developing swimming speed;

cooling off on land or in the water.

It is both possible and correct to still the learners' noticeable desire for movement at the beginning of each training unit by using more strenuous exercises and for this reason to extend the warmup period through swimming. But endurance training should not be put at the beginning of a training unit, as was commonly done in the past, followed by ball control practice.

The instructor should in each case keep *notes* on questions concerning instruction and training methods, on individual and team performance in games within the training units. They should then be summarized at the end of each main period. These notes are important because preceding development must always be analysed before the further course of action can be plotted.

7.   Basic Training in Ornamental Swimming

Ornamental swimming is a new type of sport. It received international recognition in 1952. In 1973, it was included into the programme of world championships.
Ornamental swimming consists of two disciplines,
Synchronized Swimming and
Formation Swimming
While synchronized swimming is best known on an international scale, in the German Democratic Republic formation swimming has developed as a second discipline.

(1) *On history*
The beginnings of *ornamental swimming* go back to the 19th century. In 1892, in England, championships were carried out in so-called "Scientific and Ornamental Swimming". This was cultivated in England, Canada, Holland, Germany, Belgium and France at the beginning of the 20th century. In Germany, there developed swimming in formation with Chinese lanterns and flags, and from this, there developed shape-building. From 1920, "shape-building" enjoyed great popularity, and from the thirties, it was carried out in the form of contests. *Synchronized swimming* was shown for the first time by an American sports group within the framework of the Chicago World Exhibition in 1934. Contest regulations were set up for it in 1945 only. The German Democratic Republic took over this new discipline in 1955.

The great prospects opening up for all fields of physical culture and sport in the German Democratic Republic, made a fast development for ornamental swimming possible. In the early days of swimming sports in our republic, *formation swimming* appeared at first as a marginal programme in swimming sport events. In 1952, the first central contests were organized. Since 1954, championships in formation swimming are carried out in the German Democratic Republic. In 1969, ornamental swimming was separated from popular swimming. One year later, the championship programme in ornamental swimming was extended by including Synchronized Swimming. When the German Swimming Sport Association was founded in 1958, ornamental swimming received recognition as an independent type of sport. Its task is to promote leisure sport.
Like all swimming, ornamental swimming too is very healthy and can be started in young years. The smallscale formation (in groups of 3, 4, 6) does not put too high physical demands on girls and women. Groups of 8 and 12 however, make high demands during competition. Synchronized swimming develops a sense of esthetics and requires the creative transformation of music into movement. Ornamental swimming is very popular with the public and is winning new friends for swimming. Ornamental swimming in its sports value is not inferior to any other swimming disci-

plines. The close links to aesthetics, the requirements as to rhythm, musicality, the rich variety of expression attached to movements and positions attract above all swimmers with an artistic turn of mind. The possibility of creative activity, of collective experience and education in the spirit of community life are some more valuable factors.

(2) *Material prerequisites*

Ornamental swimming can be done in both indoor and outdoor swimming pools. Indoor swimming pools are perferred for contests. Minimum requirements are to be met for contests as to size of pool and depth of water. Routine contests in synchronized swimming require a depth of 3 m with a minimum surface of 12 × 12 metres. For stunt performances in synchronized swimming at least 20 × 12 metres of surface with a depth of 2 m are needed. In the case of formation swimming, the swimming pool must have a minimum surface of 25 × 12 metres, the water must be clear and the bottom visible. Pool diagrams are necessary for the preparation of events. These diagrams must show the dimensions of the swimming pool, markings on the bottom and at the sides of the swimming pool, as well as indications about the distance from the water surface to the rim of the pool, the position of the springboards and ladders, free space for displays on land, and the position of the seats for viewers.

Training and contests require for ornamental swimming a sound equipment to transmit music from tape or records. Apart from the special technical data of the apparatus, in indoor baths the high level of humidity must be taken into account, as the quality of the tapes may be impaired. An underwater loudspeaker is required for international contests. As ornamental swimming

contests are often held in the evening, sufficient lighting must be ensured. Both participants and judges must see to it that blinding cannot occur. A special effect can be obtained in show presentations with underwater lighting and coloured light. It is advisable to provide tennis umpire chairs for the judges who are to be seated in an elevated position. The same evaluation tables can be used as for diving.

7.1. The technique of synchronized swimming and formation swimming

7.1.1. General remarks

The contests in synchronized swimming consists of a routine and a stunt score. In the routine, 5 stunts of the international table of stunts are to be performed. The mastery of the stunts, positions, twists and spins, of paddling and the layout positions are decisive for success. The stunt score contests are carried out as solo, duet or team competitions to a chosen theme. All movements are to be adapted to the theme and the music. Costumes should be adapted to the theme. The basis for the stunt score performances is provided by types of swimming, variations and combinations of stunts. The mastery of these basic skills requires that the swimmers – apart from learning and continually improving their movements – also develop their strength, speed, perseverance, adroitness and mobility to an optimum. High concentration, elegance, rhythm, musicality as well as knowledge in synchronization, choreography and interpretation are required. Once, music provided simply the background to formation swimming. In the past few years, there have been great efforts to adapt the

figures and transitions to, and synchronize them with, the music. The fundamentals for formation swimming consist in the basic positions, positions of the body and body links, paddling, the mastery of all swimming techniques, as well as in the stunts of Synchronized Swimming and in diving. Decisive for a success of a formation are the choice and composition of the elements mentioned. Figure construction begins from the centre. They are often started under the water. Every formation has a particular beginning and a final section. Both form an integral part of the formation comprising 8 figures to be chosen at liberty plus the necessary transitions. Basic training in ornamental swimming comprises two fields,
1. Basic training in swimming,
2. basic technical training.
Basic training for synchronized and formation swimming is about the same.

7.1.2. Basic training in swimming for ornamental swimming

For ornamental swimming it is necessary to have a mastery of paddling in breaststroke and backstroke, in layout position toward the head and the feet, as well as in turning. The direction of the swimmer's motion results from the position and action of her hands. In the case of paddling, the body floats on the water surface, the chin is slightly inclined, the arms are at the side of the body, with the elbows near to it, if possible. The hands perform circling movements or eights.

Stationary paddling: The basic position is the back layout position. The hands paddle just below and parallel to the water surface with the palms pointing to the bottom of the swimming pool. The width of the circular hand movements must not exceed 30 to 40 cm.

Backstroke paddling toward the head: The basic position is the same as with stationary paddling. The arms are placed along the body with the hands perpendicular to it. The palms are pointed toward the feet and are pushed in this direction when circling. The hands are at hip or thigh level and must not penetrate the water surface.

Backstroke paddling toward the feet: The basic position is the same as with stationary paddling. The arms are again placed along the body, with the hands perpendicular to it. The thumbs are pointed downward and the palms toward the head. The hands are moved circularly at thigh or hip level in the direction of the body.

Paddling with turn: Paddling with a turn can be performed in two ways: paddling with turn at full body extension and paddling with turn while the body is in tuck position. Both forms are most frequently required in formation swimming.

During the turn with the body in tuck position the layout position is the same as already described. But in this case, both hands do not work simultaneously in one direction, but one hand performs the circling movements toward the head as when paddling, and the other hand performs the movements as when paddling toward the feet, by which the turn is brought about.

The second type of turn is more frequent. From the back layout position with full body extension both knees are drawn to the chest simultaneously. The shin-bones are parallel to the water surface; the chin is slightly inclined. The body is turned around by rowing arm movements. After terminating the turn the back layout position is again taken.

Propelling: The basic position is the back layout position with full body extension. The arms are loosely stretched out behind the head. The hands are moved from the wrists. The movement is performed toward the feet.

The technique of the types of swimming corresponds essentially to the technique of sport swimming. There are differences in the following points:

1. In all types of swimming, the head is above the water.

2. All movements of the head, of the shoulders and arms should be performed rhythmically and smoothly.

3. In the stunt performances of Synchronized Swimming and formation displays all movements must be adjusted to the music. In duet and team events, the movements must be adjusted to those of the other swimmers. But that does not mean that in duet and team events the swimmers are allowed to make only the same or similar movements; on the contrary, varying movements or subsequent starts or differing performance of movements synchronized to the music can essentially enrich the choreography of the theme.

4. Another difference between ornamental swimming as opposed to sport swimming consists in the special significance of space orientation above and below water, in various positions and varying combinations of swimming, shapes and figures.

Variation, duet and team events are used in formation swimming and in the disciplines duet and team swimming of Synchronized Swimming.

The duet and group swimming is performed in line, in double line, in diagonals, in several lines and as a block. The block links can be rectangular, square, triangular, or elliptical, cf. Schöne, S.: Kunstschwimmen. Sportverlag, Berlin 1960 .

In ornamental swimming, diving is used to change places under water as quickly as possible, to cover a desired distance and in order to prepare for the new formation. For this purpose, diving is used with changing directions and paddling into position under water.

Diving as needed for formation swimming is a movement similar to the submerged phase in breaststroke swimming. When diving, the breathing must be well divided, that is, before diving the swimmer must take a deep breath, and when starting to dive, she must not fill her lungs completely. If necessary, before starting to dive, the swimmer must breathe out some air. As soon as pressure is felt during diving, part of the used air should be breathed out. This can be repeated as long as the air supply is sufficient. Another important factor in diving is orientation. It is necessary to keep one's eyes open after submersion. For the purpose of orientation, the optical, acoustic and kinesthetic analyzers are used.

As diving is required above all for transitions from one figure to another within the formations, it must be practised in training the final stages of the dolphin, dolphin foot first, flamingo stunts, and so on. If conditions and technical prerequisites are fulfilled, it is not difficult to prepare and start the figures below water level. In synchronized swimming, the swimmer's diving abilities are important for the quality of the figures. In the routine score, the diving technique corresponds to the technique of the figures. In stunt score performances, the diving technique must be adapted to the choreographic composition.

7.2. Basic technical training in synchronized swimming

7.2.1. The basic positions

– *Back Layout Position* (Fig. 101)
Full body extension
Head in line with body
Face, feet and thighs on water surface
Position of arms optional.

– *Front Layout Position* (Fig. 102)
Body extended
Head, hips and heels on surface of water
Face may be in or out of water
Position of arms optional
– *Front layout position, variant* (Fig. 103)
Body extended with back arched
One leg bent so that the foot is at the knee
or above
Position of arms optional.

7.2.2.   The positions of the body

– *Extended vertical position* (Fig. 104)
Full body extension from the shoulders to
the feet
The back must be arched in stunts like the
dolphin and the dolphin, foot first.
– *Front pike position* (Fig. 105)
Body bent at hips to form a 90° angle
Legs straight at knees and toes pointed
Head in line with trunk
– *Back pike position* (Fig. 106)
Body bent sharply at hips
Legs straight at knees, and with toes point-
ed, drawn toward chest.
– *Tuck (Front or Back)* (Fig. 107)
Body as compact as possible
Rounded back
Knees closed
Toes pointed
Heels close to buttocks
Head close to knees
– *Vertical Position* (cf. fig. 104)
Body extended vertically, head downward
Head, hips and ankles in line and perpen-
dicular
to the surface of water
Water line at any point between the ankles
and the hips
Position of arms optional.
– *Bent Knee Position* (Fig. 108)
Body extended
One leg bent in the hip and knee

Foot at the inside of the extended leg at
the knee.
– *Ballet Leg Position* (Fig. 109)
Body extended in back layout position
Head in line with the body
One leg extended perpendicular to the sur-
face of the water
The face, and the horizontal leg at the sur-
face of the water.
– *Ballet Leg, Double Position* (Fig. 110)
Extended legs with thighs perpendicular to
the surface of the water
A 90° angle between legs and trunk

Fig. 101

Fig. 102

Fig. 103

Fig. 105

Fig. 104

Fig. 106

Fig. 107

Fig. 108

Fig. 109

Toes pointed

Face at the surface of the water.

– *Flamingo Position* (Fig. 111)

Ballet leg perpendicular to the surface of the water

Non-ballet leg drawn to the chest with the mid-calf opposite the vertical leg

Foot of the non-ballet leg at surface of water

Toes pointed, face at surface of water.

– *Crane Position* (Fig. 112)

Body extended vertically, head downward

Head, hips and ankles in line with the body

The other leg is at rightangles to the trunk and parallel to the surface of the water

Position of arms optional.

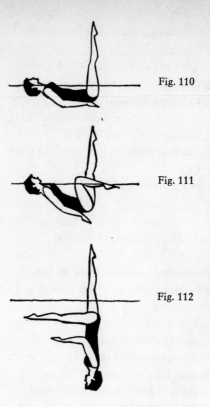

Fig. 110

Fig. 111

Fig. 112

7.2.3.   The turns of the body

– *Somersaults*

Somersaults are turns around the transverse axis of the body forward or backward.

– *Twists*

All twists should be executed in a vertical position. The body, revolving slowly on its centre axis, should remain on the same vertical line and the same horizontal plane throughout the execution of the twist. Position of arms is optional.

– *Spins* (Fig. 113)

A spin is a rapid rotation about the body axis in a vertical position head downward. All spins must be started at the height of the vertical thrust or lift of the body. A spin may be 180° or 360°. A spin of 180° may not exceed 180°. A spin of 360° may exceed 360°. In either case, the spin must be completed before the heels drop below the water line. Position of arms is optional.

Fig. 113

7.2.4. The technique of the figures in Synchronized Swimming

Below, the technique of important stunts in Synchronized Swimming will be described.

(1) Category I

101 Ballet Leg Single   – Difficulty 1.5
(Fig. 114)

This stunt is started and finished in a back layout position. The face must remain above the surface of the water all the time. One leg remains extended on the surface of the water throughout the stunt. The foot of the other leg is drawn close to the inside of the extended leg as the knee is drawn toward the chest until the thigh is perpendicular to the surface of the water. The knee is then straightened, making the entire leg perpendicular to the surface of the water. Maximum height is desirable. The bending knee and the ballet leg must not be drawn up by jerks, but smoothly. When lifting and lowering the thigh, the knee must not be moved. After keeping the ballet leg visible, it is returned downward through the bent knee position, and the stunt is finished in layout position.

103 Ballet Leg Roll, Single
– Difficulty 1.7
(Fig. 115)

This figure is started and finished in a back layout position. A ballet leg is assumed. The body is submerged to the ankle of the ballet leg. Maintaining this position, the body rotates sideways. The ballet leg does not penetrate the surface of the water lower than the ankle. The body surfaces, holding the ballet leg position. When the face is out of the water, the stunt is finished through the bent knee position.

110 Ballet Leg, Double,
Difficulty 1.8
(Fig. 116)

Like Fig. 101, to be executed only with both legs simultaneously. The water line in ballet legs, double, is between the knees and the hips.

Fig. 114

Fig. 115

Fig. 116

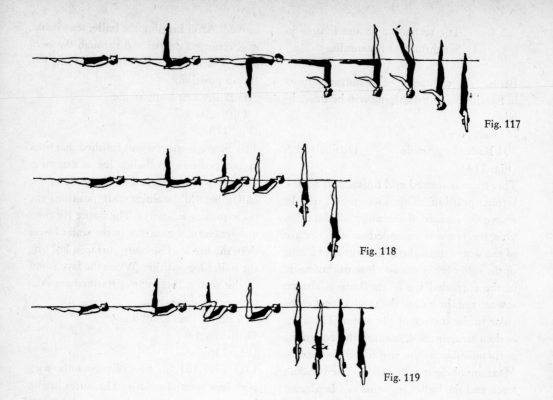

Fig. 117

Fig. 118

Fig. 119

115 Catalina – Difficulty 1.9
(Fig. 116)
This figure is started and finished in a back layout position. A ballet leg is assumed. Maintaining the vertical position of the ballet leg, the body is rotated 180°, submerging the trunk to a vertical position. During the rotation there is no loss of height, and the non-ballet leg remains on the surface of the water. Maintaining this height the non-ballet leg is then brought up to the vertical leg. This stunt is finished on submergence of the feet.

125 Eiffel Tower
– Difficulty 2.1
(Fig. 117)
This figure is started in a back layout position. A ballet leg is assumed. Maintaining this position, the body rolls sideways to the surface of the water. The trunk moves downward to a front pike position. The ballet leg is moved to the non-ballet leg.

This non-ballet leg is lifted to the vertical position. With no loss of height, the ballet leg is lifted to the vertical position, and the legs are brought together. Maximum sustained height is desirable throughout. The stunt is finished upon submergence of the feet.

130 Flamingo
– Difficulty 1.9
(Fig. 118)
This figure is carried out in back layout position. The ballet leg position is taken. Maintaining this position, the non-ballet leg is brought toward the chest (Flamingo position) and extended to the vertical position of the ballet leg (Ballet Legs, Double Position). The face is above the water. Maintaining the vertical position of the legs, and with no loss of height, the trunk is lifted to a vertical position. Maximum height must be sustained before the stunt is finished on submergence of the feet.

131 Flamingo, 1/2 Twist
– Difficulty 2.0
(Fig. 119)
The twist is to be performed slowly in vertical position.

140 Flamingo, Bent Knee
– Difficulty 1.7
(Fig. 120)
This figure is started like the Flamingo. From the Flamingo position the trunk is rolled to the rear, maintaining the bent knee. Now the bent knee is extended (vertical position). Great height is desirable. The figure is finished on submergence of the feet.

150 Submarine
– Difficulty 1.5
(Fig. 121)
The figure is started in a back layout position. One ballet leg position is taken. The body is submerged no lower than the ankle of the ballet leg. The body surfaces, holding the ballet leg position, until the face is out of water. The ballet leg is returned to the original back layout position through the bent knee position, and the stunt is finished.

160 Catalarc
– Difficulty 2.0
(Fig. 122)
This figure begins like the Catalina until the crane position. Maintaining this height, the non-ballet leg is moved in an arch over the surface of the water, passing the vertical leg, which then moves in the opposite direction. The former non-ballet leg is placed on to the surface of the water. The other leg then describes an arch over the surface of the water to meet it. Movement toward the feet is continued until the body assumes a back layout position. Maximum height is desirable.

Fig. 120

Fig. 121

Fig. 122

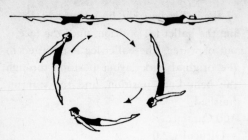

Fig. 123

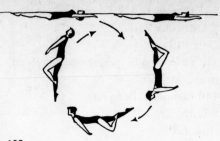

Fig. 125

(2) *Category II*
201 Dolphin
– Difficulty 1.5
(Fig. 123)
A dolphin and all of its modifications is started and finished in a back layout position. With head leading, the body follows the circumference of a circle which has a diameter of approximately 8 feet. As the body moves around the circle, the head, buttocks and feet touch the imaginary line of the circumference.

202 Dolphin, Half-Twist
– Difficulty 1.6
(Fig. 124)
This figure is started as the dolphin.
After about one quarter of the circle has been covered, the body is straightened in vertical position, feet and ankles rise above the water line. In this position a half-twist is executed. From this vertical position the dolphin is continued.

205 Dolphin, Bent Knee   – Difficulty 1.5
(Fig. 125)

This figure is started on a back layout position. With head leading, a dolphin is started. Before submergence of the knees, a bent knee position is assumed. The technical performance corresponds to Fig. 201. The bent knee is straightened as it breaks the surface of the water.

206 Dolphin, Bent Knee, Half-Twist, Difficulty 1.6
(Fig. 126)
This figure is started and finished as a Dolphin bent knee. The technical performance corresponds to Fig. 202. The bent knee position is maintained during the half-twist.

220 Knight
– Difficulty 1.9
(Fig. 127)
This figure is started in a back layout position. The ballet leg position is taken. The ballet leg remains in a relatively stable position as the back arches and the head is moved through an arch to a position under the hips. The non-ballet leg moves through

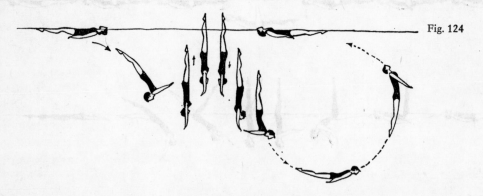

Fig. 124

210

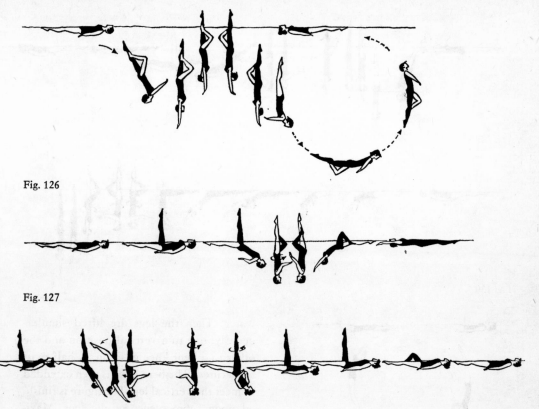

Fig. 126

Fig. 127

Fig. 128

an arch above the surface of the water to a vertical position. If it meets the ballet leg, this leg assumes a bent knee position. The body is then straightened to a vertical line, a half-twist is executed, the body arches and the extended leg moves to the surface of the water. Movement toward the feet is continued and the bent knee is straightened. This figure is finished in back layout position.

230 Castle
– Difficulty 2.1
(Fig. 128)
This figure is started in a back layout position. A ballet leg is assumed. The ballet leg remains relatively stationary as the back arches and the head is moved through an arch. The non-ballet leg moves through an arch over the water to a crane position. A

twist of 180° is executed. With a 180° rotation of the hips toward the vertical leg, the trunk rises to a horizontal position. The water level on the vertical leg remains constant during the rotation and the legs retain their respective vertical and horizontal planes. The ballet leg is then brought into the bent knee position and the figure is finished in a back layout position.

225 Reverse Crane
– Difficulty 2.0
(Fig. 129)
This figure is started as a Dolphin. After about one quarter of the circle has been covered and the feet are under water, the body is straightened to a vertical position. Then feet and ankles rise above the waterline. In this vertical position a half-twist is executed. The crane position is assumed at

Fig. 129

Fig. 130

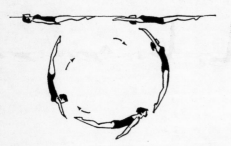

Fig. 131

the same height. In this position another half-twist is executed in the crane position at the same height. Maintaining this position, the body is turned around a horizontal axis through the hips on to the back and the stunt is finished as the submarine.

235 Albatross
– Difficulty 1.9
(Fig. 130)
This figure is started in a back layout position. With the head downward, the body begins to circumference a circle. Before the head reaches the quarter point of the circle, with the hips remaining at the surface of the water, the body is rolled onto the face, assuming a front pike position with the buttocks, legs and feet at the surface of the

water. Then the legs are lifted simultaneously, one to a vertical position and the other to a bent knee position. A half-twist is executed. The bent knee is then extended to meet the vertical leg. The figure is finished upon submergence of the feet. Maximum height is desirable.

251 Counter-dolphin
– Difficulty 1.7
(Fig. 131)
This figure is started and finished in a back layout position. With feet leading, the body circumferences a circle with a diameter of approximatively 8 feet. As the body moves around the circle, the head, trunk, buttocks, legs and feet touch the imaginary line of the circumference.

252 Counter-dolphin, 1/2 Twist
– Difficulty 1.8
(Fig. 132)
This figure is started like the Counter-dolphin. When the feet have reached the 3/4 point of the circle – with continuous motion – the body is straightened to a vertical line. A water line is established between the ankle and the hip. A twist of 180° is executed. The body submerges in

212

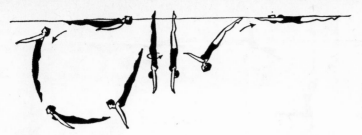

Fig. 132

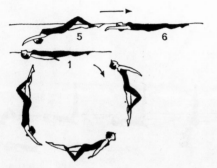

Fig. 133

vertical position. The body arches and the feet move to the surface of the water. Movement toward the feet is continued until the body surfaces in a back layout position.

255 Counter-dolphin, Bent Knee
–Difficulty 1.7
(Fig. 133)

This figure corresponds to the Counter-dolphin only toward the feet. The bent knee is assumed after the circular movement has started. When the bent knee breaks the surface of the water, this leg is straightened.

260 Counter-dolphin, Ballet Leg
– Difficulty 1.8
(Fig. 134)

This figure is started in a back layout position. A ballet leg is assumed. With the foot of the non-ballet leg leading, a Counter-dolphin is started. As the head submerges, the ballet leg is brought toward the non-ballet leg. The legs must be closed before the feet have passed the halfway point of the circle. This figure is then finished as the Dolphin, Foot First.

265 Counter-dolphin, Submarine
– Difficulty 1.9
(Fig. 135)

This figure is started as a Dolphin, Foot First, Ballet Leg. In this position the body executes a Dolphin, Foot First, toward the feet. When the body has surfaced again, the ballet leg describes an arch to meet the non-ballet leg. Movement toward the feet is continued until a back layout position is assumed.

275 Dolpholina
– Difficulty 2.1

Fig. 134

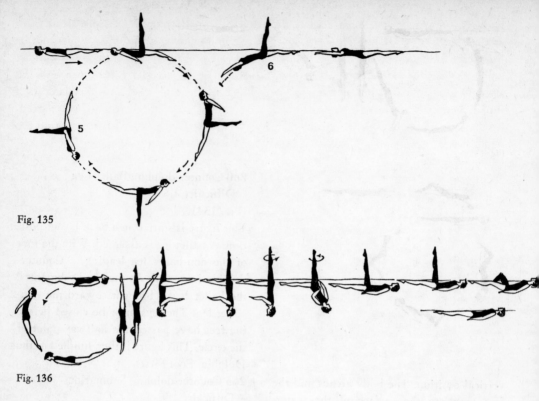

Fig. 135

Fig. 136

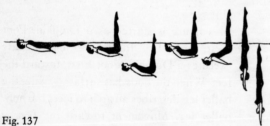

Fig. 137

(Fig. 136)

This figure is started and finished in a back layout position. The figure is started as a Dolphin, Foot First, 1/2 Twist. When the feet have passed the 3/4 point of the circle, with continuous motion, the body is straightened to a vertical line. As the toes break the surface of the water, one leg is lowered to a horizontal position. A water line is established between the ankle and the hip. In the crane position, a twist of 180° is executed. With a rotation of the hips toward the vertical leg the trunk rises to a horizontal position. The water level on the vertical leg remains constant during the rotation, and the legs retain their respective vertical and horizontal planes. The body surfaces and the ballet leg is brought to the bent knee position and the stunt is finished in a back layout position.

(3) *Category III*
301 Barracuda
– Difficulty 1.8
(Fig. 137)
This figure starts in a back layout position. The legs are rapidly raised to the vertical and a pike position is established. The

214

body is submerged no further than the ankles. The body rises until the water level is at least to the knees, the face remaining under the surface of the water. The body assumes a vertical position as the legs are thrust vertically upward. The attained height is maintained for a short time. The figure is finished upon submergence of the extended body.

305 Barracuda, Back Pike, Somersault
– Difficulty 1.9
(Fig. 138)
This figure is started in a back layout position. A partial back pike somersault is executed. As the feet break the surface of the water, the body moves to a 90° angle with the legs vertical and the water line no lower than the ankles. The further part of this figure corresponds to the technique of the Barracuda.

315 Gaviata
– Difficulty 2.0
(Fig. 139)

This figure is started in a front layout position. A partial front pike somersault is executed until the legs are vertical with the water level between the knees and the ankles. The body rises until the water level is at least to the knees. A rotation is started. Just prior to the finish of the rotation the legs are opened to a full split. The back is arched, one leg is moved in an arch over the surface of the water to meet the other. Movement toward the feet is continued until the body assumes a back layout position.

320 Heron
– Difficulty 1.8
(Fig. 140)
This figure is started in a front layout position. A partial front pike somersault is executed until the legs are vertical with the water level no lower than the ankles. One knee is brought toward the chest (Flamingo Position). The body rises until the water level is at least up to the knee of the ex-

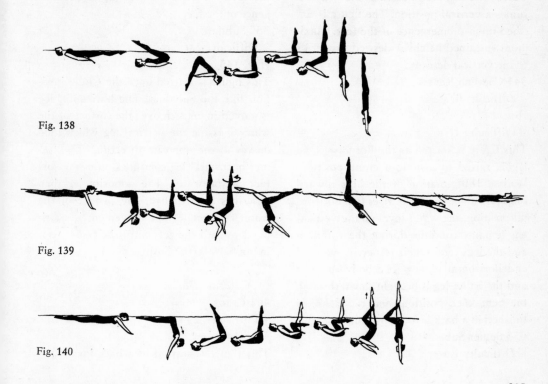

Fig. 138

Fig. 139

Fig. 140

Fig. 141

tended leg, the face remaining under the surface of the water. The trunk assumes a vertical position as the extended leg is thrust vertically upward. As the thrust is made, the foot of the bent leg is moved to the inside of the opposite leg. Maximum sustained height is desirable just prior to the vertical descent. The figure is finished upon submergence of the extended foot.

330 Porpoise
– Difficulty 1.6
(Fig. 141)
This figure is started in a front layout position. As the trunk moves downward to assume a front pike position, the buttocks, legs and feet travel along the surface of the water. The legs are raised and the body assumes a vertical position. The figure is finished upon submergence of the feet. Maximum sustained height is desired just prior to the vertical descent.

341 Catalina Reverse
– Difficulty 1.7
(Fig. 142)
– Difficulty 1.7
This figure is started as the Porpoise. One leg is raised to assume a crane position. With a 180° rotation of the hips toward the vertical leg the trunk rises to a horizontal position, the water level on the vertical leg remains constant during the rotation, and the legs retain their respective vertical and horizontal planes. The body surfaces and the ballet leg is brought down through the bent knee position, and the figure is finished in a back layout position.

355 Somer-Sub
– Difficulty 1.6

(Fig. 143)
This figure starts like a Porpoise. Maintaining the front pike position, the body is somersaulted forward until the legs are vertical to the water line. One leg is lowered parallel to the surface of the water. The body surfaces holding this position until the face is above the surface of the water. The ballet leg is then lowered to the surface of the water through the bent knee position. The figure is finished in a back layout position.

356 Subalina
– Difficulty 1.8
(Fig. 144)
This figure starts like a Porpoise. When the legs are vertical to the water line and the ankles above it, one leg is lowered to a position parallel to the surface of the water. With a strong thrust the body rises and is rotated 180°, moving the trunk to a vertical position. With no loss of height, the horizontal leg is brought to meet the vertical leg. The figure is finished upon submergence of the feet.

357 Subilarc
– Difficulty 2.0
(Fig. 145)
This figure is started until the Crane Position like the Subalina. The horizontal leg is moved in an arch over the surface of the water, passing the vertical leg which then moves in the opposite direction. The former horizontal leg continues on to the surface of the water. The opposite leg then describes an arch over the surface of the water to meet it. The movement is continued toward the feet until the body assumes a back layout position.

(4) Category IV
401 Crane
– Difficulty 2.1
(Fig. 146)
This figure is started in a back layout po-

Fig. 142

Fig. 143

Fig. 144

Fig. 145

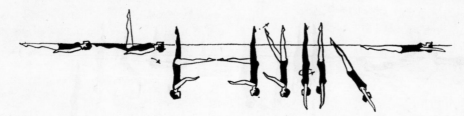

Fig. 146

Fig. 147

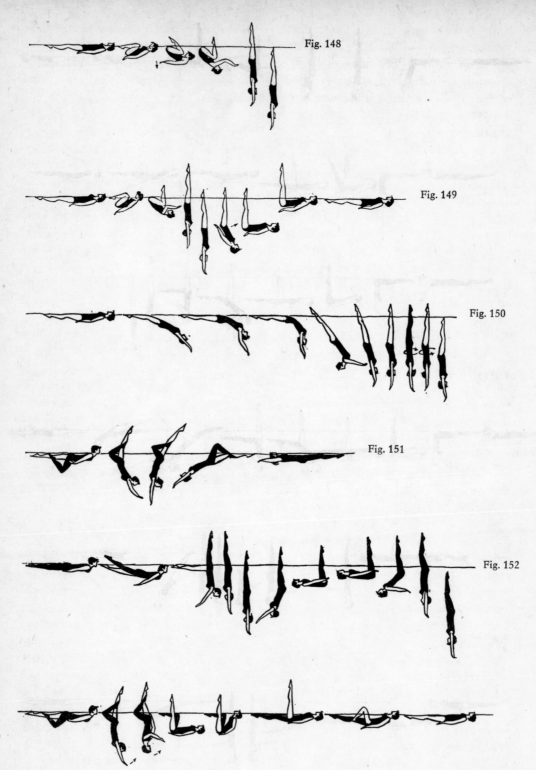

Fig. 148

Fig. 149

Fig. 150

Fig. 151

Fig. 152

Fig. 153

218

sition. A ballet leg position is taken. Maintaining this position, the body is tipped to the crane position. The horizontal leg is raised to meet the vertical leg. A second twist of 180° is executed in the same direction. The body arches and surfaces feet first in a back layout position.

402 Sub-Crane
– Difficulty 2.1
(Fig. 147)

This figure is started in a back layout position. A ballet leg position is taken. The body is submerged no lower than the ankle of the ballet leg. Maintaining the body position parallel to the surface of the water, the body rotates sideways until the ballet leg points directly to the bottom of the pool. The body moves to a vertical, head downward position. A water line is established between the ankles and the hip of the vertical leg. A twist of 180° is executed. The body arches as the vertical leg moves to the surface of the water, and the horizontal leg describes an arch over the surface of the water to meet it. Movement toward the feet is continued as the body assumes a back layout position (with optional arms).

405 Kip
– Difficulty 1.7
(Fig. 148)

This figure is started in a back layout position. The knees are drawn toward the chest with the knees and toes on the water surface. A partial back tuck somersault is executed. The trunk is straightened to the vertical as the legs are extended vertically upward. Maximum sustained height is desirable. This figure is finished upon the submergence of the feet.

411 Elevator
– Difficulty 2.0
(Fig. 149)

This figure is started like a kip. The hips are piked (submarine with double ballet legs position), in this position the body rises

to the surface until the face is out of the water. The double ballet legs are taken back through the double bent knees position and the back layout position is assumed.

455 Spiral
– Difficulty 2.0
(Fig. 150)

This figure is started in a back layout position. With head leading downward, the body begins to follow the circumference of a circle. Before the head reaches the quarter point of the circle, the legs are lifted, and the body is straightened to a vertical line, a water level is established between the ankles and the hips. In this position, four complete twists are executed. Maximum sustained height is desirable. This figure is finished upon submergence of the feet.

460 Swordfish
– Difficulty 1.7
(Fig. 151)

This figure is started in a front layout variant position. Maintaining an arched position of the body, the foot of the extended leg describes an arch to the surface of the water. Movement toward the knee is continuous and the bent knee is straightened. The body surfaces in a back layout position.

462 High Tower
– Difficulty 2.1
(Fig. 152)

This figure is started in a front layout position. The back is arched to bring the head and heels above the surface of the water. One leg is lifted to a position directly above the head. The body is then straightened to a vertical position with one leg parallel to the surface of the water. The horizontal leg is lifted to meet the vertical leg, and a water line is then established between the knees and the ankles. The hips are piked until the body assumes a right angle with the legs in a vertical position. The body rises until the water level is at least to the knees, with the face under the surface of the water. The trunk assumes a vertical position as the legs are thrust vertically upward. Maximum height is desirable. Maximum sustained height should be maintained just prior to the vertical descent.

463 Swordalina
– Difficulty 1.8
(Fig. 153)

This figure is started like a Swordfish until the head is directly beneath the extended foot. The trunk is rotated sideways into a horizontal position. As the rotation occurs, the legs change to a submerged Flamingo position. The body rises toward the surface. As the face reaches the surface, the bent knee is straightened to the horizontal line. The ballet leg is then returned to the surface of the water through the bent knee position. The figure finishes in a back layout position.

7.3. Basic technical training in ornamental formation swimming

7.3.1. The layout position

In formation swimming, the back layout position is predominant. It corresponds to the layout position in synchronized swimming.

7.3.2. The positions of the body

The positions of the body are assumed to demonstrate a variety of pictures. The various positions of the body are distinguished by differing positions of the extended arms and legs, for instance extended position of the body with straddled legs and arms extending upward at the sides.

7.3.3. The Connections

The connections have great importance in formation swimming. They have the task of keeping the various figures in a stable position. Therefore, mastery of these important connections is of primary importance for any formation swimmer. Foot connection: the connection with the feet is assumed by two swimmers lying with their feet extended to each other. Both slide their legs together up to the calves. A close connection is established by side pressure.

Foot and head connection: A swimmer connects her feet to her partner's chin.

Foot and armpit connection: A similar connection is that between the foot and the armpit. The swimmer puts her feet into the armpit of her partner.

Combined connections: A combination of foot and of foot and armpit connections is used in circling or in overturning wheels.

Hand connection: The swimmer takes her partner's hand with arm extended, if possible.

Arm connection: If the connection is to be more stable or if the partners are to be closer, a connection between upper or lower arm is established. The swimmers take each other's upper and lower arms. A similar connection is that between the shoulders. Here, the swimmers approach each other more closely. The palm of the hand is placed on the partner's shoulder.

Hand and foot connection: A further possibility of connection is that between hands or feet. The feet are held with the hands by the heel or toes.

7.3.4. Figures of synchronized swimming

Our modern Formation swimming is inconceivable without including some synchronized swimming stunts. When starting or finishing or during the transition from one figure to another, numerous elements of Synchronized Swimming are included in formation swimming. Therefore, the elementary stunts of Synchronized Swimming also belong to the repertoire of the formation swimmers.

7.3.5. Figures for small formations, including 8 or 12 swimmers

The numerous figures of formation swimming are contained in drawings, and the figures of formation with 8 or 12 swimmers, in a table of drawings.

A great number of the figures with 3, 4 and 5 or 6 swimmers are contained in the „Concise Formation Swimming Primer". The figures of formations with 8 and 12 swimmers have been collected in the patterns „Formations with 8 and 12 Swimmers". The figures of formations with 8 or 12 swimmers are subdivided into 4 groups:
1st group: Figures without any changes
2nd group: Figures with horizontal changes
3rd group: Figures with vertical changes
4th group: Figures with combined changes.

7.4. Teaching methods of ornamental swimming

7.4.1. General remarks

As the simpler forms of formation swimming are easier to learn than synchronized swimming, a method has developed for learning synchronized swimming starting from formation swimming. Wherever there are formation swimming teams this method has been applied successfully.

Once the technique of the swimming styles and of diving has been mastered, synchronized swimming can be learnt immediately. This method is to be adopted above all where there are no formation swimming teams and only few girls go in for this sport.

Training should be planned and systematic. It is necessary to coordinate learning the necessary movements, learning and improving the special technical skills and imparting the necessary fundamental theoretical knowledge. The didactic principle of proceeding from simple to complicated elements must be used in all three aspects of training.

An integrated teaching method should be used both in synchronized swimming and in formation swimming. Simple exercises are to be used as fundamental exercises for more difficult ones. For improving the technique of stunts, figures and elements, parts of figures or similar exercises of the same or other sports may serve as auxiliary exercises. Difficult figures contain several basic figures or parts of them. Therefore, the fundamental figures must be mastered with a good technique. Only then the difficult figures can be learnt and technically improved.

The following sequence is characteristic of learning the elements of ornamental swimming:
explaining and demonstrating,
preparing and exercising on land (brink of the pool, gymnasium),
exercising in shallow water,
exercises at boundaries of the swimming pool (gutters, stairs, ladders, pool bottom),
exercising with partner's help,
execution of the respective element in deep water without help.
Mastering the figures is extremely important in synchronized swimming. In the contests, 2/3 of possible scores are given for compulsory exercises. For optional perform-

Fig. 154 Example of formations with 8 swimmers

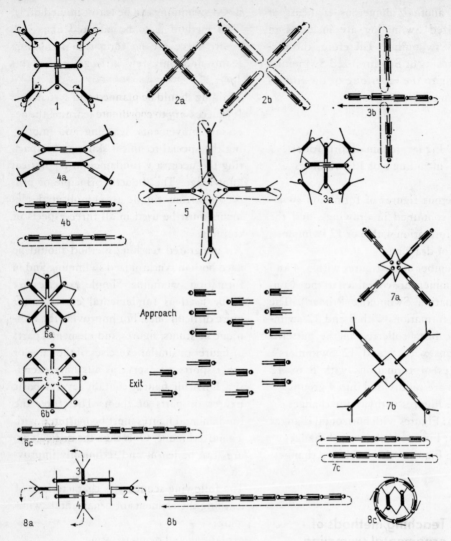

Approach:
Backstroke paddling, arm movements
Ballet legs in alternation
Backstroke crawl
Repetition
Circling movement of the arms, turning
Variable ballet leg
Double ballet leg, diving

Exit:
Surfacing from gyro-wheel
Four lines in two
Beating movements of the legs, backstroke crawl
Backward somersault
Variable ballet leg

Fig. 155 Example of formations with 12 swimmers

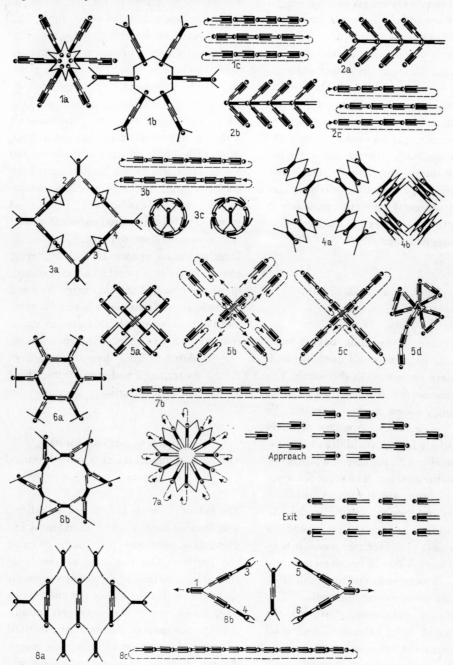

Approach:
Supine position, prone position
Supine position, arm movements
Ballet legs variable
Dolphin movement with ballet leg
Double ballet leg
Arm strokes, oyster

Exit of group:
Leg action,
Ballet leg right left variable,
Dolphin movement,
Right left ballet leg,
Two arm strokes, double ballet leg,
Spreading legs and diving

ances, the swimmers are given more points, both for the technique of swimming styles and stunts, and for variety and difficulty of the figures plus use of the pool.

So far, basic training in swimming and technique has formed the main subject of training for beginners. As musical and artistic training in ornamental swimming requires longer training, it is necessary to create the bases for optional performances at the beginning of the training already. For building up optional performances it is necessary to train ornamental swimmers regularly in rhythmical gymnastics and in the fundamentals of ballet dancing.

7.4.2.   Teaching methods of basic swimming exercises

The technique of paddling having been theoretically explained and demonstrated, exercises are performed in the water. The arm movements may be learnt in a standing or kneeling position in shallow water. To improve the technique, auxiliary exercises can be included, e. g., paddling in shallow water, possibly with the help of a partner or parallel to the pool rim. The sequence when learning paddling are: stationary paddling, backstroke paddling toward the head, backstroke paddling toward the feet, paddling with turning. To exercise more strains, greater distances should be covered in propelling or in torpedoing and in combination with synchronized swimming stunts.

In ornamental swimming, above all, the four types of sport swimming and sidestroke swimming are used, and uniform backstroke swimming and butterfly style more rarely. The type of swimming selected depends on the theme and music of the performances. Therefore, faultless mastery of all types of swimming must be demanded before optional performances are practised.

The teaching methods for the types of swimming correspond to those applied in sport swimming, bearing in mind the technical peculiarities of ornamental swimming. Active swimmers should practise as much as possible with music or rhythmic accompaniment.

Variation swimming: One should start with simple variations, e. g., backstroke crawl with simple subsequent strokes of the hands. Only when these simple forms have been mastered difficult variations such as "waltz crawling" can be learnt. If variation events have been mastered technically, exercises should be done to music.

Duet and team events: In duet and team events the point is to achieve well synchronized movements. At first, exercises should be carried out in twos, later in small groups, and later, in more difficult forms. If variation events are to be included, then it is recommendable to train them on land first. After mastering the chosen forms, these should be swum to music.

7.4.3.   Teaching methods for basic technical training in synchronized swimming

The layout positions are trained in shallow, and then in deep water. For technical improvement, temporary help can be given by the partner. The positions of the body should be practised by the active swimmers on land first. If the ideas of the movements have taken root in the swimmers' minds, then the positions of the body are practised in water in combination with easy stunts. At first, they are practised in shallow water, and if necessary, with assistance. After that, they are to be carried out and improved in deep water. The turns of the body are practised in combination with simple figures, and later with difficult ones. The turns around the transverse axis of the body are practised in combination with somersaults; twists and spins around the centre axis of the body are practised in combination with the Eiffel Tower, Porpoise, Catalina, etc.

7.4.4. The basic figures of synchronized swimming

(1) *Ballet leg*
The stages of bent knee and ballet leg position are practised on land and in shallow water. To learn the exact ballet leg movement, an assistant can hold the bent knee and give a minor assistance until the execution of the ballet leg. After that, it is recommended that the stunt be practised while putting one foot on the overflowing rim. Immediately after that, the ballet leg position can be practised with partner assistance (at the buttocks and leg) and later alone.

(2) *Dolphin*
A prerequisite for learning the Dolphin is mastery of simple stunts with twist, such as somersaults backward in tuck and back pike position. The swimmer, after assuming a back position, her feet at the rim of the pool and pressing slightly with her feet, pushes her body away from the wall. The body is extended and the head taken back, the arms are led back. With this exercise, the swimmer aquires the feeling for submersion to the Dolphin. When practising, it is to be seen to it that the knees are not bent. It is advisable to start this stunt 3 metres in front of the pool wall in the direction of the pool wall. The wall helps the swimmer to choose the correct radius, forcing her to execute the Dolphin correctly. Partner help may be given. Immediately after that, the Dolphin is practised in free water. For better orientation of the swimmers it is recommended to execute it along the pool, if possible, above a diving strip.

(3) *Counter-Dolphin*
The swimmer must master the forward and backward swingover, the Swordfish and other simple figures as well as the Dolphin before she can proceed to the Counter-Dolphin. The swimmer takes up the normal supine position at the pool wall, with his hands touching the gutter or the starting bar behind his head and pressing away from the wall. Before diving down head first, the hands move along the body to the thighs and perform vigorous swimming movements towards the head. It is advisable to have a partner support the swimmer at the hips. Once the swimmer has mastered the initial and the diving parts of the counter-dolphin movement, she can start performing the entire sequence of movements involved. Having mastered the basic movements, the swimmer can start practising the Counter-dolphin and dolphin movements towards the pool wall from a distance of about 3 metres. The swimmer can then practise the Counter-dolphin on her own using the diving marker for orientation.

(4) *Porpoise*
In shallow water, the extended breast position is taken and the trunk is bent down. One partner assists the legs from underneath in order to prevent them being pressed below the surface of the water. Bending down can be practised by putting the legs down on the overflowing rim or on a rung of a ladder. Once this stage has been mastered, the extended legs can be placed simultaneously in a vertical position, for which deeper water is necessary. The same stunt is now executed in deep water lengthwise to the pool wall. The trainer helps from the rim of the pool. After that, the porpoise can be executed in deep water.

(5) The Kip

A prerequisite for the Kip is the mastering of simpler stunts, such as the tub top, somersault backward, standing on both hands on the floor and in shallow water, furthermore, the Dolphin and the Porpoise. In shallow water, in extended back position, the drawing of the legs toward the chest is practised. Once it has been mastered technically, overturning down follows. One partner can give slight assistance from the back, aiding in the twist. After that, the swimmer takes position at the side of the pool wall in back layout position, and than carries out the Kip until overturning. In tuck position, the training master from the pool rim takes her legs and assists her in a tuck back somersault and in extending her body to the Kip. When doing so, the swimmers must watch their movements in water and toward the rim of the pool. After this, the Kip can be practised in deep water and best of all, be executed above a diving strip.

(6) Optional performances

According to the FINA regulations, optional performances are evaluated as follows:
– Execution of the types of swimming and of the figures, as well as of their constituent parts;
– variety, difficulty, utilization of the swimming pool in the course of the optional performance;
– synchronization between the swimmers and with the music;
– musical interpretation;
– type of performance.
At the same time, the evaluation points determine how the optional performances are constructed.

Synchronized swimming is an artistic sport, similar to figure skating. By combining the underlying sports movements into a harmonious whole, the performances obtain a high degree of aesthetic expressiveness. There-

fore, not only fundamental sport principles must be considered, but also those of the arts, especially of literature, music, and the fine arts.

For stunt performances, much experience can be gained by delving into the various arts. This experience should be critically examined for ornamental swimming and creatively applied in this field. The influence of the arts on the decisive factors of optional performances is shown in Chart 25.

The following should be demanded of optional performances: They are to be not a simple copy of reality, but they must reflect artistically the essential sides of selected phenomena. Therefore, not casual, but typical phenomena are to be presented.

Ornamental swimming has peculiarities of its own which must always be borne in mind. These include for instance:

optimal sports value – this must be expressed in the difficulty and technical perfection of the types of swimming and the parts;

the performances are executed in water –

Chart 25 The influence of arts on stunt performances

Decisive factor of the stunt. performance	Influence of the arts
Choreography/ interpretation	Literature (especially dramas, comedies, fairy tales) Dance (ballet, ball-room dancing, folk dances) Theatre (operetta, opera, plays, pantomime) Film
Synchronization	Music
Costumes	Literature Dance and theatre Fine arts (painting, sculpture, handicrafts)
Types of swimming, stunts and parts	Ballet, ball-room dancing, folk dances, artistic gymnastics

this must have its effect upon the choice of themes and interpretation;

the costumes must be simple, typical, and water resistant;

the themes to be shown are to be adapted to the aptitudes, skills and to the artistic level of the swimmers;

the available time of 5 minutes is to be used optimally.

Choreography and interpretation:

The presentation of the optional performance in terms of dancing is called choreography. The types of swimming, variations, transitions and their sequence are to be planned by considering the theme, the music, the number of participants, and the nature of the swimming pool. The types of movements and their sequences are to be adapted to the composition of the music and to the selected theme. In the land and water performances, the number of swimmers, the size of the swimming pool and the state of the pool are to be taken into account.

By interpretation, we understand the design of the chosen theme. The interpretation is an important element of the performance in which presentation in objective terms and faithful to the work in question and a subjective personal approach should form an artistic synthesis. The application of the method of socialist realism in ornamental swimming demands that vital phenomena of social reality be presented in concrete individual or group performances. Trainers and swimmers should try to choose interesting cultural themes present them imaginatively, thus giving the audience food for thought. The following should be considered when *choosing* and *designing themes:*

– Stunt performances must deal with a concrete subject that can be used for ornamental swimming,

– the subject and the music must form a harmonious whole,

– subjects cannot be presented solely by means of costume and make-up,

– for each theme suitable swimming, parts, variations and transitions must be chosen.

Methodical hints: There are no universally valid guidelines for the choice of themes, for interpretation and choreography. A lot of creative initiative and a vast amount of preliminary and detailed work are required from first and vague ideas up to the mature stunt performance. This means:

Making a decision in favour of a solo, duet or a team event,

– choice of a theme,

– selection of the music,

– detailed work on the theme (literary studies, collecting some experience from other arts),

– study and analysis of the music,

– drawing up the choreographic plan,

– examination of the stunt performance on land with and without music,

– practising the stunt performance in water, with and without music, possibly in individual parts, concentration upon essential problems,

– examination, alteration or supplementation to the choreographic plan,

– improvement and sophistication of the technique in water,

– once the technique has been mastered, great emphasis must be placed upon interpretation of the theme and the music,

– practising the optional performance in conditions similar to a contest.

Synchronization:

Apart from the choreography, the music is important for the value of the optional performance. We speak of synchronization if the executing of the movements by the swimmers is adapted to the music. This requires that the swimmers grasp the musical idea and creatively transform the music into movement. The chosen musical composition must be suitable for the theme of the stunt performance. This presupposes a thorough evaluation of the music and a study of the pertaining literature, if possible, also of the dates of the composer's life. Only a feeling for the music makes a good interpretation possible. Then, the swimming movements will not fail to impress the audience by their elegance, rhythm, and beauty.

The music must be suited to the training level of the swimmers, to their talents, tempers, and characters.

Predominantly, instrumental music will be used, because vocal music is unsuitable in most cases. The music can be from ballroom dancing (march, waltz, tango, rumba, etc.), classical music, light and folk music. At the beginning, to utilize slow waltzes, waltzes, tangos, and march music is recommended. Important are an even tempo and accentuated rhythm. Music that is varied in melody and rhythm is well suited. It must be recorded at a normal, constant volume and not contain any passages that are too loud or too quiet. Melody and rhythm should be easily discernible.

The development of an optional performance presupposes an understanding for the structure of musical compositions. As a rule, a composition is based on a clearly outlined theme. The swimmers must be able to recognize themes, to distinguish movements and bars of music. In the structure of the performance, the themes of the music are to be taken into account. They are not subdivided into movements that can serve as units for movement sequences. The movements are subdivided into bars. Bars of a piece of music always being of equal length, the rhythm, the interior moving force of the music always shows an infinite variety. Bars are formed by notes and rests that have a certain value (length)–e.g., semibreve note (rest), minim (rest), a crotchet note (crotchet-rest), etc. The sum of the note lengths (rests) of a bar always results in the same number. In this context, the bar becomes a common denominator for swimming. The basic units of music are sounds that are used for the movements of single parts of the body (head, arms, legs) above the surface of the water. *Beulah Gundling* recommends making a detailed analysis of the music before beginning composition of a performance. (Cf. Gundling, Beulah: Exploring Aquatic Art. IAAA Cedar Rapids, Iowa 1963.) The culmination of the music should coincide with the culmination of the optional performance. The choreographic plan must be completely tuned to the content of the music. Special effects of the piece of music must also be borne in mind. Methodical suggestions: There is no generally valid recipe either for choosing the music or for synchronization. It is necessary to practise études by including simple figures, train swimming improvisations by taking personal abilities into account, use difficult figures, variations, and combinations

Study of the music for the optional performance: The theme of the stunt performance, the skills, aptitudes, and qualities of the swimmers must be considered. Choice of music for the stunt performance: Again, the theme of the stunt performance, aptitudes, skills, character, and age of swimmers must be borne in mind. If possible, pieces that are played too often should be avoided. Either two records should be bought of the same piece of music or a tape recording should be made.

Repeated listening to the chosen music. Analysis of the music: The further way of teaching corresponds to the hints given for choreography and interpretation.

Costumes: Costumes are evaluated as an important element of „presentation". Contrary to the compulsory contests in which a dark bathing costume and a white cap are prescribed, for the optional performance the choice of costume is left to the swimmers. The choice and design of the attire depends on the theme. Specialized literature must be studied, previous experience should be included into the design and manufacturing of the costume. When designing the costume, special attention is to be given to the general impression, as well as to harmony, including the colours. A good costume can hint at the theme.

The clothing must not in any way limit the swimmer's complete mobility, it must be of good workmanship, and if possible, light and water-repellent. Ornaments, used economically, should emphasize especially the swimmer's figure. All unimportant elements are to be left out. As the arms, the head and the legs are visible from above the surface of the water simultaneously, bracelets, earrings, ribbons, and so on may be used, if appropriate to the theme. The basis for the attire is a swimming-costume or other water-resistent or synthetic materials. Most frequently, rubber or material caps are worn as headgear that are either on sale or modelled by the swimmers themselves. They must not loosen during the performance.

Types of swimming, figures and their parts:

The difficulties of the types of swimming, stunts, variations and transitions have been evaluated only since 1965 and thus the value of the optional performance increased. This has meant for our ornamental swimmers that the elements of the optional performance, apart from corresponding to the themes, must be as difficult and technically perfect as possible. After setting the theme, special subjects relevant to the theme, such as ballet, artistic gymnastics, ballroom dancing, folk dance, etc., must be studied. Types of movements are to be examined for possible use or precision move-

ments are to be chosen for ornamental swimming. Furthermore one must examine how difficult figures from the FINA table or difficult variations and combinations can be included into performances so that, if technically mastered, they give beauty and elegance to the performance.

7.4.5. Teaching methods of the basic technical training in formation swimming

(1) *The layout position*
The method of the layout position corresponds to Synchronized Swimming.

(2) *The positions of the body*
A prerequisite is technically correct mastery of the back layout position. The various positions of the body are at first explained, demonstrated, and trained on land for a brief period, and then in water. If during the performance mistakes still occur, they can be eliminated with partner assistance. The positions of the body are also to be technically correct in individual figures or when combining several compositions.

(3) *The links*
To learn the links, simple figures with two, three, or four swimmers are performed. You start with a simple connection at the feet, going over to the other connections then, by using and improving them in the various figures.

(4) *The figures of formation swimming*
The basis for the figures is mastery of the positions of the body and connections by all swimmers. All figures are constructed and prepared from the centre.
At first, the figures are practised on land. Both in the minor and major figures each swimmer is given a place number at the

beginning, and thus the task of filling her place. All figures are practised according to the same principle.

During practise in water, only minor corrections should be made. Further improvements or instructions are given only after the figure is terminated.

(5) *Building up a formation*

When composing the formations, the capabilities of the swimmers must be borne in mind. Beauty, precision and technical precision rank above insufficiently mastered difficult figures, transitions, and sequences of figures.

After mastering the figures, as well as the initial and final parts, a formation can be started. At the beginning the formation is explained on the basis of the picture pattern. Immediately after that the initial and final parts are practised on land. At first, you practise only one or two figures on land, only then is the third and fourth figure learnt. The next exercise is to combine these parts of the figure. To maintain the swimmer's interest two complexes may be practised – figures 1 to 4 and 5 to 8.

Once these complexes have been learnt they are combined. Practice in water is commenced only after the formation has been mastered on land. A stable connection and if possible, simultaneous surfacing are important when swimmers practise a new formation.

To master the formation without a flaw it is necessary to train it to music. To synchronize the formation, the type and duration of the figures must be adapted to the music.

7.5. Basic training in ornamental swimming

The aim of this basic training is to create the prerequisites for intermediate and high performance training.

Basic training is focussed on varied basic physical training, the learning and improvement of swimming skills and technique necessary for ornamental swimming.

If ornamental swimming is taken up at the age of 8 or 9, basic training takes about 4 years. At this age children are learning how to swim at school. If older children join courses in ornamental swimming, coming e. g., from sport swimming or springboard diving, the duration of the basic course is shortened.

In the basic training, education work plays an essential role. At first, a desire for regular sport activities is roused. Moral qualities, persistence and endurance are developed. The efforts aimed at conscious participation of the swimmers in the whole training plays a great role. Every ornamental swimmer must have a clear idea of the means and methods of ornamental training to enable her to develop kinetic qualities, such as strength, endurance, speed, agility, and mastery of the technical skills. Special emphasis is placed on the aesthetic education of the young girls and their feeling for music and motion must be trained. But getting familiar with contest regulations, problems of sport hygiene, and a healthy way of life also form part of the programme.

If possible, in the training, individual particularities of the ornamental swimmer are to be taken into account such as age, training years, state of training, nerve type, qualities of character, and so on.

Sports training is subdivided into a general and a specialized part. The task of general physical education consists in a comprehensive development and improvement of conditional and coordinative abilities (strength, speed, endurance, agility, feeling for movement, abilities for coordination and musicality). The means of general physical training are types of sport guaranteeing a harmonious physical development of the ornamental swimmer. To do this, those types of sport are chosen that are similar to ornamental swimming, such as artistic gymnastics, ballet, games, figure skating, gymnastics, springboard diving, and folk dancing. General training makes up about 50 to 60 per cent.

The task of special physical training consists in developing the elasticity, endurance and agility especially needed for ornamental swimming. The following types of sport or their constituent parts are appropriate for this purpose: suitable gymnastics for training agility and adroitness as well as for improving poise, ballet and rhythmical gymnastics to improve the stunt performances; swimming at varying speed, including sprints over distances of 15 to 20 metres and distance swimming for 5 minutes; individual or group swimming to music; training of figures, parts or combinations on land or in water. The special physical training amounts to about 40 to 50 per cent.

Swimming and technical training in ornamental swimming is extremely varied. It has the task of teaching the swimmers to perform the various types of swimming and the many partly difficult stunts, figures, or their combinations, to improve them so that they are mastered if possible without any flaws in the competitions.

8. Informal Swimming in Leisure and Recreational Sport

Regardless of age, sex or performance standards, swimming offers a variety of opportunities to take part in sports to all people. It is easy to arouse the interest of children and adults in popular swimming exercises. They find them enjoyable and relaxing. They give them greater confidence in water and increase their experience of moving in the water. Informal swimming is a field through which our people can be attracted to sports. Informal swimming can be engaged in facilities provided by swimming sections, schools, the armed forces, the Free German Youth or Young Pioneers groups, during weekends or on holidays. It would be a good thing if all sports teachers, coaches and organizers used swimming in their training programmes.

Informal swimming covers the whole range of swimming that is not contained in formal swimming sports, and it should be considered an independent discipline. Informal swimming can be performed both as an independent event and in combination with other swimming events.

Exercises or forms of exercises may be selected from all disciplines of formal swimming sports. A variety of opportunities for this is offered by springboard diving, water polo, sport diving, and rescue swimming.

Informal springboard diving–a part of informal swimming–will be dealt with in chapter 5.1., as it is a preliminary stage of formal springboard diving.

The various exercises during the first stage of basic training acquire particular importance in this respect. In the following, we shall consider examples from other disciplines of informal swimming. They are designed to extend the basic forms cited here by one's own activities. The exercises suggested raise no claim to completeness and they are not based on results of scientific studies, but rather on experience. Their aim is to give coaches and sports teachers some guidelines and assistance for their practical work.

8.1. Informal swimming without apparatus

8.1.1. Informal types of swimming

The informal types of swimming are not used in official contests. They can only be used in unofficial contests and are suited for all those who can swim.

(1) Informal backstroke
The swimmer is on his back. The chin is slightly drawn in towards the chest. The legs make simultaneous movements similar to those used in breaststroke. The arms, slightly bent, are moved back simultaneously close under the surface of the water up to the height of the shoulders and press-

ed down to the thighs again, now in extended position, with the palms pressing against the water. The swimmer exhales during the power phase.

(2) Backstroke with simultaneous movements

Backstroke swimming using simultaneous movements very much resembles popular backstroke. The difference is only in that the arms and upper thighs are swung out of the water during recovery phase and submersed again for the power phase.

(3) Overarm stroke

In the overarm stroke the leg movement is similar to that used in breaststroke swimming, the arm movements being the same as in crawl.

(4) Combined types of swimming

Much adroitness and a relatively high degree of feeling for the water are required for the combined types of swimming. Correctly selected and adapted to the swimmers' skills, they provide a lot of enjoyment and help improve swimming performance considerably. In the following examples an attempt is made to arrange them systematically:
– arm movements of informal backstroke combined with leg movements of the inverted crawl,
– arm movements of crawl combined with leg movements of breaststroke (this form can be practised in front and back position),
– breaststroke arm movements with crawl leg movements,
– crawl arm movements in prone and supine positions with leg movements used in the dolphin stroke.
Further combinations are possible.
Although swimming with the assistance of flippers and handicap swimming cannot be considered as belonging to informal types of swimming, they must also be named in order to simplify the systematics of this section.

(5) Swimming with flippers

Flippers can be used in conjunction with the crawl stroke, backstroke and dolphin swimming only. For beginners, flippers can be a valuable aid. The increased water pressure can be felt better thanks to the flippers' greater surface, which helps the beginner to develop a feeling for the water and to use his legs and feet effectively.

(6) Handicap swimming

This swimming exercise is suitable only for good swimmers, because movement in the water is made considerably more difficult in this manner. Thus, e. g., by taking hold of one foot the swimmer immobilizes one leg and one arm. In this position he must cover a certain distance.

8.1.2.   Group execution

In this context group execution means duet and team swimming. The uniformity and co-ordination of movements performed by two or more swimmers enhance the aesthetic effect.
A few basic combinations in this context:
– duet and team swimming without any links:
abreast and in a file with simultaneous rhythmic arm and leg movements,
– duet and team swimming with links:
Side links:
– arm links,
– lower arm links,
– upper arm and shoulder links,
– hip links (clasping the hips of the partner).
– File links:
– holding onto partner's feet,
– foot links,

– feet-and-head links,
– feet-and-armpit links.

Link combinations can be used in swimming abreast and in a file (at least 3 swimmers are needed for this).

Further combinations are mentioned in chapter 7, "Basic training in ornamental swimming".

8.2. Informal swimming with aids and apparatus

In most cases aids are used that are lighter than water, in some instances they are used for support.

Such aids include inflated objects (balls, rubber tubes, floating animals of rubber or plastic, water-wings, swimming cushions, inflatable mats) and boards or poles of wood, gliding poles of bamboo cane, aluminium or plastic tubes closed at the ends, as well as gliding boards made of plastic such as Ekazell. Objects that are heavier than water, such as solid rubber rings, plastic plates, stones well visible in water as well as washtubs, bathing tubs, umbrellas, spoons etc., can also be used for various forms of informal swimming, the most appropriate items being chosen for various types of swimming and diving contest. Such items can also be used as aids to make training work more vivid in swimming lessons for leisure and recreation.

Examples for using aids for practice:

1. A certain distance must be covered using an aid. For instance the swimmer lies on an inflated mattress and is allowed to move forward using only his arms; or he holds a ball, a toy animal or something similar, the forward movement being performed by using only his legs.

2. A floating aid (or several of them) is to be pushed over a certain distance using the head, the arms or legs.

3. Carrying an aid solely with the legs (inflated mattress, ball, inner tube).

4. Objects heavier than water must be carried over a fixed distance above or below water, e.g., carrying a brick over a distance of 25 metres or more in any chosen manner.

5. Objects that may not come into contact with the water (e.g., a spoon with a pebble, an old hat, a newspaper, etc.), are to be carried over a certain distance.

6. An obstacle swimming race is also suitable as a form of exercise. Anchored objects must be overcome or bypassed in swimming, e.g., crossing poles or ropes or diving under them, swimming around anchored floating boards, balls, buoys, and tubes in slalom.

There are various ways of using aids in contests for finding the fastest swimmer or the fastest relay team. A wide variety of tasks can be put before the participants in relay contests:

first swimmers: transporting three balls over 25 metres. Once they reach the finish the

second swimmers start: they carry a bucket each with a newspaper in it (the newspaper must not get wet); relay by the third swimmers: they must cover the distance on an inflated mattress, but are allowed to use only one arm for movement; followed by the

fourth swimmers: they carry a brick over a distance of 25 metres.

Rules for carrying out and evaluating the contest should be announced to all participants before the contest.

Anchored objects, such as the mentioned pole, a wooden cross, a raft, a roll, or old boats can be included in a popular swimming session in a variety of ways (climbing them, diving under them, climbing on them and pushing people down from them, using them in games of tag, sitting on the mat, throwing balls to the partner, and similar forms).

In all forms of exercise, steps must be taken to ensure the participants' safety; all potential sources of danger and accident must be eliminated.

8.2.1. Forms of exercise on a chute

Water-chutes are available in many open-air swimming pools; there is no reason why they should not be included in popular training. The following are a few examples of how such chutes can be used:

(1) *Individual exercises*
– in extended sitting position or in forward or backward crouch,
– in prone or supine lying position with feet or head first,
– in "rocking-horse position" (lying on the stomach, with the hands clasping the ankles),
– in sitting or lying position, with arms and legs held in different positions (e.g., arms crossed or folded, raised or held sideways, legs spread, extended or in squatting position).

Various exercises can be performed using the chute; their degree of difficulty can be varied by using other aids such as balls and rubber animals; by throwing them up and catching them or throwing them at targets such as marked circles, hoops, etc. while sliding down the chute.

(2) *Duet and group exercises*
Diving exercises are of vital importance for learning and improving the technique of swimming. Confident swimmers find diving very enjoyable. It also makes high demands on the body and calls for strength of mind and self-confidence. In the framework of informal swimming events there is a variety of ways in which diving contests with individual or team scores can be organized (see 9.6.).

There are two forms of informal diving:
1. underwater swimming,
2. deep diving.

In both forms appropriate safety precautions are essential. Divers must be able to orientate themselves under water. Diving exercises can be made even more interesting by using various aids.

(1) *Underwater swimming exercises (distance diving)*
The following are some examples of how distance diving can be used in games and contests:
(a) Distance diving: Who can dive the longest distance or cover a fixed distance (25 metres, 50 metres) in the shortest time.
(b) Diving through tunnels: In hip or shoulder deep water, two teams stand one beside the other in two files. The girl or boy behind puts his or her hands on the shoulders of the one in front. All participants straddle their legs. At a signal, the last boy or girl in each line starts, diving through the straddled legs, the others following in sequence. As they surface at the head of their respective lines they assume the same positions they held at the end of the line. The team that reaches the starting sequence first wins the game.

Another form of diving through the tunnel:
The participants in two groups stand opposite each other in two lines clasping each other's hands. The arms are held just below the surface of the water forming the "tunnel". From one end the participants start diving through this "tunnel" and line up at the other end.
(c) Diving under a ladder: The swimmers on their backs in a line with the head of the

last participant touching the feet of the one behind him (the head participant's feet touching the head of the one behind, etc.). The last swimmer dives backwards and works his way to the head of the line by remaining in a face-up position and groping along the backs of the swimmers above him using his hands and feet if necessary. On reaching the other end of the line he assumes an analogous position. He is immediately followed by the next swimmer. This exercise is also suitable as a team contest.

(2) *Deep diving exercises*

The following are a few examples of deep diving exercises:

a) Retrieving a brick: A brick is dropped into the pool. The object is to retrieve it with a minimum number of dives (also from different starting positions: while swimming, diving from the edge of the pool, from a 1 metre or 3 metres springboard). In the form of a contest, this can be carried out as an individual competition against the clock or as a team event (two bricks at about 5 metres distance).

b) Retrieving plates: It can be carried out in a manner similar to that used in diving for a brick or in a number of other ways: Distributing several plates over a limited space (about 4 to 9 square metres): The winner is the team or person that collects most plates in the shortest time. Diving for plates can also be carried out as a duet or team competition, with the partners starting simultaneously. The object is to see who or which team can bring up the most plates. Old solid rubber tyres of pramtypes are also ideally suited for this type of contest, they go down faster than plates do, are easy to see and to grasp.

c) Diving for skittles: Skittles are hooked onto a skittle board weighed down at the bottom of a swimming pool. The skittles are to be taken off the hooks by the divers. Several variations are possible here, e.g.: Several participants try to take possession of the skittle board, or attach and unhook the skittles against the clock.

Combined forms

There are also various ways of combining exercises and contests involving distance and deep diving, such as the "underwater transport". In this game, an object such as a car tyre, doll, etc., is sunk in the middle of the pool. Two teams start from opposite longitudinal or transverse sides of the swimming pool and try to get the tyre to their side. The object may be carried only under water. Mutual interference under water is not allowed.

Numerous varieties of tag can be used in combination. "Underwater tag", for instance, is very popular, especially with children and youngsters.

8.3. Swimming and springboard diving for amusement

Both in purely informal swimming and events of a more competitive character, amusement swimming, and especially amusement springboard diving performances are extremely popular. In informal swimming contests, they are designed above all to encourage more people to take part, while, in the latter case, they are used to make the event more relaxed and to enhance the programme. In both cases, however, the aim is the same: to add fun and enjoyment to swimming, to both performers and viewers.

In general, training and contest forms of amusement swimming do not call for competitive–standard performance. In amusement swimming, especially if it is performed in front of an audience, the swimmers' standard of performance must normally be higher. However, there are simpler forms to choose from here as well.

The following suggestions are given as examples. In this field, particularly, imagination and enthusiasm on the part of the coach and the participants are important ingredients of success;

a) Mirror-image swimming: Dressed ornamental swimmers wear masks at the back of their heads. They perform a few simple compositions of synchronized and ornamental formation swimming. The artificial face masks and the movement combinations can produce amusing effects that can be enhanced by suitable musical accompaniment.

b) Bath tub race: The participants should wear the most striking costumes. On a starting signal each of them tries to get into his vehicle (bath tub or wash-tub) and to cover a fixed distance by paddling. This amusing competition can also be performed as a shuttle relay.

c) Springboard diving class: A springboard diving instructor appears with his pupils in fancy dress. He performs simple springboard dives from a 1 metre or 3 metre springboard; the pupils try to imitate him, making all sorts of impossible mistakes in the process. Grotesque movements and gestures can make their dives look even funnier.

We should like to mention here that much skill is needed to do this type of diving from a 3-metre springboard and even more from a 5-metre or 10-metre firmboard. This type of diving borders on acrobatics, and performers should be warned against too much daring.

8.4.   Combined contests

It has already been suggested that the ideas from other swimming disciplines and their training and contest forms can be used for various kinds of competition in this field. Combined contests can be composed from various disciplines and contest rules drawn up according to the performance level attained by the swimmers, their age, sex and interests.

A few examples of this are:

Water polo triathlon: A combined contest based on water-polo consists of water-polo dribbling, distance-throwing of a water-polo ball, and throwing a water-polo ball at a target. An example of this type of contest is shown in section 9.6. Water polo triathlons should be carried out in the following manner:

The swimmer starts dribbling while in the water and holding on with one hand to the edge of the swimming pool. His other hand is on the ball with his arm extended. The ball should touch the water at all times when dribbling. When turning, the ball is held in both hands and tagged against the wall. The player should also touch the finishing mark with the ball once he reaches it.

The line from which the ball is to be thrown should be marked by a rope or by a beam. Each participant makes three attempts with each hand. The longest throw with each hand is measured, the distance from the throwing mark to the first splash-down is measured by using the metre markers on the edge of the swimming pool.

For throwing a water-polo ball at a target, a wooden cross should be put in the water-polo goal so as to divide it into four rectangles of equal size. The throwing mark for men is fixed at 10 metres, for woman at 8 metres. Four throws are made with the left hand and four throws with the right. All eight throws must be made in clockwise direction into the individual rectangles. The players can start throwing with either hand.

A contest is composed of elements from different disciplines and scored according to a certain system of points. The following sources can be used:

Swimming: Covering a certain distance using one or several types of stroke.

Diving: Distance diving or deep diving.

Springboard diving: Distance headers, a specified jump or an optional springboard dive listed in the table of dives with a fixed degree of difficulty can be used.

Waterpolo: One or several components can be taken from the water-polo triathlon.

Rescue swimming: Forms of swimming using specified carrying or rescue grips, in combination with swimming fully dressed;

Ornamental swimming: Performance of certain types of movements or elementary figures used in ornamental formation swimming or in synchronized swimming. When combining contests from various disciplines no more than three to five should be selected, for a greater number makes scoring more difficult and time-consuming.

Some suitable types of combination are:

Triple combination:

Swimming over 25 metres using an optional stroke, distance header,

Distance-throwing of water polo ball.

Quadruple combination (team score):

Transport swimming over 25 metres, dragging grip, diving for skittles,

Backstroke paddling over 25 metres, link between the head and foot,

Optional diving from a 3 metre springboard,

Difficulty 1.3

The choise of exercises for a combination should be based on the equipment available and on the skills of the participants. The two combinations mentioned are only two out of about two hundred possible ones.

8.5. Games in the water

The broad field of popular swimming comprises not only exercises and competitive-type training complexes, but also a variety of games that can be played in the water. Just as games on land, games in the water can be a lot of fun for children, adolescents and grown-ups, and they can stimulate more enthusiastic participation. As there are many suggestions for and examples of such games described in various publications that have appeared in the GDR, we shall not go into details here. We should like to mention the following books however: "Kleine Spiele" by *Döbler,* "100 kleine Spiele" by Rauchmaul, "69 Spiele im, am, unter Wasser" by Haase and the special issue of the Sportrevue magazine "Schwimmen sollte man können" [6, 17, 28, 61].

8.6. Organizational and methodical suggestions for popular swimming instruction

Informal swimming instruction calls for particularly thorough and careful preparation. In most cases, the groups are not so stable as in children and adolescent sport. There is also greater age variation and disproportions between the sexes. The instructor's responsibility is greater in this than in other fields of sport (danger of drowning, spreading of diseases by the water, and so on). For this reason he should bear in mind the following suggestions in addition to the usual bathing regulations:

1. The instructor should become thoroughly acquainted with the place at which instruction is to be given.

Numerous natural bathing facilities, such as lakes, gravel pits and rivers, many of which are not used at all for sports activities, are suited for popular swimming. It will be up to the German Gymnastics and Sports Federation (DTSB of the GDR), the Confederation of Free German Trade Unions (FDGB) and sports teachers to make better use of such facilities for popular sports. But there are also dangers that must be borne in mind when swimming in lakes and rivers. In principle, it is not advisable to bathe in water with so-called creeping aquatic plants, muddy soil, or sedge. Bathing and swimming near piers, bridges, quays, weirs, and ferries is prohibited, as whirlpools and cold currents often occur in such places.

2. Every sports teacher or instructor should try to get to know each participant as well as possible before commencing instruction. The better he knows his group, the better he can adjust his instruction. It is particularly important for him to know the ages and state of health of the learners, because it is essential to appraise the performance standard of the group in order to choose the right exercises and exercise workloads.

3. It is advisable to subdivide the participants into performance groups as soon as possible. The roughest subdivision would be into swimmers and non-swimmers. In the case of non-swimmers it is suggested to choose exercises from the complex of the first stage of basic swimming instruction, e. g., exercises designed to accustom the learners to water, to feel and utilize water resistance and static and dynamic buoyancy, breathing and diving exercises, etc. In the case of swimmers, existing motion skills can be reinforced and improved by selecting appropriate exercises.

4. It is good to know the inclinations and interests of the participants. Experience shows that better results can be achieved if the sports teacher manages to take individual or collective wishes of his group into account when organizing training sessions or meets.

5. Simple and common exercises should be chosen for instruction purposes. Above all, preference should be given to exercises in which as many learners as possible can take part, gradually raising the demands as the learners develop.

6. Groups of equal performance standard should be matched when organizing contests. It is very important that this rule be observed, for great superiority of one team often has a discouraging effect on the other.

It is also important that the instructor should draw up simple rules for the games and contests so as not to complicate things unnecessarily.

7. The instructor should make sure that he is heard well by all members of the group and that his instructions are brief and easy to understand. This is also important in order not to prolong unduly the time the learners have to keep still in the water listening to his instructions.

8. The duration of each session should be adjusted to the air and water temperature. The colder the water, the shorter the training time, and the higher the intensity of the training session.

To conclude this chapter, we should like to sum up by saying that the wide range of possibilities offered by popular swimming should serve above all to help those taking part enjoy themselves and relax while gradually aquiring more and more confidence and a wide range of movement skills and to improve their qualities of movement and character.

9. Applying Competition Rules of the German Swimming Sports Association of the GDR

In the statute of the German Swimming Sports Association of the GDR (DSSV), which belongs to the German Gymnastics and Sports Federation (DTSB of the GDR), and elsewhere it is stated that the DSSV must conduct its activities in the field of swimming sports (swimming, springboard diving, water-polo, and ornamental swimming) in the German Democratic Republic in accordance with the Olympic idea on the basis of the statute of the DTSB of the GDR. The DSSV is a member of the "Fédération Internationale de Natation Amateur" (FINA), the international swimming sports organization, and of the "Ligue Européenne de Natation" (LEN), the European Swimming League.

The tasks set forth by the DSSV in its statute include "Drawing up uniform contest regulations and rules for swimming sports in the GDR based on international competition rules;

organizing contests, championships, cup competitions and international events; making arrangements for participation in international contests; granting permission for, and monitoring all sports relations with other Federations affiliated to FINA."

The contest regulations of the DSSV have a two-fold purpose:

Firstly, they provide guidelines for all athletic activities and relations in the GDR. This is covered in part 1, "General provisions". Secondly, they must be in compliance with the valid FINA regulations.

This means that competition rules cannot be rigid and immutable. They must depend on the prevailing social conditions and on the level of development in swimming sports. Thus, e.g., there is *no* provision in the FINA rules for protecting juveniles from excessive strain, harmful influences of the weather, or for looking after juvenile sport swimmers. In the contest regulations of the DSSV, however, there is an extensive section devoted to provisions for the protection of juveniles. These apply to all young people up to 18, that is to say, until they are mature. In this way youngsters are given comprehensive protection from potential harm and from impediments being put in the way of their development. In socialist society, in which young people are given all forms of social care and promotion, this cannot be otherwise.

We should like to refer to another example illustrating how competition rules are influenced by the evolution of sports and sport techniques:

From the possibilities left open by the international rules of competition there developed, in about 1930, the butterfly stroke, in which the straddling positions of the legs used in "orthodox" breaststroke was combined with a forward overwater simultaneous arm swing and vertical thigh movement. It was at first sharply criticized by many "experts", but then it gradually began to find general acceptance under the English name of "butterfly", as better results could be obtained with this technique than with "orthodox" breaststroke movements. In 1935, FINA had to approve an application made for permission to use the butterfly technique in breaststroke swimming competitions. Some more reflections and experiments revealed that better times still can be achieved by using the dolphin movement, coordinated with the butterfly stroke. Rejected initially, this technique of butterfly swimming was admitted in 1953 and thus became a stroke in its own right.

From that time on, FINA granted recognition to the butterfly stroke as a swimming style of its own and records began being kept. The butterfly event was put on an equal footing with other swimming events as an independent discipline for the first time in the 1960 Olympics. This goes to show that rules of competition can be changed with a view to promoting a certain positive development or to checking a negative one. This evolution is also illustrated by the fact that there was a transitional period in the GDR when the name "dolphin" was used instead of "butterfly" and "inverted crawl" instead of "backstroke" in the GDR in German championships and in test meets in children, juvenile and adult classes. This has led to the gradual disappearance of the obsolete technique known here as "butterfly with breaststroke leg kick" and "backstroke with simultaneous movements".

Another change made in competition rules serves to illustrate how the development of sports, which is often tempestuous, makes it necessary to change or supplement existing regulations: In the competition rules for swimmers that came into force in 1962 for events sponsored by the DSSV, there was no age group subdivision into Children Group B (up to the completed 12th year of age) and Children Group A (up to the completed 14th year of age). Wider participation and a remarkable rise in performance led to the introduction, in 1967, of age subdivison for children taking part in swimming sports according to age and school year (see section 9.2.2.).

These examples show that competition rules ar no immutable dogma: they are designed to ensure orderly contests held under the auspices of the DSSV and to allow athletes of all age classes and groups to measure their skill and strength in fair competitions. They also show that rules of competition should be applied in a sensible manner. They apply in full to swimming events that are sponsored by the DSSV for the age classes and age groups specified. In all other swimming events that are organized by schools, for popular participation or in the military services they should serve as a guideline. In events of this kind, the rules covering stroke execution, turns or the approach used in springboard dives can be declared non-binding. In this case, there would be no officials judging turns or swimming judges. In meets between schools, Young Pioneers or Free German Youth groups, the subdivision by age groups should be replaced by other regulations (e.g., class formations). For waterpolo games, changes in the duration of a game or of the team strength are conceivable.

The examples mentioned in the foregoing are but a few ways of adapting competition rules to participants and existing conditions. In general, competition rules for the sports events of the DSSV in the German Democratic Republic remain in force for about four years. The rules valid at present are subdivided into six main sections.

(1) *General provisions*
Rules in this section are mandatory for all events sponsored by the DSSV.

(2) *Swimming competition rules*

(3) Diving competitions rules

(4) Water polo contest rules

The definitions and regulations for swimming, springboard diving and water-polo are based essentially on the international FINA rules. In addition, they also cover all the problems that are important for the sport relations within the discipline concerned in the DSSV.

(5) Competition rules for synchronized swimming and ornamental formation swimming

Contest rules for synchronized swimming as part of ornamental swimming are also based on FINA rules. Ornamental formation swimming not in use in international contests has been adapted to these rules wherever possible.

Examination regulations for officials judging contests are formulated in swimming and springboard diving contest rules. These rules, with the necessary adjustments, should also be used for examining officials judging water polo and ornamental swimming events.

Examinations for judges are subdivided into the following groups:

Group 1: Swimming sports
Group 2: Diving
Group 2a: Ornamental swimming
Group 3: Water polo
Group 4: For judges officiating in events of the discipline concerned
Group 5: For judges officiating in international events.

(6) Rules and regulations for the Olympic Games

This section deals with the FINA provisions contained in FINA articles 169 to 184, which cover management, organizing competitions, submitting of entries and score-keeping in Olympic contests in swim-ming sports, springboard diving and water-polo.

The instruction manual to hand does not contain detailed competition rules. Only the essential points are dealt with that are useful for understanding the valid composition rules and their practical application. In addition, some recommendations are given for informal swimming.

9.1. General provisions

The general provisions deal with fundamental questions of competitions held within the framework of the German Swimming Sports Federation (DSSV).

They cover the following complexes:
Eligibility
Officials
Provisions on the protection of children and young people
Sports dress
Legal provisions
Disciplinary provisions
Regulations on procedure and judicial bodies of the DSSV

9.1.1. Eligibility

The introductory provision must be observed in general: To become eligible to take part in regular contests of the DSSV the following prerequisite must be fulfilled: the person in question must be a member of the DTSB and belong to the swimming section of a primary organization. Furthermore the participants must be amateurs according to the FINA definition, i.e., they must not practise their sport for money.

The concept of "egilibility" is subordinate to "authorization to participate". A sportsman has the right to take part for a sports club only if he can present a valid membership card of the DTSB at the contest. Detailed provisions cover various questions involved in the case of changing sports clubs.

9.1.2.   Officials

Apart from organization, the success of a match depends to a great extent on the standard of work of the referee panel. There should be close cooperation between the referee court and the organizational management. The composition of these bodies depends on the event. The referee as chairman of the panel is the officer responsible for maintaining a high standard of sportsmanship and discipline among the contestants. He is the person exercising the highest authority over the participants and he is the only person that has the right to decide in cases of doubt.

This means that not only competence, but high moral qualities are required for officiating as a referee.

Before every sport swimming event a meeting of the referee panel assigned to the contest is held at which all members of the referee panel, the members of the organizational management and the representatives of the participating clubs are present.

If several disciplines are involved in an event, then a jury must be formed.

9.1.3.   Regulations for the protection of children and young people

We have already mentioned that the regulations for the protection of children and young people reflect the level of social development, which is a determining factor in sports in the German Democratic Republic. The purpose of competitive sports is to help children and adolescents get more enjoyment out of life and to help them develop good physical and character qualities. Therefore any elements that might impair any side of the overall personal development must be eliminated.

For this reason, there are certain provisions for protecting juveniles from physical overburdening; moreover there are also provisions that take into account the work of young people at school and at their place of employment and that – if correctly implemented – help prevent an undesirable development.

In the regulations for the protection of children and young people there are included above all the obligations incumbent upon sports clubs sponsoring swimming events and working with children and young people. A few important aspects are stressed in these provisions: There is a maximum number of times a contestant can take part in any one competition;

children in the 7 to 15 age group may not take part in swimming competitions if the water temperature is below 16 °C or in springboard diving and water-polo competitions if the temperature is below 18 °C.

Training sessions must be organized in such a way that children can leave the swimming pool by 8 o'clock p.m. and juveniles by 10.00 p.m. at the latest. This ruling also applies to meets. Examinations by sports physicians have to be carried out at least once a year, and for diving, every six months. The persons in charge of sports clubs will be made liable for any infringements of the regulations for the protection of juveniles.

9.1.4. Sports dress

Certain guidelines are given by FINA regulations for the sports dress that is to be worn when participating in any international swimming event. Generally these regulations are mandatory also for sports activities in the GDR. The referee has the right to exclude from the contests athletes wearing swimming dresses not in compliance with these regulations.

The purpose of the regulations is to prevent the wearing of improper swimming attire in events and during training.

9.1.5. Legal and disciplinary provisions, standing operating procedures

The meaningful application of legal and disciplinary regulations plays an important part in educating the athletes and officers of the DSSV. It promotes honesty and fairness of competitions and helps to conduct them in keeping with the Olympic spirit, to establish an atmosphere of comradeship among the sportsmen and to every official feeling responsible for the education of the young generation. It is particularly important that the disciplinary regulations should not be interpreted exclusively by the letter, but that they should act as an instrument of education in keeping with socialist morals.

Legal regulations should be consulted for deciding on the penalty to be meted out in cases of violation of the rules of competition. If a violation of the contest rules is established, an "objection" is submitted to the referee for *his ruling*.

Any ruling can be appealed to the responsible legal commission.

To prevent abuse of the right of appeal a certain amount of money is to be paid with each appeal. If the objection or appeal is granted, this sum is refunded, if not, the sum goes to the legal commission treasury.

Disciplinary regulations are applied in cases of infringement of sports discipline. Decision about penalties are taken by the competent legal commission of the district or county committee or by the presidium of the DSSV. Penalties decided upon come into force as soon as the decision has been made. An objection raised against them does not postpone the penalty.

Operating procedures cover the procedures of the legal bodies of the DTSB. Such legal bodies are:

– At highest level (Republic level): commission on legal problems to the presidium of the DSSV of the GDR

– At county and district level: legal committees of the competent county and district committees

– At events: The jury, the objection commission, or the tournament committee.

– Types of procedure: the objection procedure, procedure for the establishment of facts, the protest procedure, and the disciplinary procedure. As legal remedies there are available the appeal procedure, appeal to higher authorities and objections.

9.2. Rules of swimming competition

Sixteen complexes are dealt with in section 2:

Events
Age classes
Referees
General regulations for referees officiating at contests
Types of stroke

Start and contest
Types of contest and distances
Championships and test competitions
Amateur world records
GDR records
Lists of the best athletes
Evaluation in friendly contests
Records and awards
Swimming pool
Examination regulations for referees at contests
Conditions for awarding the official swimming sports badge of the DSSV
Some of these complexes will be commented upon in the following:

9.2.1.   Events

A distinction is made between *official* events and *unofficial* ones. Official events include championships, test competitions, team tests, tournaments and championship games. They are sponsored by the presidium of the DSSV or by the county or district sport discipline committees. Unofficial events are contests at invitation and friendly competitions, "open" events, and advertised events.

All unofficial events have to be approved by competent bodies of the DSSV (district sport discipline committee, county sport discipline committee, general secretary).

Every sports teacher, trainer and coach should be familiar with the procedure for orderly preparation and holding of a swimming event. The invitation plays an important role here. It must include:

Time, place and type of event,
type and sequence of the contests,
age classes, if necessary, compulsory times for every contest,
sports facilities to be used,
opening and closing date for entries,
entry fees and penalties, if applicable the signature of the organizer and approval endorsement.

Entries must be submitted by the date indicated on the invitation by using official entry forms. The club submitting the entries must check them for correctness, and rubber-stamp and sign them.

9.2.2.   Age classes and age groups

The following subdivision into age classes (AC) is valid in sport swimming within the DSSV:

AC 7 = 7 years
AC 8 = 8 years
.
.
.
AC 15 = 15 years
Junior class
Adult class.

The effective date for age classification is 1 June. The change into the next age class is effected on 1 September. In this manner, the subdivision into age classes is geared to the normal school years (up to the 9th grade), so that the start of the training year coincides with the first day of school, which is 1 September.

The junior class comprises athletes who complete their 16th to 18th by 31 May of the current year.

The adult class comprises athletes who have completed their 19th year on June 1st of the previous year and older athletes.

In general, proficiency in sports begins to decline after a certain age. For this reason the DSSV has formed *age groups* for adults starting from the completed 30th year of age. Here, transition from one group to the next is effected every five years (beginning with group A), the birthday being the reference date.

9.2.3.   Judges, officials and their tasks

The rules of competition of the DSSV comply with the corresponding FINA articles in all questions of adjudication.

Officials must be present to carry out at least the following functions:

1 referee
1 starter
1 lane timer
1 finish judge
1 turn judge
2 swimming judges
1 secretary.

It is also advisable to have officials for lining up the contestants, an announcer, a head timer and an evaluator in order to prevent undue confusion during events.

The referee bears overall responsibility, he decides in all douptful cases where no consensus can be achieved among the judges.

The *starter* acquaints the participants with the command (an acousti or flag signal). After the referee has given the signal to start, the starter instructs the participants to take their places (starting positions), and then gives the starting signal. If there has been a false start he recalls the contestants by blowing the whistle or shooting several times in succession.

With the aid of a precision stop-watch that has been previously checked, the *timer* times the swimming in the lane assigned to him. The timer measures the time from the instant he hears or sees the starting signal to the time the swimmer touches the finishing mark. In competitions involving distances in excess of 400 metres he gives the contestant in his lane an acoustic signal indicating the beginning of the last 100 metres. The timers are headed by a head timer who makes spot time checks and submits the recorded results to the referee. As the development of technology progresses, more and more of the time measurement previously done by hand is being done electronically.

The *finish judges,* independently of each other, state in writing the sequence in which the participants arrive at the finishing mark. If their statements are unanimous, then the decision is incontestable. If their opinions differ, the referee must make a decision.

Another function of the finishing judges is to check if turns and relays are executed properly and to watch the lanes. If there are three false starts, the finishing judges must identify the swimmer or swimmers starting too early.

The activity of the finish judges and of the turn judges is coordinated and supervised by the head finish judge. He passes the results and any objections on to the referee.

It must also be pointed out that in the case of differing results between the times and the finish judges as to the sequence in which the contestants reached the finish, the decision of the finish judges is final provided that it is unanimous. (This regulation does not apply if an electronic time measuring system is used.)

The *turn judges* check whether the turns are made in compliance with the rules for the discipline in question. Objections must be made immediately in writing via the finish judge to the referee. In contests involving distances in excess of 400 metres they signal to the contestants the number of the tracks still to be swum.

The *swimming judges* are responsible directly to the referee; they check whether the execution of the stroke is in compliance with the rules (important in breaststroke events). They are allowed to walk back and forth along the edge of the pool.

9.2.4. Swimming strokes

The definitions of the competition rules of the DSSV that are valid at present do not differ from those of FINA. The execution of movements in breaststroke, butterfly, and backstroke swimming is laid down therein. Freestyle is not mentioned at all, as the term "freestyle" expresses that the choice of technique is optional. In practice, however, the crawl stroke is used almost exclusively where freestyle is allowed, as the highest swimming speeds can be achieved with this style.

In medley relays and in medley races freestyle means that the swimmer may use any swimming style with the exception of breaststroke, backstroke or butterfly.

Turns become necessary in swimming contests if the distance to be swum is several lengths of the lane. The swimmer changes his swimming direction by 180 degrees each time he executes a turn. Infringements of the valid rules occur most frequently when making turns and when making the finishing touch. This is particularly true in the case of breaststroke and butterfly. In the case of either stroke, the swimmer's hands must touch the wall simultaneously and at the same level when making a turn or touching the finishing mark. It should also be borne in mind that the swimmer must maintain the backstroke position until he touches the wall with one hand and that he must resume it after his feet push off from the pool wall. In the case of the freestyle turn, the swimmer must touch the pool wall but he can do this with any part of his body.

9.2.5. Start and competition

The racing dive is used in crawl, butterfly and breaststroke events. In backstroke events the swimmers are in the water facing the starting-wall when starting. After being signalled by the starter to get set the swimmers must remain motionless in the starting position until the start signal is given.

In relay contests the provision mentioned last applies only to the first swimmer in the relay team. The relief swimmers may start winding up with his arms before jumping off. The rule concerned in the contest regulations requires that the feet of the relieving swimmer may leave the starting-block only after the incoming team-mate has touched the wall. If this happens before this time a false start is called. This rule applies analogously to letting go of the hand rail in backstroke starts.

For holding the contest, there are rules covering interference or blocking, assignment of lanes for the preliminary heat, intermediate heat and final heat, the fastest swimmer (in the case of 6 lanes) being assigned to lane 3, the second-fastest swimmer to lane 4, the others in descending order of their speed to lanes 2, 5, 1 and 6; in the case of 8 lanes, the fastest swimmer starts on lane 4 and the rest follow in analogous order.

9.2.6. Contest types and distances

The fast development of children's performance in swimming has been taken into account in laying down rules for contest types and distances; apart from the usual Olympic distances, 25 metres and 50 metres distances have been included in individual and relay meets.

9.2.7. Championships and test matches

Championships and test matches are included in official events in sport swimming.
The German Championships highlight the

swimming sports events at the association level. They are held only on 50-metre lanes suited for such events and in pools having at least eight lanes. County and district championships in adult, junior and children's classes are held in analogous manner. Championships are also held for the individual age classes at county, district and GDR levels under a championship programme.

The sequence of competitions is published by the general secretary of the DSSV in the Association's periodical for every competition season. County and district level invitation competitions should conform with this pattern if possible, deviations being made if required by local conditions.

Test matches are sponsored by the Association's presidium, county or district championships by the sports committees according to the existing tasks and requirements. They serve primarily to check the performance of certain groups of sportsmen.

9.2.8.   Records

DSSV and GDR records are generally kept in compliance with FINA regulations.

To focus attention on certain fundamental problems of the development of sports, the presidium of the DSSV may include additional distances or groups of athletes in the standard programme of records. Thus, for instance, to promote juveniles, records are kept for certain age classes.

A record can be recognized only if the venue, the referee panel and the keeping of the records fully comply with the relevant provisions.

9.2.9.   Lists of best athletes

Lists of best athletes are kept with a view to observing development trends and site provisions that serve to promote athletic performance and to reach top performance levels on a world scale. They also make it possible to compare the performance of individual athletes in various disciplines and between similar sports clubs.

The official lists of best athletes of the DSSV are kept for the record distances determined by the Association, broken down by age classes. There is also an overall list of best sportsmen comprising all age classes.

9.2.10.   Awarding points at matches

Matches between clubs and town, district, county or national teams are extremely popular in swimming sports and they are held frequently. Two methods of awarding points at such matches can be used:

(a) Awarding points according to time
This includes the "100 points scoring method" and scoring with the aid of the points table of the DSSV.

(b) Awarding points according to placing
The European Cup evaluation can be used as an example of these methods (Chart 26).

In the case of the first system mentioned under (a) the winner of a competition is awarded 100 points. Whoever is next has 1 point subtracted for each additional second (1/10 of a second = 1/10 of a point). The match is won by whoever gets the

Chart 26

Place	Individual competition	Relay competition
1	9 points	18 points
2	7 points	14 points
3	6 points	12 points
4	5 points	10 points
5	4 points	8 points
6	3 points	6 points
7	2 points	4 points
8	1 point	2 points

maximum aggregate number of points scored in individual competitions.

Chart 27 shows that the result of a friendly match depends not only on the performance of the athletes, but also on the system of awarding points.

The example shows how either team can be regarded as the winner of a match, depending on whether time or placing is used as the criterion for awarding points. From these results, the conclusion can be drawn that the choice of contestants for such meets is a question of tactics and that it depends considerably on the method of awarding points agreed upon in each case.

9.2.11. Records and awards

A record should be kept of every swimming event. Three copies of the record should be sent to the general secretary of the DSSV, and in the case of events at county level, to the competent county sports committee. In the case of district-level events the record is sent to the competent county and district sports committees. Each participating sports club is also given a copy of the record.

Certificates, badges, souvenirs, token gifts, and challenge trophies may be awarded as a mark of distinction.

9.2.12. Swimming facilities

The organizer must see to it that the pool earmarked for a swimming contest is in a good condition for holding contests in an orderly manner. The referee should check the facility thoroughly to make sure that it meets the requirements.

Swimming facilities with lane lengths of $12 \frac{1}{2}$, $16 \frac{2}{3}$, 20, 25 and $33 \frac{1}{3}$ and 50 metres are suitable for events held under the auspices of the DSSV.

For international competitions and for GDR championships as for world, European and GDR records to be recognized, only facilities with lanes 50 metres long and with equipment that is in compliance with FINA regulations are admitted.

Chart 27 Two methods of awarding points

Contest	Team A				Team B			
(Relays)	Place	Points	Time	Points	Place	Points	Time	Points
4 × 100 Breast-stroke	2	14	6:00.2	98.2	1	18	5:58.4	100.0
4 × 100 Freestyle	1	18	5:16.5	100.0	2	14	5:24.0	92.5
4 × 100 Medley	2	14	5:40.1	96.1	1	18	5:36.2	100.0
Total		46		294.3		50		292.5

Winner in scoring according to time: Team A
Winner in scoring according to placing: Team B

9.2.13. Conditions for obtaining the official swimming sports badge of the DSSV of the GDR

To promote a wide range of swimming instruction, especially among young people, binding regulations for the official swimming sports badge of the DSSV have been drawn up on the basis of an agreement between the Ministry of Education and the German Swimming Sports Association. The badge is awarded to children, juveniles and adults in the field of popular swimming. Because of the great importance of the badge, the conditions for gaining it have been included in the contest regulations.

9.3. Competition rules for diving

Competition rules for diving comply with the "General provisions" in dealing with general problems.
The provisions for each diving discipline are subdivided as follows:
Events
Judges and examination regulations for judges
Age classes/age groups
Venue
Holding of events
Methods of judging, execution of the dives, competitions
Tables of springboard and firmboard dives.

9.3.1. Events

The "General provisions" are considered with reference to diving and explained in this chapter. They apply, among other things, to "official" and "unofficial" events, to methods of awarding points in meets and to invitations and entries.

9.3.2. Judges

The referee panel for diving must be composed of officials to handle the following functions:
1 diving judge
1 announcer who also keeps the score
5 or 7 judges
2 officials in charge of the lists of divers
1 record keeper and
typists.
At international events a scoreboard must be kept on which the number of every jump to be performed, and its execution and the diver's name must be clearly displayed.
Examination regulations for competition judges set forth the preparation and holding of the examinations for judges of groups 2 and 4 b. An examining board of the competent county sports committee is responsible for group 2, while for group 4 b examinations the swimming sports council is the competent body.

9.3.3. Age classes/age groups

Athletes taking part in diving are classified into three age classes:
Children's class
Junior class
Adult class.
Children are subdivided into groups corresponding to groups 1 to 8 to the school grades 1 to 8 (provided that the children in question began their education at the prescribed age and did not repeat or skip any years). The junior class is subdivided into group B (15 to 16 years of age) and group A (17 to 18 years on age). From 18 years onwards, athletes belong to the adult class.
The reference date for all age classes of children and juniors is September 1st. The change into the next higher age class is

effected according to the calendar age (cf. section 9.2.2.).

For men and woman over 30 years of age, the regulation is analogous to that of sport swimming: The age groups are arranged at 5-year intervals, with the birthday being the effective date.

Competition programmes are adapted to the different age classes and age groups based on FINA regulations and on the performance of the class or group in question.

9.3.4.   Diving facilities

All facilities for springboard and firmboard diving must comply with the requirements and provisions of the competition rules. This is essential in order to ensure the safety of all participants during training and in competitions and in order to create the necessary conditions for diving.

In the following we shall briefly review the rules and regulations that currently apply to diving facilities. It is particularly important to bear them in mind when designing new diving facilities or when selecting a venue for a swimming sports event which is to include diving contests.

(a) Facilities for springboard diving

Springboard:

Minimum length 4.80 metres

Minimum width 0.50 metres.

Height above water level 1 metre or 3 metres.

The front edge of the board must extend at least 1.80 metres beyond the edge of the pool. Minimum depth of water under the 1 metre springboard must be 3.40 metres, and 3.80 metres below the 3 metres springboard.

The safety distances between the front edge of the board and the opposite and side walls are as follows:

Opposite wall:

1 metre springboard = 6.00 metres
3 metres springboard = 6.00 metres
Side walls:
1 metre springboard = 2.50 metres
3 metres springboard = 3.25 metres.

The upper surface of the springboard must be skid-proof; for this purpose it can be covered with coconut-matting.

(b) Firmboard diving facilities

Firmboard:

Minimum length 6 metres

Minimum width 2 metres

Height above water level 5 metres, 7.50 metres or 10 metres.

The front edge of the firmboard should extend at least 1.50 metres beyond the edge of the pool. If several firmboards are superimposed, then the front edge of the next higher platform must extend at least for 0.75 metres beyond that of the lower one. The minimum depth below the 5 metres and 7.5 metres firmboards is to be 4 metres, below the 10 metres platform, 4.50 metres.

The safety distances are as follows:

 5 metres firmboard =   6.00 metres
10 metres platform = 12.00 metres.

Distance at each side of the vertical line:

 5 metres platform = 4.25 metres
10 metres platform = 5.25 metres.

There are further provisions covering the distances between the rear and opposite pool walls, between adjoining firmboards and ceiling heights in indoor swimming-pools. Each firmboard that must be covered with coconut-matting over its entire length for reasons of safety and fitted with handrails on either side and at the rear must also have a staircase (or a small ladder) leading up to it. The firmboard must have a resilient wooden topping.

9.3.5. The holding of events

Binding regulations for international events and for events sponsored under the auspices of the DSSV are contained in this chapter. They cover the sequence in which the participants compete, the orderly keeping of lists of divers and the sequence of the events, announcement and display of dives, the start of a jump after the starting-signal of the referee and other points.

9.3.6. Methods of awarding points

The referee panel officiating at diving competitions carries out its activities in accordance with the regulations on the composition and procedure.

After a dive and a signal from the referee, the judges announce their judgements independently of each other. The dives are judged by awarding marks of from 1 to 10 points, half points may also be awarded. The judgement begins after the participants have assumed the starting positions; the approach (if required), the takeoff, the height of the jump, execution and grace of the jump in the flight phase and the entry are judged.

The highest and lowest marks given by the judges for each dive are cancelled and the remaining ones are multiplied by the degree of difficulty. This gives the number of points of the dive. The athlete is placed on the basis of the sum of points he scores for the individual dives.

Execution of the dives

The execution and evaluation of the dives is done according to certain international principles. Thus, for instance, every athlete taking part in a diving event is required to assume a starting position in dives from standing position (with the body erect, head raised, arms at the sides of he body or raised and legs kept together) or, in the case of dives with an approach, to perform this approach elegantly and in a straight line, without hesitation and using at least four approach steps.

In all springboard dives the takeoff is performed simultaneously with both feet, whereas in firmboard diving single-footed takeoffs are also allowed. Each dive should be performed boldly, confidently and the diver should always try to jump as high as possible.

The attitude of the body in the flight phase of the dive determines the type of execution of the dive. Thus, for instance, the same dive (the same dive number) can be executed in a number of different ways, many of which have different degrees of difficulty.

The type of execution of a dive or jump can be:

straight

(execution type a): The body must be kept completely straight without any bending of the hips or knees;

piked

(execution type b): The hips are flexed during the dive, the legs must remain extended;

tucked

(execution type c): The hips and knees are bent, the body is, so to speak, rolled up; the feet remain extended;

optional position

(execution type d): The position is optional.

Competitions

Every diving competition is subdivided into a series of compulsory dives and into a series of optional dives. The numbers assigned to the compulsory dives is the same for all age and performance classes; a compulsory series is composed of five dives, i. e., of one from every group of dives, the number of the dive is compulsory, the execution optional. The number of compulsory and optional dives varies for the children's age groups, but it is the same for the junior and adult classes. There is also a difference between the number of dives that have to be performed by male and female divers. Thus, the competition programme for women consists of a total of 10 dives, and for men of 11 dives. Five compulsory dives are included in both programmes.

The compulsory dives are laid down by the FINA diving committee for a period of 4 years, they may be changed each time after the Olympic Games. At present, the following dives are compulsory for men and women:

1. Forward dive
2. Back dive
3. Reserve dive straight
4. Inward dive
5. Forward dive half-twist.

Execution type being optional in dives 1 to 4, the fifth dive must be performed in execution type a) (straight).

Optional dives are chosen by athletes from the table of dives according to their level of performance. Each dive should be taken from another dive or jump group, with the exception of optional men's springboard dives, where two dives are to be chosen from each group.

The firmboard competition programme is composed of 8 dives for women and of 10 dives for men. Instead of the compulsory dives, the athletes may choose 4 dives from the 6 dive groups whose sum of difficulty is not to exceed 7.5. The remaining dives (four for women and six for men) are then without any limitation of difficulty; however they must be taken from different dive groups.

A springboard and firmboard competition consists of a preliminary contest and a final contest. The full programme of dives is performed in both parts of the contest.

The eight best divers of the preliminary contest compete in the finals; the winner of the meet is the diver with the highest number of points scored in the final contest.

9.3.7.   Tables of dives

Springboard and firmboard dives are arranged in groups according to takeoff, direction of spin and to starting position.

In springboard diving there are five groups of dives:

Group 1:
Forward dives – from standing position or with an approach

Group 2:
Back dives – backwards

Group 3:
Reverse dives – reverse dives (gainers), from standing position, or with an approach

Group 4:
Inward dives

Group 5:
Spin dives or dives combined with spins, from standing position or with an approach.

The same subdivision applies in firmboard diving, but another group of dives is added:

Group 6:
Handstand dives

A number and a degree of difficulty has been assigned to each of the dives admitted in official contests and they are included in the tables of dives.

The tables of dives are drawn up by the FINA Diving Council and remain in force for a certain period of years, mostly for four years.

9.4. Water polo competition rules

Contest rules for water polo competitions sponsored under the auspices of the DSSV are based on the "General Provisions" and on special provisions, which are in compliance with international water polo rules. These rules are laid down by the FINA Water Polo Council for a certain limited period of time.

The water polo provisions valid at present for the GDR contain the following essential sections:

Events
Classification
Championships and tournaments
Rules of the game

9.4.1. Events

"Official water polo events" are tournaments and elimination matches for GDR or county championships that are fixed by the responsible authorities of the German Swimming Sports Association (DSSV) or of a competent county sports committee. International games sponsored by FINA or LEN are also considered official events. All other water polo tournaments or friendly games are considered "unofficial events".

In the section entitled "Holding of events" are contained all details that are necessary to ensure that the contests or tournaments take place without any snags. They cover above all the obligations of the club entrusted with carrying out the event. This section also contains instructions on the keeping of records, the calculation of points for placing the teams, and the settlement of any refereeing problems that might crop up.

Referees and team managers should pay special attention to the compliance with the regulation calling for a minimum water temperature of 18 °C when official matches are held.

9.4.2. Classification

Teams are classified every year by a competent commission according to the results of the championship games. At present, water polo is played in the GDR by males only.

The adult class (men) is subdivided into
a) the federation division
b) the first division
c) the county division
d) the district class.

The German Youth Championships, Boys' Championships of the GDR and the championships in the counties are organized on the basis of invitations supervised by the game commission. Promotion and relegation are covered by provisions adopted by the presidium of the DSSV.

9.4.3. Championships and tournaments

The system of championships and tournaments is organized periodically according to requirements. Its purpose is to help continually improve the standards of waterpolo in the GDR.

Championships, matches of the GDR's 1st division and the German Youth Water Polo Championships are carried out with teams of seven swimmers each. Exchanging players during breaks in the game is allowed; a total of eleven players may take part in the course of a game. County matches may be carried out with teams of 5 players each if local conditions do not permit another solution.

9.4.4.   Rules of the game

According to water polo regulations or men's and juvenile teams) the playing field has to have the following dimensions: Distance between the two goal lines: maximum 30 metres, minimum 20 metres.

Distance between the two side lines: maximum 20 metres, minimum 8 metres. For boy's water polo games, the maximum dimensions are 25 × 17 metres.

An imaginary line clearly defined by marks on either side of the playing field passes 2 metres in front and parallel to the goal line over the whole width of the playing field (2 metres line), a second line is 4 metres in front of the goal line (4 metres line). The centre line must also be clearly marked at the sides.

The goal has the following dimensions: Width (inner edge of the goalposts) 3 metres, height (water level to the bottom edge of the crossbar) 0.90 metres, if the pool is less than 1.50 metres deep, then the lower edge of the crossbar should be 2.40 metres above the pool bottom. Goal depth (goal line in the rear net) at least 0.30 metres.

The ball must have a self-closing nipple, be water-tight, round, and firmly inflated. Its circumference must be not greater than 71 centimetres and not less than 68 centimetres. Its maximum weight is 450 grammes, minimum weight 400 grammes and it must not be coated with grease.

The referee panel in water polo is composed of the referee, two secretaries, two timekeepers and two goal-line judges. These officials have certain rights and obligations, excerpts of some of them are given in the following.

The referee has unlimited control of the events in the game and also over the players. He uses a flag-pole with a white flag attached to the one end and a blue flag to the other; these colours correspond to those of the caps of the two teams. By raising the flag of the appropriate colour the referee indicates which of the two teams decision applies to.

The secretaries have the following functions:

– Keeping a record of all players, goals and of all serious faults (time, colour of the cap, and its number),

– signaling the third fault made by the same player by raising a red flag,

– keeping track of the penalty times of players taken out of the game and authorizing their re-entry into the game after the penalty time has elapsed (signal with a flag according to the colour of the respective player's cap),

– signaling any player's entry into the game contrary to the rules (consequence: immediate interruption of the game).

The head timer keeps track of the prescribed "pure playing-time", the length of the three breaks between the quarters and the penalty time of players that had to leave the field after committing serious faults. He announces the end of every quarter of the game by blowing a whistle. To enable the timer to fulfil his tasks properly he must be provided with a water polo watch or a stop-watch. The 2nd alternate timer sees to it that neither team keeps the ball for more than 45 seconds without taking a shot at the goal.

Every goal-line judge is given a white and a red flag. During the game he sits at the imaginary extension of the goal-line and signals goal throws, corner throws, and goals scored. He raises the white flag to indicate a goal throw, the red flag to indicate a corner throw and both simultaneously to indicate a goal.

The duration of a water polo game for adult and juniorclass teams is 20 minutes of pure playing time, which means that the time-keeper stops the time whenever there is an interruption and lets it run on when it is over. The playing time is subdivided into four quarters of 5 minutes each, with 2-minute breaks between quarters. The pure playing time for boys' teams is 12 minutes (4 × 3 minutes with 2 minutes breaks in between). Each team participating in a water-polo game must wear caps of uniform colour (dark blue or white that must have clearly visible numbers (from 2 to 11). The goalkeepers always wear red caps with the number 1. A fixed system of rules corresponding to the international water polo rules in all respects provides the necessary framework and guide-lines for holding water polo matches. It allows the referee to conduct and control the game properly. Among others, questions like "minor faults", "serious faults", goals, goal throws, corner throws, free throws, penalty throws meting out penalty times to players and prolonging the game to make up for interruptions are dealt with. But all the rules not withstanding, it is first and foremost the fair and comradely attitude of every participant that will determine whether a water polo game becomes a memorable experience for the player and for the viewer and whether it will promote the game.

9.5. Competition rules for synchronized swimming and for ornamental formation swimming

In the still relatively new discipline of ornamental swimming, not so much experience has been gathered as yet as in the other swimming sports that have been Olympic disciplines for a long time already. Therefore, changes will have to be made in the course of further development.

The regulations valid at present for the sub-disciplines of synchronized swimming and ornamental formation swimming are arranged in the following sections, which apply to both of them:
Competitions
Referee panels
Entries
Methods of awarding points
Table of the internationally valid groups of formations (only for synchronized swimming).

9.5.1. Holding of events

In the GDR, contests in ornamental swimming are open only to female participants. In synchronized swimming, the contests consist of solo, duet and team events (4 to 8 participants). Contests in formation swimming are exclusively team competitions that are held in official championships as formation with 8 and 12 swimmers. Show performances given by groups of 16 or 24 swimmers also enjoy great popularity among spectators.

To carry out events in ornamental swimming properly, the place of the event and equipment must meet certain standards. Thus, the area of the swimming pool (or of part of it) in which a synchronized swimming event is to take place must be at least 12 × 12 metres, and the pool must be 3 metres deep; for an event in ornamental formation swimming, the swimming pool should be at least 25 metres long. The water should be clear enough to enable the spectators to see the bottom of the swimming pool.

A record player, a tape recorder, an underwater loudspeaker and underwater lighting are part of the technical equipment.

9.5.2. Contests

Every contest in ornamental swimming consists of a compulsory part and an optional one. In the compulsory part of synchronized swimming, each participant must execute 5 compulsory figures. The participants must wear dark swimming-costumes and white caps. Optional movements can be chosen from the table of optional figures. With their aid and with freely chosen figures the participants should perform a selected theme to musical accompaniment; the attire should also be adapted to the theme.

In ornamental formation swimming, the participating teams also choose 8 optional compositions. It should be borne in mind that their maximum difficulty prescribed by the regulations must be observed (for formations of eight swimmers 16.5, for formations of twelve swimmers 20.0). The entry and exit are also part of the formation swimming contest.

The time limits for the various contests are also defined in the contest regulations. Thus, for instance, an optional synchronized swimming performance must not exceed 5 minutes. A composition with 8 swimmers in ornamental formation swimming must not exceed 12 minutes, including the entry and exit parts; a maximum of 16 minutes is allowed for a composition with 12 swimmers.

9.5.3. Referee panel

The referee panel in formation swimming is made up of:
1 referee (in synchronized swimming there is also an assistant referee)
5 or 7 judges (in some circumstances, 3 judges are also sufficient in ornamental formation swimming)
1 time-keeper (for synchronized swimming, 2 time-keepers)

1 record keeper with 2 or 3 secretaries
1 announcer.
Sound engineers, technical managers and evaluation officials also belong to the referee panel.

9.5.4. Entries

In addition to the regulations relating to the submission of entries and to the opening date for the submission contained in the section "General provisions", a few particular points should be borne in mind for ornamental swimming contests. They concern mainly the submission of the evaluation forms, their number and how they should be filled in.

9.5.5. Methods of awarding points

The awarding and calculation of points won during synchronized swimming and ornamental formation swimming contests correspond in principle to the methods used in diving.

The following aspects are essential for awarding points for optional synchronized swimming figures:

Synchronization between music and movements

Choreography (including the use of formations and different strokes)

Interpretation of the music (performance and originality of style)

Performance of the different strokes, of formations and their components.

9.5.6. Table of formations

The table of synchronized swimming formations is similar to the table of dives. The formations are subdivided into four categories according to the determining elements of the movements involved in the formations. Each formation has a number and a degree of difficulty assigned to it.

9.6. Competition rules for informal swimming

Although the contest rules of the DSSV valid at present do not contain any rules for popular swimming, we believe that it would be appropriate to give some suggestions for this field of swimming sports. Popular swimming is gaining in importance as a leisure activity. Contests take place either within the framework of other swimming events, in which case they are designed primarily to promote the event and to contribute to a more relaxed atmosphere, or as events in their own right.

Popular swimming events should be included in athletic contests held at enterprises, schools, colleges, universities and recreation centres. Popular swimming contests are not subject to such strict contest regulations as the sports disciplines and allow combinations between individual sports disciplines and techniques according to the principle of combined events. They can be held as individual events or as team events. Preference should be given to the latter.

9.6.1. Types of contest

Diving, underwater swimming exercises in which adults and juveniles can take part, water polo triathlon in which adults, juveniles, and children can participate, are some of the general types of contest.

The first group comprises:
Underwater swimming (compliance with safety rules is essential)

diving for plates
diving for skittles
distance headers
water-polo triathlon includes:
ball dribbling over 50 metres
throwing a water polo ball for distance
throwing a water polo ball at a target.

9.6.2. Awarding points

The following system of awarding points can be used:

Diving exercises
a) Underwater diving
50 metres (maximum permissible distance) = 20 points, each 1 metre less = 1 minus point
b) Diving for plates: Number of plates = 20. Each plate retrieved = 1 point
c) Diving for skittles:
Unhooking skittle 1 to 4: 1 point each = 4 points.
Unhooking skittles 5 to 8: 2 points each = 8 points
Unhooking the 9th skittle: 3 points = 3 points
Bringing the skittle board up: 5 points = 5 points;
a total of 20 points.

Distance header
The distance from the starting wall below the jump-off to the soles of the feet is measured, as soon as the participant raises his face above the water. Each half metre scores a point.
Each participant gets three tries, the points scored at each try being added up. The total number of points scored in the three attempts determines the winner and the order of those after him.

Water polo triathlon
The water polo triathlon consists of 50 metres dribbling, the distance throw and the target throw.

a) 50 metres ball dribbling

The contestant starts in the water with one hand on the edge of the pool, the other hand on the ball. He may not lift or throw the ball; at the finishing mark, the ball must be taken with both hands and tagged against the finishing wall. The time is measured from the start signal to the touching of the finishing wall with the ball.

Men: 50 metres in 50 seconds = 0 points
Women: 50 metres in 60 seconds = 0 points

Every second below the fixed time = 1 plus point
Every second above the fixed time = 1 minus point.
Tenths of a second are rounded up.

b) Throwing a water-polo ball for distance

Marked throwing lines. Every participant gets 3 tries with each hand, the type of throw being optional. The longest throw with the right hand and with the left hand is evaluated. There must be clearly visible metre marks along the edge of the pool.

Men:

| strong hand | – 15 metres = 0 points |
| weak hand | – 9 metres = 0 points |

Women:

| strong hand | – 12 metres = 0 points |
| weak hand | – 7 metres = 0 points. |

Every metre above the standard value = 1 plus point
Every metre below the standard value = 1 minus point
Fractions of metres are always rounded off to the next lower whole number (e.g., 16.7 metres = 16 metres).

c) Target throwing

A wooden cross is put into a water-polo goal so as to form 4 square fields of equal size.

From a marked throwing line–men: 9 metres, women: 7 metres–each contestant throws the ball with each hand trying to hit each one of the four squares in clockwise direction (a total of 8 throws). Every correct hit without touching a post scores two plus points, if the ball touches the post, 1 plus point, in all other cases, 0 points. The total number of points scored determines the winner of the water polo triathlon and the order of those after him. If the number of points scored is equal, the player with the better time in ball dribbling wins the game.

The system of awarding points given here as an example can be enhanced and supplemented by including other popular swimming varieties such as obstacle swimming races, popular diving, etc., in the contest programme.

Definition of some Terms used in the Book

CIRCUIT TRAINING, training in which all swimmers exercise simultaneously at different stations, changing their stations in rapid succession. The aim is to carry out a fixed amount of exercises in the shortest possible time or to do a maximum number of exercises in a fixed period of time.

DISJOINTED TRAINING, form of training in which the swimmer increases and decreases his swimming speed according to a fixed pattern.

ENDURANCE, the ability to resist physical stress over prolonged periods of exercise. In sports involving cyclic movements a distinction is made between the following types of endurance:

ENDURANCE, LONG-TERM, this type of endurance is required for distances which it takes more than eight minutes to cover.

ENDURANCE, MEDIUM-TERM, endurance required for distances which it takes two to eight minutes to cover.

ENDURANCE, SHORT-TERM, kind of endurance needed for distances which it takes 45 seconds to two minutes to cover.

ENDURANCE, SPEED, the body's resistance to fatigue in exercises involving sub-maximum to maximum stress intensity and mainly anaerobic energy generation (important in sprints and in intermediate and final spurts).

FEELING FOR THE WATER, term used to denote the feeling a swimmer develops for the water on the basis of certain coordination abilities. The main components involved are regulation ability, rhythmic movement, differentiation and sense of orientation in the water.

GLIDING POLE, a pole whose full length is put in the water and which is used as an obstacle, for practising leg movements, performing breathing exercises or other exercises.

PROGRESSIVE OVERLOAD SWIMMING, form of disjointed training in which speeds at which a swimmer is supposed to cover certain distances are periodically increased.

REACHING POLE, a pole handled by the instructor to give the beginner confidence and support. The reaching pole should be light, about two metres in length and it should have a ring about 30 to 40 cm in diameter attached at one end for the beginner to hold on to.

SPRINGINESS, ability of the nerve-muscle system to overcome resistance at high speeds (in swimming this ability is particularly important for executing starts and turns).

STAMINA, the body's ability to resist stress in doing sustained strength exercises (in the case of swimming, for instance, this means overcoming the resistance posed by the water).

STATION EXERCISES, exercises in which small groups of swimmers change stations in a fixed sequence. At the stations the athletes independently perform co-ordinated sets of exercises designed mainly for developing physical abilities.

TURNS, HIGH, turns executed with the trunk in erect position, the swimmer can inhale while performing these turns.

TURNS, DEEP, turns in which head and trunk are submerged while the legs are swung towards the wall above the water. The swimmer cannot inhale while executing these turns.

TURNS, FLAT, turns during which the swimmer's head and upper part of the body remain in horizontal position on the surface of the water. The swimmer can inhale through the hollow behind the bow wave formed in front of his head during this turn.

Bibliography

(The numbers listed in the book in brackets refer to the numbers listed in this bibliography)

1. Anordnung zur Regelung des Freibadewesens vom 18. 5. 1956, Gesetzbl. der DDR I, Nr. 50, vom 6. 6. 1956

2. Aschoff, J.: Der Wärmehaushalt im Wasser. In: „Sportmedizin und Schwimmen", special issue on Sportmedizin of „Theorie und Praxis der Körperkultur", 1958

3. Autorenkollektiv: Die Grundausbildung im Schwimmen und das volkstümliche Wasserspringen, 4th ed., Sportverlag, Berlin 1964

4. Autorenkollektiv: Kurzer Abriß der Geschichte der Körperkultur in Deutschland nach 1800, Berlin 1952

5. Autorenkollektiv: Moderner Schwimmunterricht, Berlin 1960

6. Autorenkollektiv: Schwimmen sollte man können. Special issue of Sportrevue, Sportverlag, Berlin 1962

7. Baade, G.: „Lauterbach" – „Thiessow" und Freiwasseranlagen. In: „Deutscher Schwimmsport", Berlin 9 (1962) 5

8. Badeordnung für Gruppen von Kindern und Jugendlichen in Gewässern und Schwimmbädern. In: Gesetzblatt der DDR Sonderdruck, Nr. 514, S. 23

9. Barthelmes, G.: Wettkampfbestimmungen von gestern bis heute. In: „Schwimmsport" 2 (1955) 22, 25, 26

10. Bauhofer, R.: Geschichte der Lehrweisen des Schwimmens von den Anfängen bis heute, doctoral thesis, Vienna 1944

11. Bernadi, O. de: Vollständiger Lehrbegriff der Schwimmkunst, auf neue Versuche über die spezifische Schwere des menschlichen Körpers gegründet, Weimar 1797

12. Butovich, N. A.: Plavanye (Swimming), Fiskultura i sport, Moscow 1963

13. Bykow, K. M.: Lehrbuch der Physiologie, Berlin 1960

14. Delitzsch, H.: Terminologie des Wasserspringens. In: „Schwimmsport", Berlin 8 (1961) 37

15. Delitzsch, H.: Untersuchungen über Schwierigkeit und Reihenfolge der Sprünge im Anfangsstadium der Ausbildung von Wasserspringern, doctoral thesis, Leipzig 1963

16. Delitzsch, H.: Zentralnervöse Steuerung beim Wasserspringen. In: „Schwimmsport", Berlin 8 (1961) 37, annex of Schwimmsport-Forum

17. Döbler, E. und H.: Kleine Spiele, ein Handbuch für Schule und Sportgemeinschaft, Berlin 1963

18. Farfel, W. S.: Fiziologya sporta (Physiology of Sports), translation DHfK (996) 1961

19. Fechner, B.: Die Entwicklung des Schwimmsports in der Sektion Schwimmen im Deutschen Sportausschuß (1948–1952), thesis, DHfK, Leipzig, 1964

20. Festschrift zum 75jährigen Bestehen des DSV, Idealismus trägt das große Werk, West-Berlin 1961

21. Filin, W. P. (Filin, V. P.): Über die Perspektivplanung des Trainings für Leistungssportler. In: „Beiträge zu Trainingsfragen", Berlin 1960

22. Frey/Gellert: Unsere Gegner, Band I, Leipzig 1926/27

23. Fritzsche, K.-H.: Haltungsfehler und Haltungsschäden bei Kindern und Jugendlichen, Berlin 1958

24. Fulda, K.: Philonexia, 2nd ed., Leipzig 1914

25. Gräfe, H.-K.: Optimale Ernährungsbilanzen für Leistungssportler, Berlin 1964

26. GutsMuths: Kleines Lehrbuch der Schwimmkunst zum Selbstunterricht, Weimar 1789

27. GutsMuths: Gymnastik für die Jugend, Schnepfenthal 1793

28. Haase, J.: Spiele im, am, unter Wasser, Sportverlag, Berlin 1979

29. Hammer, H./Wünsch, D./Jähnig, W.: Die schwimmbegeisterten Halloren und ihr Einfluß auf die Ausbreitung des Schwimmsports in Deutschland. In: „Theorie und Praxis der Körperkultur" 11 (1962) 8

30. Harre, D.: Trainingslehre, Sportverlag 7th ed., Berlin 1977

31. Henatsch, H.-M.: Allgemeine Elektrophysiologie der erregbaren Strukturen. In: Landois-Rosemann „Lehrbuch der Physiologie", Munich-Berlin 1962

32. Hentzschel, W./Standke, A.: Empfehlungen für den Unterricht mit Schwimmanfängern unter Tiefwasserbedingungen. In: Körpererziehung, Heft 3/1970

33. Hirtz, P.: Zur Bewegungseigenschaft Gewandtheit. In: „Theorie und Praxis der Körperkultur" 13 (1964) 8

34. Höhne, E.: Zur Frage der didaktischen Prinzipien und ihrer Anwendung im Unterrichtsfach Körpererziehung. In: Körpererziehung 14 (1964) 6

35. Homagk, Ch.: Zur Trainingsplanung der Gemeinschaften ohne Winterbad, state examination, DHfK, Leipzig 1962

36. Kapinos, H.: Die geschichtliche Entwicklung und kritische Betrachtungen der Schulmethodik im Schwimmen, thesis, DHfK, Leipzig 1958

37. Kefer, H./Lechnir, J.: Die Schule des Wasserspringens, 3rd ed., Frankfurt/Main 1952

38. Kleine Enzyklopädie Körperkultur und Sport, 3rd ed., Leipzig 1965

39. Kozlik, H.: Die Bildung der Bewegungsfertigkeiten in Abhängigkeit von der Zeiteinteilung des Übens. In: „Jugend und Sport", special issue of „Theorie und Praxis der Körperkultur", 1957

40. Krestownikow, A. N.: Physiologie der Körperübungen, Berlin 1953

41. Ladebeck: Ladebecks Schwimmschule, 3rd ed., Leipzig 1885

42. Lechnir, J.: Handbuch des Wasserspringens, Hof 1930

43. Lewin, G.: Das Hallen-Training des Leistungsschwimmens unter besonderer Berücksichtigung der Vorbereitungsperiode. In: „Theorie und Praxis der Körperkultur" 6 (1957) 2

44. Lewin, G.: Das Training des Leistungsschwimmers in der Freiwasserschwimmzeit. In: „Theorie und Praxis der Körperkultur" 6 (1957) 6

45. Lewin, G.: Methodisch-organisatorische Hilfen für die Grundausbildung im Schwimmen unter Tiefwasserbedingungen. In: Körpererziehung 23 (1973) 5

46. Lewin, G.: Schwimmausbildung für Kinder im Vorschulalter, doctoral thesis, Leipzig 1963

47. Lewin, G.: Schwimmen mit kleinen Leuten, Sportverlag, Berlin 1975

48. Lorentz, F.: Gesundheitswert der Sportarten, Stuttgart 1938

49. Marhold, G.: Der Absprung vom Turm und die Gestaltung des Sprunges und des Eintauchens; eine biomechanische Betrachtung. In: „Schwimmsport", Berlin, 7 (1960) 29, 30, annex of Schwimmsport-Forum

50. Matveyev, L. P.: Kak stroit' kruglodivnuyu trenirovku (How to build up a year-round training schedule). In: „Teor. i prakt. fiz. kult.", Moscow 27 (1964) 5

51. Matwejew, L. P. (Matveyev, L. P.): Die Periodisierung des Trainings. In: „Beiträge zu Trainingsfragen", Berlin 1960

52. Meinel, K.: Bewegungslehre, Versuch einer Theorie der sportlichen Bewegungen unter pädagogischem Aspekt, Berlin 1966

53. Mellerowicz, H.: Herz und Blutkreislauf beim Sport. In: Arnold, A. „Lehrbuch der Sportmedizin", J. A. Barth, Leipzig 1960

54. Mellerowicz, H.: Herz und Kreislauf beim Schwimmen. In: Supplement Sportmedizin der „Theorie und Praxis der Körperkultur", 1957

55. Mezö, F.: Die modernen Olympischen Spiele, 2nd ed., Berlin – Budapest 1959

56. Müller, E. A.: Physiologie der körperlichen Leistungsfähigkeit. In: Landois-Rosemann „Lehrbuch der Physiologie", München–Berlin 1962

57. Osolin, N.: Das Training des Leichtathleten, Berlin 1954

58. Paerisch, M.: Der dynamische Stereotyp und seine Bedeutung für Training und Wettkampf. In: „Theorie und Praxis der Körperkultur" 8 (1959) 6

59. Rajki, B.: Die Technik des Sportschwimmens, Berlin–Budapest 1956

60. Rajki, B.: Das Wasserballspiel, Budapest 1959

61. Rauchmaul, S.: 100 kleine Spiele, 5th ed., Sportverlag, Berlin 1958

62. Reindell, H.: Das Intervalltraining, Munich 1962

63. Röblitz, G./Schwidtmann, H.: Pädagogik, tutorial instructions for correspondance course students, DHfK, 1960

64. Rossier, P. H./Bühlmann, A./Wiesinger, K.: Physiologie und Pathophysiologie der Atmung, Berlin–Göttingen–Heidelberg 1956

65. Rudik, T. A.: Psychologie, Berlin 1963

66. Schnurpel/Stahn: Rettungsschwimmen, Berlin 1960

67. Schöne, S.: Die Orientierung im Wasser. In: „Schwimmsport", Berlin, 7 (1960) 15, annex of „Schwimmsport-Forum"

68. Schöne, S.: Kunstschwimmen, Sportverlag, Berlin 1960

69. Schuchardt, P.: Das Training an Land im Trainingsjahr der Gemeinschaften ohne Winterbad, thesis, DHfK, Leipzig 1964

70. Strubbe, A. B. P.: Ursprung und Entwicklung des Kunstschwimmens. In: „De Zwemkroniek" (Netherlands), 23 (1958) 6

71. Unser Bildungssystem – wichtiger Schritt auf dem Wege zur gebildeten Nation. Staatsverlag, Berlin 1956

72. Wagner, Chr.: Auswahl und Anwendung von Hilfsgeräten im Vorschulschwimmen, state examination, DHfK, Leipzig 1962

73. Wagner, Chr./Müller, Chr.: Rahmen- und Stoff-verteilungspläne für die Grundausbildung im Schwimmen. In: „Theorie und Praxis der Körperkultur" 16 (1967) 8

74. Weimann: Colymbetes – der Schwimmer oder die Schwimmkunst, reprint, Berlin 1937

75. Weißhuhn, Ch.: Die geschichtliche Entwicklung des Schulschwimmens in Deutschland und besondere Betrachtungen des Schwimmunterrichts in Leipzig, state examination, Karl-Marx-Universität, Leipzig 1958

76. Wettkampfbestimmungen des Deutschen Schwimmsportverbandes der Deutschen Demokratischen Republik, Berlin 1970

77. Wiessner, K.: Natürlicher Schwimmunterricht, 4th ed., Wien 1950

78. Verfügungen und Mitteilungen. Richtlinien für den Arbeitsschutz in den Ausbildungs- und Erziehungsstätten der DDR, Ministerium für Volksbildung, 15. 4. 1964

C